Grassroots Struggles for Sustainability in Central America

Grassroots Struggles for Sustainability in Central America

LYNN R. HORTON

UNIVERSITY PRESS OF COLORADO

© 2007 by the University Press of Colorado

Published by the University Press of Colorado
5589 Arapahoe Avenue, Suite 206C
Boulder, Colorado 80303

All rights reserved
Printed in the United States of America

 The University Press of Colorado is a proud member of
the Association of American University Presses.

The University Press of Colorado is a cooperative publishing enterprise supported, in part, by Adams State College, Colorado State University, Fort Lewis College, Mesa State College, Metropolitan State College of Denver, University of Colorado, University of Northern Colorado, and Western State College of Colorado.

∞ The paper used in this publication meets the minimum requirements of the American National Standard for Information Sciences — Permanence of Paper for Printed Library Materials. ANSI Z39.48-1992

Library of Congress Cataloging-in-Publication Data

Horton, Lynn, 1964–
  Grassroots struggles for sustainability in Central America / Lynn R. Horton.
    p. cm.
  Includes bibliographical references (p.) and index.
  ISBN 978-0-87081-872-1 (hardcover : alk. paper) 1. Sustainable development — Central America — Citizen participation — Case studies. 2. Sustainable development — Costa Rica — Osa Peninsula — Citizen participation. 3. Sustainable development — Nicaragua — Miraflores (Chinandegas) — Citizen participation. 4. Sustainable development — Panama — Ipetí — Citizen participation. 5. Rural development — Central America — Case studies. 6. Cuna Indians — Panama — Ipetí — Economic conditions. I. Title.
  HC141.Z9E547 2007
  338.9728′07 — dc22
                                                                              2007003905

Design by Daniel Pratt

16 15 14 13 12 11 10 09 08 07   10 9 8 7 6 5 4 3 2 1

Contents

List of Figures, Tables, and Maps / vii
List of Acronyms / ix
Preface and Acknowledgments / xi

1. Contested Visions of Sustainability / 1
2. Poverty and Forests: Development and (Dis)empowerment in Central America / 19
3. "All The Land Belongs to the Foreigners": Ecotourism and Sustainability / 41
4. "Nature That Gives Them Life": Grassroots Sustainability on the Osa Peninsula / 51
5. "Right Behind Him Are the Campesinos with Axes": Developing the Estero Real / 69
6. "He Has Been Taught Not to Be Afraid": Grassroots Sustainability in Miraflores / 79
7. "Before, There Were Only Kunas": The Struggle for the Comarca / 97
8. "There Are No Poor People Here": Grassroots Sustainability in Ipetí / 109
9. Bringing the Case Studies Together / 127
10. Conclusion / 145

Appendix / 157
Notes / 167
Bibliography / 187
Index / 211

Figures, Tables, and Maps

Figures
1.1. Discourses of Sustainability / 3

Tables
1.1. Comparison of Discourses of Sustainability / 5
1.2 Contested Components of Sustainability / 9
2.1. Basic Indicators: Miraflores, Nicaragua, 2001 / 23
2.2. Central America: Gross Domestic Product, 1960–2001 / 23
2.3. Central America: Distribution of Rural Families by Size of Property, 1970 / 24
2.4. Central America: Poverty, 2001 / 24
2.5. Basic Indicators: Ipetí, Panama, 2000 / 29
2.6. Central America: National Forest Cover and Annual Deforestation, 1990, 2000 / 33
2.7. Central America: Changes in Land Use, 1972–1987 / 33
2.8. Basic Indicators: Puerto Jiménez, Costa Rica, 2000 / 36
2.9. Central America: Protected Areas, 2002 / 37
6.1. Major Development Projects: Miraflores, Nicaragua, 1984–2003 / 84
7.1. Bayano Land Use, 1980–1997 / 99
8.1. Development Projects: Ipetí, Panama, 1993–2003 / 120

FIGURES, TABLES, AND MAPS

9.1. Community Visions of Sustainable Development / 129
9.2. Engagement with Dominant Policies of Sustainability / 133
9.3. Community Empowerment / 139
A.1. Interview Data / 160

Maps
2.1. Chinandega Province, Nicaragua / 22
2.2. Bayano Region, Panama / 28
2.3. Osa Peninsula, Costa Rica / 35

Acronyms

ADPESCA (Nicaragua) Adminstración Pesquera (Fishery Administration)

AECO Asociación Ecologista Costarricense (Costa Rican Ecological Association)

ANAM (Panama) Autoridad Nacional del Ambiente (National Environmental Authority)

ANCON (Panama) Asociación Nacional para la Conservación de la Naturaleza (National Association for the Conservation of Nature)

BDA (Panama) Banco de Desarrollo Agropecuario (Agricultural Development Bank)

CAS (Nicaragua) Cooperativa Agrícola Sandinista (Sandinista Agricultural Cooperative)

DANIDA Danish International Development Agency

FSLN (Nicaragua) Frente Sandinista de Liberación Nacional (Sandinista National Liberation Front)

GDP gross domestic product

GEF Global Environmental Facility

GNP gross national product

ICD Integrated Conservation and Development

Acronyms

IDA (Costa Rica)   Instituto de Desarrollo Agrario (Agrarian Development Institute)

IDB   Inter-American Development Bank

IFI   international financial institution

IRENA   Instituto Nicaragüense de Recursos Naturales y del Ambiente (Nicaraguan Institute of Natural Resources and Environment)

INRENARE (Panama)   Instituto Nacional de Recursos Naturales Renovables (National Institute for Renewable Resources)

IRHE (Panama)   Instituto de Recursos Hidráulicos y Electrificación (Institute of Hydraulic Resources and Electricity)

ISI   import substitution industrialization

ITCO (Costa Rica)   Instituto de Tierras y Colonización (Land Colonization Institute)

IUCN   World Conservation Union

MAG-FOR (Nicaragua)   Ministerio Agropecuario y Forestal (Ministry of Agriculture and Forestry)

MARENA (Nicaragua)   Ministerio de Ambiente y Recursos Naturales (Ministry of Environment and Natural Resources)

MIDINRA (Nicaragua)   Ministerio de Desarrollo Agrario y Reforma Agraria (Ministry for Agrarian Development and Reform)

MINAE (Costa Rica)   Ministerio de Ambiente y Energía (Ministry of Environment and Energy)

MIRENEM (Costa Rica)   Ministerio de Recursos Naturales, Energía y Minas (Ministry of Natural Resources, Energy, and Mines)

NGO   Nongovernmental Organization

OFP   Osa Forest Products

SAP   structural adjustment program

SINAC (Costa Rica)   National System of Conservation Areas

SIPRAICO (Costa Rica)   Sindicato de Productores Agrícolas Independientes del Cantón de Osa (Union of Independent Agricultural Producers of the Osa Canton)

UNAG (Nicaragua)   Unión Nacional de Agricultores y Ganaderos (National Union of Farmers and Ranchers)

USAID   United States Agency for International Development

Preface and Acknowledgments

I first met Santiago[1] in the late 1980s, soon after he had been recognized as a full member (*militante*) of Nicaragua's revolutionary Sandinista National Liberation Front (FSLN). A tall man with an untrimmed beard and hands calloused from work in the fields, Santiago and his *compañera*, Ana, joined the cooperative Miraflores[2] in 1983 as part of the FSLN's agrarian reform program. That evening in 1988, we sat outside their two-room cinderblock house and swatted away insects. Nicaragua's civil war was in its eighth year, but the running community joke was that any attempted attack on Miraflores by the anti-Sandinista "contra" rebels would be driven away by the swarms of mosquitoes and gnats from the nearby estuary, the Estero Real.

Santiago explained that during the 1978–1979 uprising against the Somoza family dictatorship, he had hidden grenades for the Sandinista guerrillas in his home. After the FSLN took power, Santiago was mobilized half a dozen times in Nicaragua's mountainous interior war zone as part of the Sandinista Army reserves and often wore his olive fatigues and army boots to work in the fields. Santiago saw in Nicaragua's revolutionary process of the 1980s an opportunity to radically transform the fabric of social life in his province and nation. He believed land would be taken from the large landowners (*terratenientes*) and distributed to the rural poor like himself and that the campesino would no longer be seen as "common" and "vulgar" but would become an equal, with dignity and a voice.

For Santiago and most Miraflores residents, the 1990 FSLN electoral defeat brought profound changes to the community, including the parcelization of land once held collectively. Over a decade later, I had another opportunity to visit with Santiago. He reiterated his support for the FSLN, at that point an opposition party, and then spent the next several hours discussing his participation in a series of new, externally funded sustainable development projects. Santiago demonstrated techniques he had recently learned to make natural pesticides from the neem seed and recalled with chagrin his earlier years of "ignorance" when he had cut down trees without thought and handled agrochemicals with little understanding of the risks to himself or the environment. Santiago no longer dressed in military clothing or owned an AK47 rifle to defend his community against a possible contra or U.S. invasion. By the early 2000s, confronted with an unfavorable national political context and responsive to the new interests of international donors, Santiago's activism had shifted to protection of the neighboring Estero Real mangrove forest and maintenance of a community nursery of tree seedlings as part of a European Community–financed reforestation project.

This transformation of Santiago and Miraflores activists from revolutionaries in the 1980s to participants in sustainability practices in the twenty-first century reflects broader regional trends. The social upheaval and violence of earlier decades in Central America, as well as leftist efforts to build and consolidate broad coalitions to address the region's profound structural inequalities and seize control of the state, have abated. Instead, an ideologically diverse set of institutions—ranging from conservative to progressive—as well as numerous community activists such as Santiago, are dedicating time, funds, and effort to smaller-scale, localized change in the name of "sustainable development."

Adams (2001) has stated of sustainable development that "more and more has been added to the concept, until it groans under the weight of ideas not only about the environment, but about equity, democracy, openness, and freedom" (369). An exploration of concepts of sustainability can seem a frustratingly unwieldy struggle to understand the linkages among these complex economic, social, and environmental processes. Yet I suggest that sustainability also offers a unique opportunity to conceptualize social change in a more holistic manner, to combine knowledge and theory, and possibly to move beyond the impasse of development (Adams 2001; Schuurman 1993). This book incorporates three case studies from rural Nicaragua, Costa Rica, and Panama. It applies a broad, working understanding of sustainable development in these settings as a process of beneficial change, as defined and guided by empowered communities in three key areas: (1) the meeting of basic material needs and economic accumulation; (2) social equity, cultural rights, and participation; and (3) environmental conservation.

A key premise of this book is that all discourses of sustainability are inherently political in the sense that they are built on underlying assumptions and values (e.g., material, emotional, spiritual, aesthetic) that cannot be predetermined through scientific methods or technical analysis. Rather, these intrinsic normative elements of sustainability discourses are the product of collective political processes that range from imposition by a small group of elites to democratic forms of decision making and that can take place at levels from the local to the transnational (Bryant and Bailey 1997; Goldman 1998b, 1998c; Rocheleau, Thomas-Slater, and Wangari 1996a; Peet and Watts 1996b; Moore and Schmitz 1995). In addition, development discourses and associated policies have inherent material and distributional consequences, benefits, and costs. They impact distinct groups in society differently, producing winners and losers. Development discourses, I argue, are a product of power relations and in turn influence relations and distribution of social, political, and discursive power.

While this book focuses on sustainable development discourses and practices as experienced and mediated at the local level, sustainability is in many senses a globalized set of discourses, understood here as "shared meanings of a phenomenon" whose intellectual and institutional origins are located largely outside the Central American region (Adger et al. 2001). The transnational origins of sustainable development discourses are multistranded, linked to environmental movements that emerged in the United States and Europe in the 1970s, to growing social justice critiques of neoliberal development policies, and to more recent policy shifts by international financial institutions (IFIs) such as the World Bank and the Inter-American Development Bank (IDB) (Wade 2004; Boas and McNeill 2004a; Fox and Brown 1998).

This recent institutional adoption of a discourse of sustainability can also be located within the broader rubric of globalization, a contested set of processes occurring at the levels of economics, technology, polity, culture, and consciousness.[3] McMichael (2000) describes the globalization project as "an emerging vision of the world and its resources as a globally organized and managed free trade/free enterprise economy pursued by a largely unaccountable political and economic elite" (348). A second premise of this book is that the discourses of sustainable development produced and reproduced by IFIs and associated policies are compatible with, and indeed may advance, the top-down globalization project identified by McMichael.

At times, institutional adopters of sustainability and some of their critics blur sustainability discourse into an undifferentiated whole, a seemingly monolithic construction based on universal economic principles or the machinations of development elites in the post–World War II period (Nustad 2001; Nederveen Pieterse 2000). I suggest, however, that precisely because development discourses have embodied implications for collective identities, ways of life, and the distribution of material costs and benefits, they are inherently contested. Sustainable development, I argue, likely holds very different meanings for a Central American peasant and a World Bank official. A priori assumptions that all actors share the same understanding of the term and a focus only on dominant constructions exclude more critical and potentially empowering alternative conceptualizations of sustainability. While recognizing the economic and institutional power of the dominant project, this book also focuses on points of opening and spaces of potential resistance to explore the conditions under which alternative and potentially empowering discourses and practices of sustainability may be produced and appropriated from below.

These efforts to unpack the concept of sustainable development are not merely semantic debates but hold more profound importance for the lives of Central America's poor majority, given that development discourse "promotes and justifies very real interventions and practices, and is inextricably linked to sets of material relationships, to certain kinds of specific activities and to the exercise of power" (Crush cited in Adams 2001:6). In rural Central America, hunger, sickness, social marginalization, and lack of access to land are lived experiences and pressing issues for the majority of the rural population (Proyecto Estado de la Nación 2003). Under these circumstances, I believe an ethical imperative exists to further explore short- to medium-term intermediate processes of sustainable development, as shaped and guided by empowered communities. The question of how or if relatively autonomous spaces of collective action can be achieved in practice, particularly within the context of the seemingly inexorable expansion of globalization, mass media, and legal-bureaucratic regimes into the most geographically remote zones Central America, is an important one.

A third premise of this book is that grassroots perspectives and contextualized local histories are critical to help us better delimit both the possibilities and the limitations of grassroots agency in globalized processes of sustainability. To this end, I examine sustainability in a grounded context, seeking to identify the potential mediating effects of nation-states and local histories, as well as social locations of class, ethnicity, and gender. A focus on geographically limited communities with relatively small populations offers the advantage of allowing a more holistic exploration of the interactions of economic, social, and environmental processes of sustainability.

A substantial body of literature offers excellent comparative insights into Central America's experiences with traditional development, highlighting regionally common patterns of economic and political dependence, deep inequality, civil wars, and, most recently, "low-intensity" democracy. A number of the seminal works on the region rely largely on macroeconomic data (Brockett 1990; Bulmer-Thomas 1987; Williams 1986) and interview data gathered from Central American elites (Paige 1997). Other studies have explored political violence in the region (Brockett 2005), as well as peasant mobilization within a context of civil war (Wood 2003; Horton 1999) and as part of transnational social movements (Edelman 1999). Likewise, studies of sustainability in Central America have provided valuable insights into the underlying dynamics of environmental destruction in the region and the implementation of development interventions within previously determined rubrics of sustainability (Danielson and Dijkstra 2001; Stonich 2000; Hatch and Swisher 1999; de Groot and Ruben 1997; Utting 1996; Leonard 1987). Few studies though, have explored in depth the very concept of sustainability as envisioned from rural, grassroots perspectives.

To address this issue, three rural and indigenous communities in Nicaragua, Costa Rica, and Panama were selected on the basis of a sociological comparative logic that sought research sites with common theoretically significant elements, as well as key differences. All three case study communities are located in geographically isolated regions, on the "periphery of the periphery," only in recent years linked more deeply to expanding global market forces. Second, these three communities are located on the border of environmentally fragile zones that in recent times, in the name of sustainability, have shifted from open commons to state-designated and regulated protected areas. Third, and most important, these case study communities were selected because they all have a trajectory of resistance and mobilization that offers a gateway to examine the conditions under which communities act as empowered agents of sustainability. As will be explored, however, the communities vary in their particular pathways to self-guided sustainability, with distinct groundings in class-based, environmental, and ethnic discourses. In these case studies, I also seek to strike a balance between overly structuralist approaches to the region—which may unintentionally disempower and reinforce resignation in the face of powerful global economic trends—and a naive rural populism by highlighting both the agency of grassroots actors and the internal and external constraints that limit them.

The primary fieldwork for this book was carried out over an eighteen-month period from 2000 to 2001, in the communities of Miraflores in northwestern Nicaragua, Ipetí in the Bayano region of eastern Panama, and Puerto Jiménez on the Osa peninsula of southern Costa Rica, with follow-up visits to Panama (2004) and Nicaragua (2006). I conducted a total of ninety-two formal interviews with community members, as well as nongovernmental organization and government personnel who have worked in the communities. In addition, I carried out participant observation and held ongoing conversations with key informants to construct a narrative of the communities' recent histories. Further details on the selection of interview subjects and country-specific methodological issues are provided in the appendix.

The discussions of sustainability that follow are not an attempt to bring an externally defined concept of development in through the back door, with an assumption that it is a necessary option for local communities. Rather, in all three case study communities, including the most isolated and tradition-bound community—the Kuna community of Ipetí, Panama—community members identified a series of needs and problems they face and supported forms of change, with the important condition that change be controlled by the communities and coincide with their particular vision of improved quality of life. The case studies explore these specific local visions of sustainability, highlighting the ways in which they overlap with or challenge dominant discourse of sustainability.

A second area explored in this book encompasses the multiple strands of dominant sustainable development discourse and policies—neoliberal reforms, sustainable development interventions, and environmental protection. The book considers the ways in which these multiple fields of the dominant project of sustainability undermine communities or provide new economic, cultural, and political opportunities for the rural poor and indigenous peoples. A third major theme explored in this book involves processes of community empowerment, which I define as pathways that reinforce the power, meaning, and integrity of local settings, enabling communities to collectively articulate and put into practice local visions of sustainability while contributing to broader social and structural transformation processes.

I would like to express my deep appreciation to the research participants, colleagues, friends, and family who helped make this book possible. I am particularly grateful to Antonio Ugalde and Bryan Roberts for their guidance, support, and valuable theoretical insights. I thank Christine Williams for her continued encouragement and enthusiasm for this project. Much of the funding for the fieldwork behind this book came from the Andrew W. Mellon Foundation. I greatly appreciate their generosity and Peter Ward's help in facilitating the funding process. I also gratefully acknowledge the funding and other support provided by Chapman University for later stages of this research.

I owe a very deep debt to the many people in Nicaragua, Costa Rica, and Panama who shared their stories and opinions with me. I greatly appreciate their time, patience, and understanding, and I have tried to do justice to what they shared with me. I found much hope and inspiration in the lives of the people I met through this research, and I have deep respect for those women and men who, in places far from the centers of power, carry out the daily, indefatigable "work of ants" in favor of sustainability and social justice. I acknowledge in particular Orlando, Alvaro, Doricita, María, Julio, Juan Felipe, and most of all Marta for their generous assistance and friendship during my fieldwork. I am appreciative of the Rojas-Ríos family for their warmth, which made Panama my second home, and for our barbeques in Torrijos-Carter. I thank my mom, Randy, and Deepa for their positive attitude and support over the years. Rigoberto has also accompanied me on this journey with his encouragement and deep affection for the region and *"la tierra prometida,"* Chiriquí.

Finally, I would like to recognize three special individuals who passed away while I was writing this book. Mary McKenna and Martha Goldsboro were strong and independent women before their time and always gave generously of themselves to others. I was privileged as well to have known Valentín Ríos Quintero, a *panameño* who worked and loved the land. He struggled through poverty to raise a large, loving family, with wisdom about life well beyond anything formal education can provide. Don Vale embodied much of what I admire most about rural Central America, and he will be greatly missed.

Grassroots Struggles for Sustainability in Central America

CHAPTER 1

Contested Visions of Sustainability

In 2002, the 180 nations participating in the Johannesburg World Summit on Sustainable Development reaffirmed a "collective responsibility to advance and strengthen the interdependent and mutually reinforcing pillars of sustainable development—economic development, social development and environmental protection—at local, national, regional and global levels" (United Nations Division for Sustainable Development 2002:1). Yet even before the conference had concluded, environmental, social justice, and women's rights nongovernmental organizations (NGOs) and activists were denouncing the summit's outcomes as vague, nonbinding, and ineffective (Von Frantzius 2004; Middleton and O'Keefe 2003). They expressed frustration that in areas such as energy policy, the precautionary principle, and northern government funding, the summit appeared to be retreating from, rather than advancing toward, sustainability.

The 2002 Earth Summit experience highlights the parallel processes of the early twenty-first century—global convergence toward a discourse of sustainable development and simultaneous underlying conflicts over the meanings, policies, and practices of sustainability. In Central America as in the rest of the developing world, policy papers from the World Bank and the Inter-American Development Bank (IDB), project descriptions from the United States Agency for International Development (USAID), and

1

annual reports of NGOs are filled with references to sustainable development.[1] As one Costa Rican NGO program director acknowledged in an interview, "Whether they really believe in it or [engage in it only] by force, everyone is doing sustainable development. A project will never get funded if it is not 'sustainable.'"[2]

DEFINING SUSTAINABLE DEVELOPMENT

Originally conceptualized primarily in environmental terms, sustainable development discourses have come to encompass complex interlocking values and goals, unarticulated assumptions, and both descriptive and normative elements. While dozens of definitions of sustainable development have been proposed (see Bowers 1995), the most widely cited definition comes from the 1987 Brundtland Commission report that defines sustainable development as development that "meets the needs of the present without compromising the ability of future generations to meet their own needs" (World Commission on Environment and Development 1987:43).[3] Definitions of sustainability generally incorporate three central components—economic, social, and environmental—maintained or improved over some medium- to long-term period. One way to conceptually sort discourses of sustainability is to consider which of the three components is prioritized (implicitly as well as explicitly) and placed as the underlying normatively positive force that should drive sustainability. I have termed these the institutionally "dominant," people-centered or "livelihood," and "ecocentric" discourses, respectively (see Figure 1.1). By the term *discourse,* I refer to broadly shared meanings of a phenomenon that are closely linked to policy sets (Adger et al. 2001).[4] Discourses also serve an explicit or implicit instrumental function for the groups that develop and propagate them.

These discourses differ in the way the relationships among economic, social, and environmental goals of sustainable development are conceptualized. Goals can be viewed as either positive and mutually reinforcing or negative and "zero-sum," in which gains in one area imply less gain or negative tradeoffs in another area. Thus, for example, the ecocentric model envisions a direct (indeed, normatively unacceptable) negative tradeoff between maximizing economic growth and social and environmental sustainability.

OVERVIEW OF SUSTAINABILITY DISCOURSES

Rather than advancing or receding purely on the basis of their technical and scientific merits, discourses of sustainability are embedded within broader relations of power and receive (or fail to receive) economic, polit-

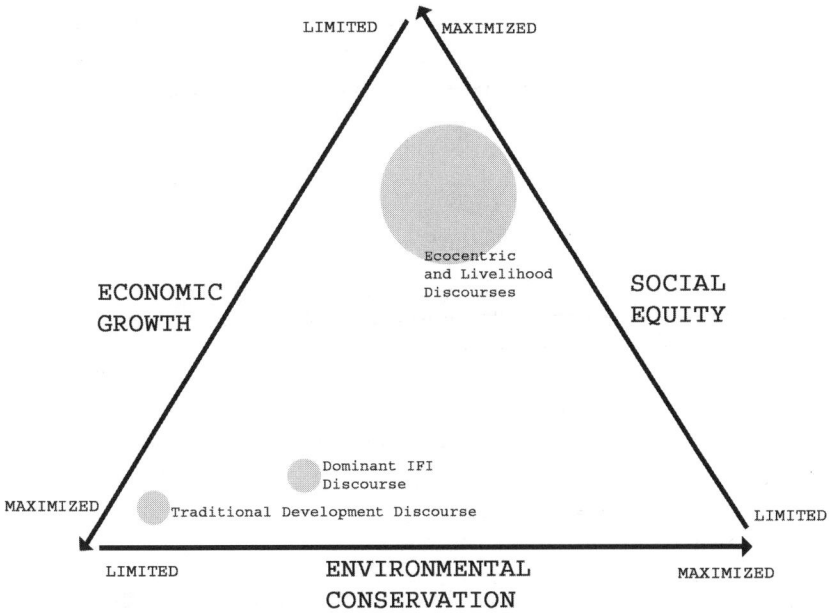

1.1. *Discourses of Sustainability*

ical, and institutional support from specific sets of actors and interests (Adams 2001). In the 1990s, institutions that had previously supported the traditional economic growth model—the World Bank, the IDB, and other international financial institutions (IFIs); donors such as USAID; and certain NGOs—moved their discourse toward a "post-Washington Consensus" that encompassed sustainable development (Onis and Senses 2005).[5] Of these institutions, the World Bank has made the greatest effort to articulate this perspective for a broader, non-economist audience. The World Bank also increasingly identifies itself as a transnational "knowledge bank" and contains possibly the world's largest collection of comparative data on developing countries (Lera St. Clair 2006:78). For these reasons, my discussion of dominant sustainability discourse draws primarily on more general World Bank policy documents and reports, as well as Central America–specific World Bank documents. This sustainability discourse and linked policy orientations place their greatest emphasis on economic accumulation and efficiency as the driving force behind sustainability (World Bank 2003d). I refer to this as the dominant discourse because it has been reproduced and transmitted by powerful international financial institutions and national donor agencies and is embedded in their development policies and practices (see Table 1.1).

This market-focused approach contends that economic growth at the macro level is essential for human well-being and quality of life and is the central means by which poverty, social inequity, and environmental deterioration can be reduced over the medium to long term. Dominant sustainable development posits a long-term "win-win-win" correlation among the economic, social, and environmental components of sustainability.

The livelihood or people-centered discourse of sustainable development contends from a normative perspective that social justice and empowerment of local communities should be the driving force of sustainability constructed from below. This discourse, which has its origins in communities in the global South, grassroots organizations, and NGOs, values place-based ways of life (Guha and Martínez-Alier 1998; Friedmann and Rangan 1993). It seeks to deepen and expand cultural diversity and democratic rights and thereby to strengthen the capacity of communities to act as caretakers of their local environments.

The third broad discourse of sustainability, with a stronger presence in Europe and the United States than in the Third World, is the ecocentric or deep ecology discourse of sustainable development, which places its greatest value on the natural world and perceives nature not as socially constructed but rather as having an intrinsic value in and of itself. In contrast to dominant sustainability discourses linked to modernization theory, science, and rationality, ecocentric discourse draws on romantic, transcendentalist, bio-ethics, and utopian worldviews (Adams 2001). Deep ecology models often draw on a vision of a past "Arcadian golden age of human harmony with nature" that has been lost through the formation of social hierarchies, capitalism, or patriarchy as forms of human domination of humans and nature (Benton 1994:39). Some deep ecologists reject anthropomorphism and posit a biospherical egalitarianism that places all life forms on a par with each other (Bryner 2001). Others emphasize that the emotional and spiritual, as well as material, well-being of human society is inextricably linked to the well-being of nature (Adams 2001). This discourse prioritizes the environment and posits a negative tradeoff between its ecological goals and economic growth, which is to be constrained or, in more radical discourse, halted altogether. Because ecocentric discourses and practices have a limited presence in Central America, the following sections focus primarily on dominant and livelihood discourses of sustainable development.

DOMINANT SUSTAINABILITY DISCOURSE

The shift of dominant institutional discourse toward sustainability in the 1990s was linked to protests and lobbying campaigns carried out by

Table 1.1 Comparison of Discourses of Sustainability

Component of Sustainability		Discourses of Sustainability		
		Dominant	Livelihood	Ecocentric
Overview	Origins and key proponents	IFIs, USAID, mainstream NGOs	grassroots movements in the South; some NGOs; political ecologists	grassroots movements in the North
	Core value(s)	economic growth	equity, diversity, and empowerment	nature has intrinsic value
	Epistemology	scientific, rational	ethical, social justice	emotional, spiritual, ethical
	Scope	narrow technocratic, small fixes to existing institutions	broader structural transformations	broader structural transformations
Economic component	Economic growth	neoliberal reforms to promote economic growth	a qualitatively different form of growth	limited or no economic growth
Social equity component	Poverty	economic growth reduces poverty	economic growth may exacerbate poverty	economic growth may exacerbate poverty
	Participation	instrumental project participation, good governance	local empowerment; decentralized, diverse governance; substantive democracy	local empowerment, substantive democracy
Environmental component	Causes of environmental destruction	the poor, government policies	wealthy classes, transnational corporations	wealthy classes, transnational corporations, population growth
	Environmental conservation	expansion of protected areas; buffer zones, small-scale ICD projects	community control of natural resources	community control of natural resources, transnational environmental institutions

increasingly global environmental and human rights NGOs and grassroots organizations in the 1980s, which were critical of the negative social and environmental consequences of the traditional development projects funded by these agencies (Wade 2004; Sindzingre 2004; Fox and Brown 1998; Bryant and Bailey 1997).[6] Economists and financiers who have played a central role in developing dominant institutional analysis and policies place less emphasis on these political processes and instead make claims for validity through technical discourses of econometrics and cross-country regressions (Sindzingre 2004).[7] This dominant model of sustainability is reformist rather than transformational and is compatible with and indeed may advance ideological and economic projects of globalization from above and economic liberalization. An examination of the reports and directives of these institutions suggests that many of the values and assumptions of the traditional development model—especially economic growth, free markets, efficiency, rationality, and individualism—remain at its core, even as development is now redefined as sustainable (World Bank 2006a, 2003d; Adams 2001; Fox and Brown 1998; Warford, Munasinghe, and Cruz 1997).

Economic Component

If one asks what is essential to improve human welfare and happiness, what drives sustainability, the answer first and foremost is material accumulation—optimizing income flows while maintaining human-made and natural capital stocks.[8] The overall tone of this discourse is optimistic. If a packet of neoliberal reforms is correctly and consistently applied, the argument goes, economic growth will follow, and this expanding "economic pie" will alleviate problems of poverty in the medium to long term (Collier and Dollar 2002; Wodon and Ayres 2000).[9] This discourse, while acknowledging potential negative social and environmental consequences of traditional development interventions, ultimately relies on a managerial optimism that believes negative consequences can be minimized through the use of mitigating measures (World Bank 2004a, 2003d, 1999a).

In its economic component, the dominant discourse draws on neoliberalism, a revival of nineteenth-century liberalism that holds that the optimizing efforts of self-interested entrepreneurs and efficiently coordinated self-regulating markets produce economic growth (Hartwick and Peet 2003). The application of neoliberal policy reforms in Latin America dates from the region's accumulation of external debt in the 1970s and the subsequent emergence of the Washington Consensus and loan conditionality among IFIs (Boas and McNeill 2004b; Chase 2002).[10] Neoliberal policies favor an outward-oriented export economy and typically include a diminished the role for the state, reduced fiscal deficits, privatization of publicly owned enterprises, deregulation of domestic labor markets, trade and interest rate liberalization, tax reforms, secure property rights, and free capital flows to support long-term economic growth (Chase 2002).[11] To date, proponents have credited neoliberal reforms in Latin America with bringing hyperinflation under control, increasing capital flows in the region, modernizing governance structures, strengthening property regimes and opportunities for small-scale entrepreneurship, and expanding nontraditional manufacturing exports (Collier and Dollar 2002; Gwynne 1997; Bulmer-Thomas 1996; Lustig 1995).[12]

Social Component

By the 1990s, however, World Bank analysts had come to acknowledge critics' claim that Latin America's historically high levels of inequality, combined with the negative impacts of macro-economic shocks, have thwarted more rapid poverty reduction in the region (Wodon and Ayres 2000). IFI discourse has shifted to give greater emphasis to the second component of sustainability: social and economic equity. It now promotes "pro-poor" growth that seeks to improve the overall investment climate and empower poor people by investing in their assets, particularly education and health care (World Bank 2006a; Sindzingre 2004).[13] Dominant discourse also argues that markets are distorted by rent-seeking state elites and now recognizes a need for "good governance" (World Bank 2006a, 2003d; Mosse 2004; Wodon and Ayres 2000). A government that practices good governance is transparent and accountable, with limited functions, including the regulatory oversight of privatization and liberalization of financial markets. Good governance, in other words, is not seen as an end in itself but rather as a means to create and maintain the conditions for effective functioning of markets and economic growth (Onis and Senses 2005; Taylor 2004).

Similar to traditional development discourse, the new dominant vision still seeks to facilitate the integration of individuals into competitive market relations (Onis and Senses 2005).[14] An increased role for organized civil society has been added, however. Civil society is now charged with the provision of services no longer covered by the state and is given the more political role of restraining and demanding accountability from state elites to protect the neutrality and benefits of markets (World Bank 2006a). As will be further explored in Chapter 3, dominant institutions have also adopted the language of empowerment of their critics, defined in one World Bank study as the ability to make effective choices linked to agency and opportunity structures (Narayan 2005:5).

Environmental Component

The environmental component of dominant discourses can be termed eco-capitalism or "light green" environmentalism to distinguish it from more radical deep ecology perspectives. It "predicates environmental protection on the promotion and maintenance of a liberal economic order" and favors market incentives over state regulation as tools to bring about positive environmental outcomes (Bernstein 2001:4). This discourse highlights the mutual, potentially positive relationships between economic growth and environmental conservation (Collier and Dollar 2002).[15] As with good governance, the new discourse focuses not on potential damaging impacts of market forces but rather on government interventions, inefficiencies, and subsidies, which, it is argued, distort land and natural resource markets and lead to environmental deterioration (World Bank 2001b). In Central America, the World Bank has funded programs to both expand and improve administration of environmentally protected areas and to strengthen private property regimes in zones deemed environmentally vulnerable (World Bank 2003c, 1998).[16] Originally, the model's "light" environmentalism was associated with the policing approach to protected areas in which local populations, viewed as environmentally predatory, were physically excluded from lands and natural resources now declared under the control of the state. By the early 2000s, however, from an anti-statist and instrumentalist perspective, dominant sustainability had shifted to a discourse of local participation in environmental conservation measures (Collier and Dollar 2002; Peet and Watts 1996b).[17]

CRITICAL PERSPECTIVES

Critics have interpreted these institutional shifts in discourse and policy from a range of perspectives (see Table 1.2). The more optimistic end of the critical continuum interprets the adoption of sustainability as a product of institutional reassessment and a genuine effort by IFIs, particularly the World Bank, to learn from past errors and to respond and be accountable to their NGO and grassroots critics. A slightly different analysis suggests that IFIs have responded reluctantly to their critics' growing transnational organizational and political power and therefore seek to limit change to the level of discourse and resist putting the new policies into practice in meaningful ways.[18] In other words, in this analysis, dominant institutions such as the World Bank still prioritize the traditional development goal of maximizing economic growth. To the degree to which social and environmental considerations appear to constrain this goal, such measures will be implemented minimally in practice or be ignored altogether (Fox and Brown 1998; Dore 1997; Peet and Watts 1996b; Yearly 1996).[19] Both of these outlooks imply that IFIs' new focus on the environment, par-

Table 1.2 Contested Components of Sustainability

Dominant IFI Discourse	Critical Responses
Economic component	
"Pro-poor" economic growth reduces poverty	Market reforms increase poverty and inequality
Targeted support during transition periods protects those most vulnerable	Transitional, targeted support for the poor is inadequate
Investment in human assets	Also need redistributive measures, profound economic transformation
Social component	
Ideologically neutral and apolitical	Dominant discourse is a disguised ideological project
Increased spaces for participation	New spaces for participation are largely symbolic, constrained; may disempower participants
Good governance and accountability	Excludes alternative forms and roles of the state from democratic debate
Environmental component	
Support for expansion of protected areas and indigenous collective land rights	Such measures undermined by broader model of economic liberalization
Increased economic growth reduces poverty and pressure on environment	Current forms of economic growth expand/intensify unsustainable resource use

ticipation, and good governance is at least potentially beneficial to the rural poor, in that institutions may offer material resources, new spaces for grassroots voice and participation, and mitigating measures against environmental deterioration.

At the other end of the continuum, critics contend that this dominant shift in discourse toward sustainability does not simply represent a defensive concession to pressures from below. Rather, it is seen as a "greenwash," an elite project to silence and demobilize critics and "to accommodate crisis ridden capitalism" by advancing a project of global economic liberalization and extending hegemonic control over physical and social spaces once distant from bureaucratic and state elites (Sachs 1999; Goldman 1998c:23; Rahnema and Bawtree 1997; Escobar 1995). In this interpretation, dominant sustainability is not simply a cosmetic institutional slight of hand but a more pernicious project.

Political economy critiques of IFI approaches to sustainability have found theoretical expression in the new academic field of political ecology, characterized by Peet and Watts (1996b) as a "confluence between ecologically rooted social science and the principles of political economy" (6).[20] Political ecology attempts to bring together a crisis of development and an environmental crisis that have been distant in concept and practice, to argue that Third World environmental crises cannot be understood in isolation from political and economic contexts, specifically contexts of power and distribution (Adams 2001; Bryant and Bailey 1997). Political ecology explores such topics as ideological orientations toward resource use, internal interests, the role of the state, class structure, market relations, and subsistence and market production (Schmink and Wood, cited in Stonich, Bort, and Ovares 1999).

The political ecology critique suggests that the pro-poor measures of dominant sustainability—targeted programs to cushion the most vulnerable and help them develop human capital—are insufficient and ultimately undermined by the broader policies of economic liberalization supported by dominant institutions (Utting 1996). This process may also represent a further extension and deepening of transnational market relations into what were once geographically remote zones (Robinson 2003). Political ecology contends that rather than facilitating economic growth, policies of economic liberalization that remain at the center of dominant policy reinforce historical patterns of inequality, poverty, and social marginality among the poor, indigenous peoples, and women in particular (Adams 2001; Bryant and Bailey 1997; Peet and Watts 1996b). Any benefits from state- and NGO-sponsored sustainability projects, what Hickey and Mohan (2004b:10) term "imminent development," are overwhelmed by historical processes of social change linked to economic liberalization, or immanent development. Critics contend that the negative distributive impacts of the expansion and intensification of market relations fuel processes of environmental destruction, both directly and indirectly (Utting 1996; Painter and Durham 1995; Stonich 1993; Faber 1993). Environmental damage may occur directly as particular forms of economic growth promote the unsustainable expansion and intensification of natural resource extraction activities by national and transnational corporations. The increased inequality and subsistence insecurity may also intensify unsustainable use of land and natural resources by the poor (Utting 1996; Faber 1993).

In addition to the political ecology literature, a loose body of postdevelopment literature offers a strong ideological critique of dominant sustainability.[21] This literature draws on Foucault and discourse analysis to question the embedded Eurocentric assumptions and representations of mainstream development. Some of the postdevelopment literature rejects development altogether, calling for an alternative to development (Escobar 1995). Many postdevelopment scholars characterize IFI policy shifts as a project of cultural homogenization and expansion of power by northern elites and bureaucracies (Nustad 2001; Sachs 1999). Newer environmentalist institutional bodies such as the Global Environmental Fund designate the atmosphere and biodiversity in Third World tropical forests as "global commons" and thus override historical local access and claims to natural resources (Hildyard 1993).[22] Ferguson (1990) asserts that even when development interventions "fail" to meet their self-defined project goals, they may still succeed in expanding and entrenching bureaucratic state power.

In addition, postdevelopment analysis contends that under conditions of formal democracy, sustainable development interventions form part of a more insidious, palliative process to depoliticize and demobilize the radical potential of grassroots organizations (Goldman 2005, 2001, 1998a; Escobar 2000, 1995; Sachs 1999, 1993; Rahnema and Bawtree 1997; Ferguson 1990). Critics contend that IFIs have co-opted the language of participation, empowerment, and environmentalism as a means to obfuscate the continuation of unsustainable projects and make it more difficult for activists and NGOs to oppose such policies (Fox and Brown 1998; Dore 1997; Peet and Watts 1996b; Yearley 1996).[23] Similarly, Goldman (1998b) suggests that dominant sustainability discourse is an ideological project to scientize and depoliticize sustainability debates, framing the values and claims of limited elite groups as technical and universal truths. Markets, for example, are naturalized, while regulatory interventions are represented as "distortions" (Deininger and Binswinger 1999). The de facto effect of such a "nonpolitical" epistemology, critics believe, is to limit articulation and consideration of alternative discourses of development or alternatives to development. In Central America, for example, dominant discourse essentially removes from the table "political" issues of structural inequalities, such as unequal landholding patterns and power that is maldistributed, even under formal democracy. It also excludes a series of distributive policy measures—land reform, state subsidies, collective land management, and debt relief (World Bank 2006a, 2003c, 1998).

Dominant institution sustainability discourse now incorporates policies to create or expand spaces for community participation, promote the development of social capital, and strengthen grassroots collective action (World Bank 2006a). Critics suggest, however, that this does not represent additive or new spaces for mobilization and empowerment but is rather an elite attempt to control and "deradicalize" grassroots groups, shifting their more transformative claims, time, and energy to more manageable, small-scale project activities (Goldman 2005, 2001; Ferguson 1990). Participation in development projects may be highly manipulated, as power relationships are disguised, and it may reinforce institutional, financial, and ideological dependencies or co-opt leaders (Brown 2004). More broadly, dominant discourse envisions a specific form of democracy, or good governance, in which states should be transparent and accountable and provide for market stability through sound fiscal and monetary policies and a stable regulatory framework (World Bank 2006a). Demmers and colleagues (2004b) suggest, however, that this predetermined, normative model of the state excludes the inherently political processes of collectively determining states' scope and functions.

Political ecology and postdevelopment critiques, I believe, offer several suggestions on how Central American community experiences of sustainability should be approached. First, we need to be particularly sensitive to the inherent issues of power and inequality and concealed values and assumptions of development discourses. Similarly, sustainable development cannot be understood from a narrow, technical perspective or from a singular focus on the seeming proximate agents of environmental destruction: the rural poor who cut down the rain forest along the agricultural frontier in Central America and other regions. Rather, studies of sustainability need to examine the complex links among affluence, accumulation, poverty, and the environment. Nonplace actors must also be incorporated into analyses of community and the ways globalized discourses and practices may be relocalized, reworked, engaged, and transformed in local arenas of social encounters (Long 2000). Third, sustainable development should be considered not only in its imminent forms of planned interventions but also as embedded in broader immanent processes of economic liberalization and the expansion and deepening of capitalism (Hickey and Mohan 2004b).

Critical perspectives of dominant discourses and practices of sustainable development should not, I argue, be equated with normative support for the status quo—conditions of hunger, morbidity, exclusion, and repression among rural populations of Central America—or with a belief that traditional and indigenous societies should (or even somehow could) be essentialized and frozen in time. Rather, I suggest that mirrored in these critiques is an implicit foil of the dominant construction, a vision of social change emerging from the perspectives, experiences, and creativity of those same communities now targeted by development institutions. In this sense, those who seek to qualitatively transform processes of development and those who reject it altogether coalesce in support of a qualitatively different form of social change. This form of change is bottom-up and small-scale, supports appropriate technology and self-sufficiency, and gives special recognition to traditional and indigenous place-based actors, including small farmers, shifting cultivators, fishers, and hunter-gatherers (Bryant and Bailey 1997; Moffat 1996).

LIVELIHOOD ALTERNATIVES

I broadly refer to alternative forms of sustainability that prioritize sociocultural values of diversity, equity, and way of life as livelihood discourses.

This discourse is suspicious of both globalized markets and transnational regulatory structures that impede local access in the name of a "global" environmentalism. Livelihood discourse focuses on the control of land and resources by diverse, place-based grassroots actors and a more profound empowerment of local communities (Bryant and Bailey 1997; Peet and Watts 1996a; Redclift 1987). Scholars suggest that such livelihood movements of the poor have emerged as localized responses to processes of economic globalization—the extension and deepening of market forces, modernizing development projects, and penetration of transnational capital and multinational corporations into once remote spaces—that threaten both the environment and the livelihoods of traditional and indigenous peoples (Guha and Martínez-Alier 1998; Bryant and Bailey 1997).[24]

In contrast to the scientific and technocratic approach of dominant discourse, livelihood discourses of sustainability recognize multiple epistemologies, in particular traditional knowledge systems developed not necessarily through experimentation and replication but through observation and localized experiences. Dominant discourse places at its center human beings whose interactions with the environment can be understood primarily through universal applications of cost-benefit analyses (Guha and Martínez-Alier 1998; Peet and Watts 1996a; Friedmann and Rangan 1993). In contrast, the livelihood perspective views rural residents and the indigenous as deeply embedded in community structures and influenced by shared beliefs and norms. Community in a weaker sense may be instrumentalist, a group of people bounded by geographic space at a particular point in time who form a committee to participate in a particular sustainable development intervention. The livelihood model, however, implies a qualitatively different conception of community. In the case studies, I follow this lead and consider community to be a bounded group that constructs, negotiates, and defends common identity and shared interests. Communities in this sense also often have unique historical, religious, and cultural relationships with their surrounding natural environment.

The livelihood perspective also challenges the mainstream characterization of the poor as environmentally destructive, elite representations of "dark and poor peasant masses destroying forests and mountainsides with axes and machetes" (Escobar 1995:51). As Chambers states, "The poor are not the problem, they are the solution" (cited in Adams 2001:370). While acknowledging that the poor do at times, under pressure, act in environmentally destructive ways, proponents of the livelihood discourse argue that poor and indigenous communities with strong placed-based identities are more likely to serve as environmental caretakers, protecting intact ecosystems and playing a critical role in the recuperation of degraded areas. Local communities are not simply reactive, the argument goes, but

13

knowledgeable, concerned, and active (Peet and Watts 1996a; Friedmann and Rangan 1993; Reilly 1992; Korten 1990). This perspective suggests that communities have developed often complex, informal, locally appropriate norms that govern the sustainable use of natural resources. Cultural diversity, linked most commonly to place and ethnicity, is not only seen to hold intrinsic value but is also critical for long-term environmental conservation. As will be explored in Chapter 3, livelihood discourses place a deeper form of community empowerment as a central and critical element of sustainability.

ALTERNATIVE PATHWAYS TO SUSTAINABILITY

Critical approaches to date have been weaker, however, in delineating pathways through which local communities and larger human societies might move toward empowerment and alternative practices of sustainability. The dominant discourse, with its fundamental optimism that sustainability can be achieved through technological advances, global markets, and targeted project interventions, requires relatively minor fixes to existing social and economic structures. In contrast, alternative models of sustainability must grapple with more transformative forms of economic and social change and the strong resistance such change will likely engender. The critical scholarship would benefit from further clarity in terms of which social groups are to lead the struggle toward empowered sustainability and how the formation of such social groups might occur. Earlier Marxist theory saw the working class as the agent of social transformation. The livelihood literature falls back on more ambiguous and fluid coalitions of the poor and lower middle classes, similar to the popular classes Central American revolutionaries sought to mobilize in the 1970s and 1980s.

Much of the critical literature locates traditional rural communities and indigenous peoples at the vanguard of struggles for sustainability, arguing that such communities are driven by cultural, spiritual, and social justice values to defend their unique ways of life that are deeply embedded in the surrounding natural environment (Peet and Watts 1996a; Friedmann and Rangan 1993; Reilly 1992). A weakness of this approach, however, is its tendency to draw a dichotomy between undifferentiated, virtuous local communities, with their traditional knowledge and epistemologies that function in harmony with the natural world, and the environmentally destructive external forces of modernization. This dichotomy seems to mirror the universalizing assumptions of dominant discourse by removing local peoples from their specific historical, social, and cultural contexts. It may simplify or even romanticize local communities, and it highlights the necessity of moving beyond stereotypes of "predatory" states and transnational corporations pitted against "eco-friendly" NGOs and locals (Bryant and Bailey 1997:25). Representations have polarized, for example, between Central America's poor as environmental destroyers who need to be taught environmental management skills by outside experts and the poor as "natural" environmental stewards.

I argue that we need to consider Central America's poor not as predetermined actors but rather as groups whose relationships with the environment, ideological perspectives, and organizational forms are mediated through a range of factors—including specific community histories, subcultures, and social locations (such as class, gender, race/ethnicity)—as well as broader structural transformations linked to globalization. Rather than assume a priori that Central America's rural poor will, if allowed, act as agents of sustainability, I believe we need to explore the specific contexts under which such empowerment may occur. I suggest that empowerment—which I define as pathways that reinforce the power, meaning, and integrity of local settings—is an intrinsically valuable process. It may also enable communities to collectively articulate and put into practice local visions of sustainability while contributing to broader social and structural transformation processes.

The postdevelopment literature, in its call for community withdrawal from participation in dominant economic and social institutions, implies that empowerment is fundamentally an organic, internal process (Sachs 1999). Embedded in this approach is an assumption that communities collectively hold, to some degree intact, alternative visions of society that draw on localized subaltern histories, ethnic traditions, and gender-specific experiences and contrast sharply with dominant constructions of the "good life." In essence, the global is equated with hegemonic discourse, the local with counterhegemonic discourse. Community in Central America is a complex and diverse phenomenon, however, particularly given recent migratory patterns and longer-term influences of transnational processes (Edelman 1999; Robinson 2003). Alongside relatively intact, traditional communities that may draw upon unique collective histories are communities long penetrated by dominant institutions not only in economic and political terms but also at the level of culture and consciousness.[25] There is a need to expand our understanding of the ways more fragmented, mobile communities, influenced by dominant practices and discourses, may construct or reconstruct alternatives to dominant perspectives. Under these circumstances, the struggle for locally based sustainability is more complex than simply maintaining the knowledge and practices of intact communities.

Likewise, the global-local relationship is more complex than unambiguous local resistance to global processes. Communities may find empowerment not from withdrawal but rather by engaging with globalized and dominant discourses and practices, attempting to appropriate them and draw out their more radical potential (Bebbington 2000, 1999). This book takes the latter approach to explore ways in which selective engagement with globalized discourses and practices of sustainability, under conditions of community strength and outward unity, may open spaces for both autonomy and participation. I argue that the expansion of dominant sustainability in Central America does not imply an inevitable and universal breakdown of local practices. In essence, just as it is possible for community-state-NGO interactions to perpetuate a downward spiral of cooptation, division, and disempowerment, so is it possible that selective engagement can provide communities with material and organizational resources, as well as opportunities to explore and appropriate critical discourses. Sustainable development discourses and policies form a field of struggle within which community residents have appropriated class, ethnic, and ethically based identities to draw boundaries of commonality, negotiate and articulate collective interests, and make claims toward the state and other external actors.

In addition, the critical literature highlights issues of power, inequality, and distribution as key to more profound sustainability. I believe it is important to consider these dynamics not only at the international and national levels but also at the local level. Inequalities of class, gender, ethnicity, age, and so forth also permeate everyday community life. While these case studies focus on relatively empowered and democratic communities as social actors, this is not meant to suggest that these communities hold predetermined common perspectives or interests. In fact, the case studies explore the ways discourses of sustainability prioritize certain types of claims over others. Likewise, community empowerment, while providing certain collective benefits, is also an internally partial and unequal process.

OVERVIEW OF THE BOOK

Dominant sustainable development is a multistranded process that incorporates a range of institutional actors and interlocking policies operating at the global, national, and local levels whose impacts may be mutually reinforcing or contradictory. The case studies that follow incorporate these multiple fields of community-state-NGO interaction—neoliberal economic reforms, the extension of environmental regulations, and sustainable development projects—to explore the implications of the new dominant discourse and policies for the empowerment of communities as active agents of sustainability. In particular, I seek through these grassroots experiences to identify conditions that facilitate the upward spiral of empowerment described earlier.

Chapter 2 introduces the three case study communities and provides an overview of their post–World War II histories, exploring regional traditional development patterns of agro-export-led growth, state-led modernization, and the more recent challenges of top-down environmentalism. The chapter links these experiences of traditional development in Central America to community empowerment, in particular the emergence of critical consciousness and community control of material resources that underlie community mobilization. Chapter 3 is the first of three chapters that explore a set of activities—ecotourism, nontraditional exports, and indigenous collective land titling—that have been promoted by dominant institutions as a pathway to sustainable development. It analyzes the economic, sociocultural, and environmental impacts of Costa Rica's ecotourism boom on the Osa peninsula. Chapter 4 explores three key themes of the case studies: the emergence of community discourses of sustainability and the ways they overlap with or challenge dominant discourse; the impact of environmental protectionism, sustainable development projects, and neoliberal reforms on community empowerment; and factors that undermine communities' ability to act as agents of sustainability.

The focus shifts in Chapters 5 and 6 to the Nicaragua case study, first exploring the expansion of nontraditional exports—in particular shrimp production—and claims that this market activity advances social and environmental sustainability. Similar to the earlier chapter on Costa Rica, Chapter 6 examines Nicaraguan local visions of sustainability, interactions with state agencies and NGOs, and dynamics of community empowerment.

Chapter 7 is the first of two chapters that explore the experiences and perceptions of the Kuna Indians of Panama. It details the ways the Kunas have been able to appropriate a shift in the global discourse toward support for collective, indigenous land rights among development institutions to advance their local claims for legal recognition of semiautonomous *comarca*. Chapter 8 parallels earlier chapters in probing in greater depth Kuna discourses of sustainability, state-NGO interactions, and local experiences of empowerment.

Chapter 9 summarizes, in a comparative framework, the main findings from each of the case studies, while Chapter 10 draws linkages between these findings and the broader theoretical debates on sustainable development.

CHAPTER

2

POVERTY AND FORESTS

Development and (Dis)empowerment in Central America

The history of Central America reflects a complex interplay of convergences linked to global processes and divergences mediated by nationally and locally specific historical trajectories.[1] Just over half of Central America's 33 million inhabitants live in poverty, and approximately one in four live in extreme poverty (Proyecto Estado de la Nación 2003:47). Central America's high levels of poverty and inequality are linked to the region's insertion into a mercantilist and, later, capitalist global economy as an exporter of primary products. Following formal independence in the 1820s, the expansion of coffee exports drew the small, open economies of Central America more deeply into world markets (Paige 1997). In the post–World War II period, subsidized infrastructure development and growing U.S. demand led to a further expansion of agricultural exports of beef, sugar, cotton, and bananas (Robinson 2003; Paige 1997; Brockett 1990; Bulmer-Thomas 1987). While limited industrialization took place during the Central American Common Market of the 1960s and 1970s and later in the 1990s, agriculture has continued to play a key role in the region's economy. In the twenty-first century, almost one-third of the region's population still works in agriculture (Proyecto Estado de la Nación 2003).

In addition to its dependent and highly unequal historical model of economic development, Central America has been subject to strong external military and political interventions and pressure from the United States over the past century.² In the post–World War II period, such interventions supported the model of agro-export-led economic development, described earlier, and helped exclude, often through support of anti-leftist state violence, alternative conceptualizations and practices of economic and social organization. Authoritarian rule prevailed in El Salvador, Guatemala, Honduras, and Nicaragua through the 1980s as nationally specific paths influenced elites to opt for repression over incorporation of popular classes (Paige 1997). In contrast, Costa Rica's democracy, dating from 1948, has been characterized by relatively high levels of legitimacy and a fairly strong social safety net (Seligson 2003; Edelman 1999; Watson et al. 1998). Panama, in turn, experienced military populism and more limited political repression from the 1968 coup of General Omar Torrijos to the U.S. invasion in 1989 (Elton 1997; Zimbalist and Weeks 1991; Priestley 1986; Ropp 1982).

EMPOWERMENT

The remainder of this chapter introduces the three case study communities in Nicaragua, Panama, and Costa Rica and explores the ways Central America's traditional development patterns have impacted communities, in particular their capacity to act as empowered agents of sustainability. As with sustainable development, the discourse of empowerment has been adopted by a wide range of institutions and actors and has a series of meanings (Rowlands 1997). In its weakest sense, "empowerment" may refer to little more than passive approval and participation in projects predesigned by outside agencies, as well as the instrumental use of community voluntary labor to reduce project costs (Long 2001; Pretty and Chambers 2000). Other scholars such as Rowlands (1995), however, identify more profound forms of empowerment as processes "by which people become aware of their own interests and how those relate to others, in order to both participate from a position of greater strength in decision making and actually influence such decisions" (107).³

Definitions of empowerment typically encompass several common elements. First, empowerment involves critical consciousness, an awareness and ability to articulate collective interests, as well as a degree of autonomy, in the sense that consciousness is not easily manipulated or controlled by external actors or institutions with hegemonic perspectives. Empowerment is also less a static condition than a process of interaction and learning. It implies an individual and collective capacity to influence wider decision-making processes and advance social justice and environmental sustainability (Hickey and Mohan 2004b; Korten 1990). An additional element, which I argue is particularly significant in regions such as

Central America, is access to a material base of support. Unless peoples are able to meet at least basic needs—food, shelter, health care, and education—meaningful empowerment cannot occur.

MIRAFLORES, NICARAGUA

The first case study community, Miraflores, is located in the southern portion of the province of Chinandega, one of Nicaragua's most agriculturally productive zones, with deep, friable soil of recent volcanic origin and high organic matter content (Williams 1986). To the west of Miraflores lies a chain of volcanoes, including the Casitas volcano, where deforestation contributed to a deadly mudslide during Hurricane Mitch in 1998. Miraflores is also located on the southern edge of the Estero Real (Royal Estuary), a protected 46,000-hectare (ha) mangrove ecosystem that plays a key role in the life cycles of a number of marine plants and animals, particularly shrimp (IDR and CATIE 1999). Miraflores's twenty-three households live in a cluster of two- and three-room cinder block houses and farm 162 ha of land. The community is just above the Nicaraguan poverty line, with an average yearly household income the equivalent of US$429 and infrastructure that includes unreliable electrical service, an elementary school, and a day care center (Morales, Aburto, and Aburto 1999).[4] The nearby town of Tonalá offers access to a health clinic, a high school, and public transportation over dirt roads to the provincial capital, Chinandega city (see Map 2.1, Table 2.1).

While Miraflores is a relatively new community, established in 1980 as part of the Sandinista National Liberation Front's (FSLN's) agrarian reform program, residents have long-term ties to the region and retain individual and collective narratives of the earlier era of the Somoza family dictatorship, which extended from 1937 to 1979. In the first half of the twentieth century, Chinandega produced high yields of corn for national and regional markets, while more marginal lands were used as pasture and kept forested (Barahona Najlis and Mendoza 1999). Growing markets in the United States, combined with support from regional governments and international financial institutions (IFIs) in the form of infrastructure projects, subsidies, and financing, led to the rapid expansion of agro-exports of cotton, sugar, and cattle along Central America's Pacific Coast in the 1950s and 1960s (see Paige 1997; Brockett 1990; Stonich 1993; Williams 1986; Biderman 1982). Under traditional development criteria and at the macro level, the agro-export booms were a success in that they propelled Central America's high economic growth rates, which averaged 6.2 percent in the 1960s and 1970s (see Table 2.2).[5]

Studies suggest, however, that the economic benefits of the region's agro-export booms were captured largely by large landowners (Enriquez

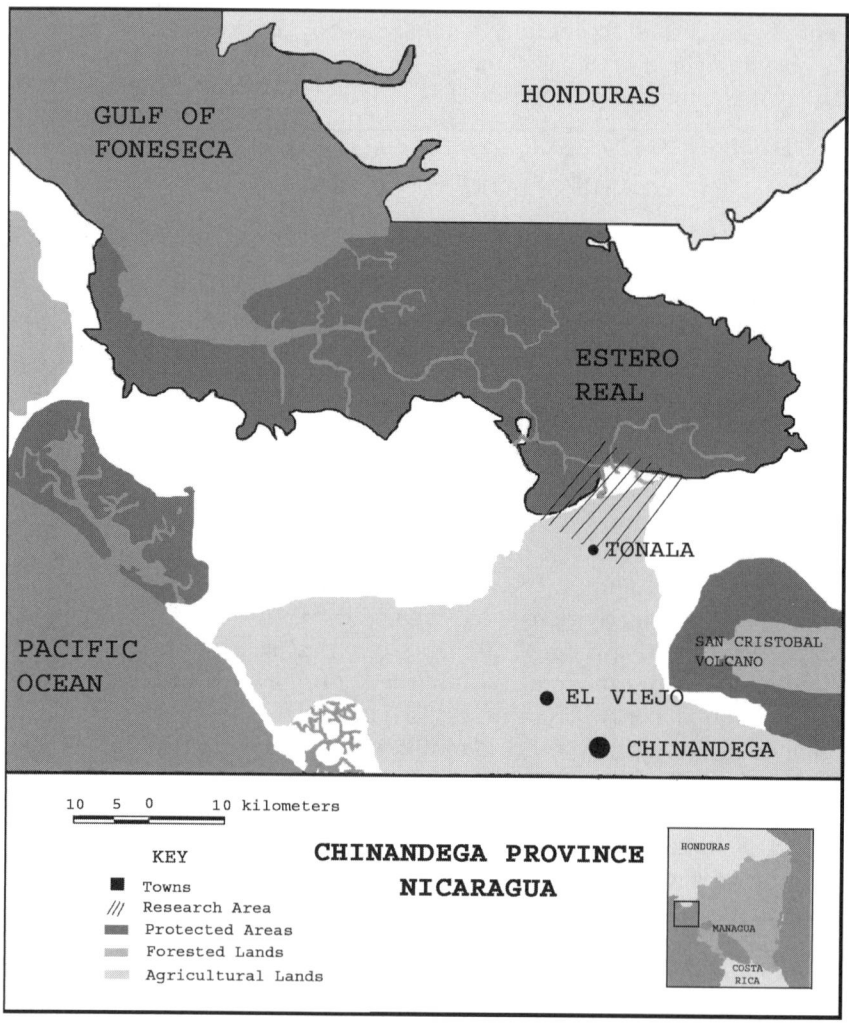

2.1. Chinandega Province, Nicaragua

1991; Williams 1986; De Janvry 1981).[6] Export crop production intensified land use on Central America's Pacific coastal region in particular (Gould 1990; Williams 1986). As a consequence, the rural poor lost access to increasingly expensive land, and their status shifted from smallholders to agricultural workers, forced to rely on seasonal cotton harvest labor to sustain their families. In 1970, at the height of the region's agro-export boom, 78 percent of rural Central American families owned insufficient land (less than 7 ha) to meet their subsistence needs or owned no land at all (Table 2.3).

Table 2.1. Basic Indicators: Miraflores, Nicaragua, 2001

Households: 23
Total population: 119
Mean annual household income: $429
Population living at or below the poverty line: 100%
Total landholdings: 232 mz/162.4 ha
Basic services:
  elementary school, yes
  potable water, no
  electricity, yes
  access to health care, yes (basic)
Protected area nearby: the Estero Real (46,000 ha)

Sources: Community field notes; Morales, Aburto, and Aburto 1999.

Table 2.2. Central America: Gross Domestic Product (GDP), 1960–2001 (average annual percentage change)

	1960–1979*	1980–1990	1991–2001
Costa Rica	6.3	2.2	4.6
El Salvador	5.9	–0.4	4.1
Guatemala	5.6	0.9	3.9
Honduras	5.5	2.4	3.2
Nicaragua	6.3	–1.5	3.3
Panama	4.1†	1.4	4.2
Region	6.2	0.8	4.1

Sources: 1960 to 1979, Brockett 1990:61; 1980–1990 and 1991–2001, ECLAC 2001.
Notes: * GNP.
† 1960–1975.

Stonich (1993) argues that the export-led model of development of this era contributed to declines in per capita food production, growing food imports, balance-of-payment difficulties, high levels of external debt, under- and unemployment, and increased poverty and malnutrition. Over three decades later, 68 percent of the region's rural population still lived in poverty, one-third of that number in extreme poverty (Table 2.4).

In the Nicaraguan province of Chinandega, the rapid expansion of cotton production, while driving high national economic growth rates of 6.3 percent, appears to have brought limited economic benefits to the poor majority. In fact, in many cases the cotton boom was a disruptive and exclusionary process that deepened economic inequality and social polarization. Large landowners, or *terratenientes*, expanded their cotton production by deforesting land they already owned, by purchasing land,

Table 2.3. Central America: Distribution of Rural Families by Size of Property, 1970 (percentages)

Country	Property size (hectares)						
	No land	Less than 0.7	0.7–4	4–7	7–34	35–350	350+
Costa Rica	26.3	32.2	13.1	4.8	14.6	8.3	0.7
El Salvador	26.1	24.4	36.2	6.2	4.9	2.0	0.2
Guatemala	26.6	15.0	42.3	6.9	57.4	1.4	0.4
Honduras	31.4	10.3	24.1	11.9	18.1	3.9	0.3
Nicaragua	33.8	1.5	24.2	7.9	18.1	13.5	1.0
Region	28.1	16.8	32.6	7.4	10.7	4.0	0.4

Source: Utting 1996:41.

Table 2.4. Central America: Poverty in 2001 (percentages)

Country	Poverty			Extreme Poverty		
	TOTAL	Urban	Rural	TOTAL	Urban	Rural
Costa Rica	23	19	29	7	4	11
El Salvador	46	35	60	20	11	32
Guatemala	56	27	75	16	3	24
Honduras	72	63	79	53	33	70
Nicaragua	46	30	68	15	6	27
Panama	41	23	69	27	11	52
Region	51	34	68	23	11	35

Source: Proyecto Estado de la Nación 2003:53.

and by extra-legal means.[7] In the municipio of Puerto Morazán, on the eve of the revolution, seventy-seven farms ranging in size from 700 to 1,750 ha occupied 49 percent of the area, while 41 percent of rural families owned less than 3.5 ha of land—one of the highest levels of land concentration in Nicaragua (Barahona Najlis and Mendoza 1999; Nitlapán 1990; MIDINRA 1980). These patterns of land concentration were in turn reinforced by political exclusion. With economic and military support from the United States, the Somoza family dictatorship used repression by the National Guard to dampen political and social dissent, retain power for over forty years, and amass wealth and property (Knut 1993).

In the 1970s, approximately two-thirds of Miraflores residents worked as landless day laborers on the cotton haciendas of the Tonalá zone. These former day laborers almost unanimously emphasized the rural poor's inability to meet their basic needs, largely because of the seasonal nature of cotton work, the high price of land in the cotton zones, and the deep economic and social polarization between "rich" landowners and the poor.[8] Miraflores resident Yolanda remembered lines of displaced rural families, "dirty, shoeless, hungry, sick," waiting for work outside the Chinandega railroad station. Each December Yolanda, her *compañero*, Eusebio, and their five children joined as many as 200,000 rural workers to pick cotton at piece rates, earning in the 1970s seven to eight *cordobas*, about a dollar a day (Biderman 1982). Yolanda's son Santiago stated, "Work was abundant but poorly paid. They [the large landowners] paid what they wanted. . . . [Y]ou worked for two weeks picking cotton and all you could afford to buy with your earnings was your food because at that time no campesinos grew corn. Only the rich could sow the land, or they brought food in from other places." Another community member, Celso, raised by a single mother, first worked in the cotton fields at age seven. He explained:

> You'll hear a lot of people around here say that their boss (patrón) was a good patrón. There were a lot like that, but others gave their workers no incentive, no bonus at Christmas. They wouldn't lend [the workers] money. They would run a worker (*mozo*) off their property like a dog. The mozo then had hatred in his heart and wouldn't forget. Until one day the people of Nicaragua exploded. It would have been better if all the patrones had been good, had given a little more. So many people would not have died.

Scholars suggest that such dynamics of social and economic dislocation, decreased subsistence security, and political repression were underlying grievances that contributed to increased peasant mobilization in Central America from the 1960s through the 1980s (Brockett 2005; Robinson 2003; Wickham-Crawley 1992; Williams 1986). Peasants participated in both nonviolent mass movements and in leftist-nationalist guerrilla movements in Nicaragua, El Salvador, and Guatemala in particular. Brockett (2005) provides evidence from El Salvador and Guatemala indicating that favorable configurations of political opportunities have also been crucial in the emergence, trajectories, and outcomes of contentious movements in Central America.[9]

In their narratives, Miraflores residents characterize the Somoza era as a very unfavorable political opportunity context—activism on land issues was met with arrest and state violence, and few external allies were available.[10] Despite these unfavorable conditions, however, the Tonalá zone became an epicenter of collective campesino resistance against expanding cotton haciendas, and as many as 10,000 people participated in land invasions in the 1960s and 1970s (Gould 1990). Half a dozen of the founding members of Miraflores participated in such land invasions and were beaten and jailed by Somoza's National Guard. Through this process of mobilization, community members developed a more autonomous and critical consciousness, a class-based discourse that emphasized conflicts of interest between the wealthy and the poor and made social justice arguments for land rights of the poor.[11] These patterns of critical consciousness and organized peasant resistance were not universal in the cotton zones, however. A number of Miraflores residents engaged in what I term "active accommodation," seeking individual and household openings within existing social, political, and economic structures. Community member Ignacio explained, "I earned 30 to 40 *cordobas* daily working on different haciendas and was able to save money. Only a few others did this. Others liked to drink, but I wanted to be free. With my savings I bought [3.5 ha] of land to grow corn, wheat, and sesame. In Somotillo it was possible to buy land. Here in Tonalá, no. The rich bought it all to grow cotton."

The northern sector of Chinandega province, unsuitable for cotton production, served as a type of internal agricultural frontier for poor peasants. National lands like these, largely unregulated and unoccupied ecosystems, subsidized the broader development model, as the environmental losses their settlement entailed were "externalities" not taken into account in measurements of national gross domestic product (GDP). In deeply stratified societies such as Nicaragua, these frontier regions also played a political function, diffusing individual and organized land claims and demobilizing the population to a degree (see Horton 1999; Maldidier 1996). The Miraflores families who purchased land in the northern zones of the department suggested that with less contact with the landless worker movements of the Tonalá zone, they maintained a more dependent consciousness. In other words, although they established a degree of economic autonomy through the purchase of land, socially and ideologically they were still enmeshed in the patron-client ties and ideological dependencies on elites common in the more remote, agricultural frontier zones of Nicaragua (Horton 1999). Men, and to an even lesser degree women, did not view themselves as autonomous, knowledgeable political subjects in the Somoza era. Miraflores resident Raimundo recalled, "There were elections and we all voted for Somoza. It was the custom. We saw Somoza as the administrator of the country." Residents described themselves as "asleep," unseeing and unaware of the social reality that surrounded them and without voice, until participation in revolutionary movements "awakened" them to a more critical class consciousness in the late 1970s.

In addition to these social transformations, the expansion of cotton production in the provinces of León and Chinandega also brought negative environmental consequences (Faber 1993; Brockett 1990; Williams 1986).[12] Longtime residents of the Tonalá zone recalled that in the years before the cotton boom intensified land use, most haciendas still kept much of their land in forest. Animals such as iguanas and deer were common, and the mangrove forests of the Estero Real were largely intact. Local people accessed the Estero Real, at that time unregulated national land, for small-scale commercial activities—artisan shrimp cultivation and the extraction of tannin from mangrove bark—and to meet subsistence needs (Paniagua and Aguilar 1996). As cotton production expanded, deforestation in the province accelerated, signifying a loss of shade for the population and contributing to the ecological deterioration of surrounding lands as winds and rains, no longer blocked by stands of trees, swept away topsoil with high organic matter content.[13] This destruction of habitat, combined with hunting by local residents, has also contributed to the sharp decline of wildlife such as the green iguana and deer in the area.

Another direct negative environmental consequence of the cotton boom has been high levels of pesticide contamination in the region. Levels of DDT in mother's breast milk in Nicaragua's cotton zones, for example, have been found to be 42 to 185 times above safe levels and among the highest rates of pesticide contamination in the world (Faber 1993:103). Data are not available on the impact of this pesticide contamination on human health, but in the late 1980s, when crop duster planes sprayed the cotton fields, doctors reported that an average of three to five people per day visited the Tonalá health center to be treated for symptoms of pesticide poisoning. As can be seen, the cotton boom in Chinandega propelled a traditional model of development that led to high levels of economic growth on a national scale even as it undermined social and environmental components of sustainability. From the perspective of Chinandega's rural poor, this state-supported, market-driven model intensified historic conditions of inequality and exclusion and caused direct and indirect ecological damage.

IPETÍ, PANAMA

Miraflores residents have for many decades been deeply engaged with global markets on the edge of Nicaragua's agricultural heartland. In contrast, the Kuna members of the community of Ipetí lived on the rural periphery and deliberately avoided interaction with much of Panama's broader development model until the 1970s, when modernization literally arrived at their doorstep in the form of a hydroelectric dam project. Ipetí is one of twelve indigenous Kuna communities that form part of the *comarca*, or semi-autonomous indigenous territory, of Madungandí in eastern Panama (see Map 2.2).[14] Ipetí is the largest community in the *comarca*, with around forty-five households and a total population of 365 people (Contraloría General de la República de Panamá 2000). Ipetí is also the most easily accessible community in the *comarca*, located on the edge of the dirt and gravel Pan-American Highway, approximately 150 km east of Panama

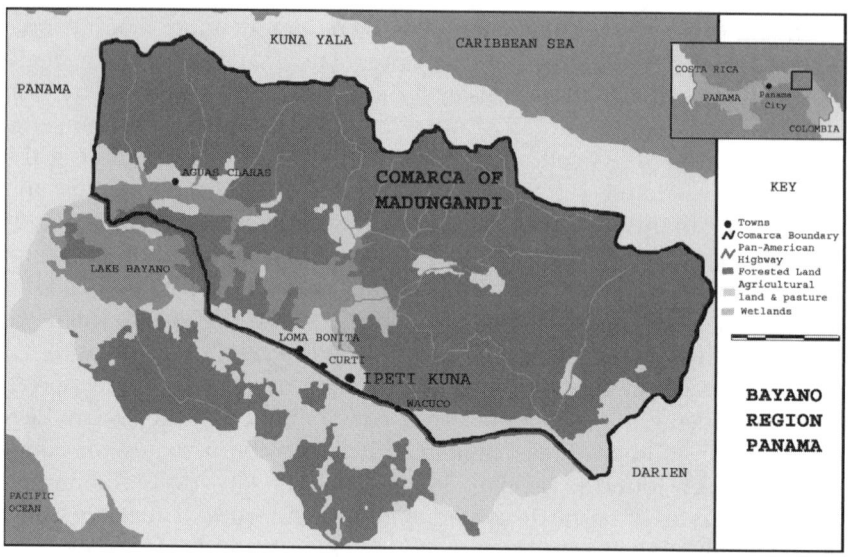

2.2. *Bayano Region, Panama*

City. Close to the Kuna community of Ipetí are two other communities: Ipetí Embará, an indigenous Embará community, and a non-indigenous community known locally as Ipetí colono.[15]

Of the twelve Kuna communities located in the *comarca* of Madungandí, Ipetí has been the most strongly influenced by Panama's broader social and economic institutions (see Table 2.5). A constant stream of non-indigenous visitors enter Ipetí: government teachers, professionals from the health ministry combating malaria, police officers, lottery ticket vendors, missionaries, and NGO technicians. The majority of the men in Ipetí speak at least some Spanish, and some have spent extended periods outside the community. The community has a small school where classes are conducted in Spanish, although 41 percent of Ipetí residents over age ten are illiterate (Contraloría General de la República de Panamá 2000). At the same time, the linguistic and cultural markers that distinguish this indigenous community from Panama's dominant culture are immediately apparent. Women and girls wear traditional hand-sewn clothing—blouses made of *molas* (embroidered cloth panels), wrap skirts, red and gold head scarves. They wrap *wini* beadwork around their legs and arms and paint their faces with *jagua* dye. Before the nightly congresses, men don traditional bright yellow, blue, and green shirts and elaborately woven straw hats. The Kunas practice a rich ceremonial life that focuses on "protection from supernatural danger, creation of community, [and] their destiny as a chosen people" (Howe 1998:17). The Ipetí calendar is filled with commu-

Table 2.5. Basic Indicators: Ipetí, Panama, 2000

Households: 45
Total population: 365
Population living at or below the poverty line: 100%
Mean annual household income: $2,772
Total landholdings (all communities of the *comarca*): 180,000 ha

Basic services:
  elementary school, yes
  potable water, no
  electricity, no
  access to health care, yes (basic)

Protected area nearby: Comarca of Madungandí (180,000 ha)

Sources: Contraloría General de la República de Panamá 2000; field notes.

nal activities such as the milling of sugarcane to prepare for puberty rite celebrations (*innas*), healing ceremonies, house buildings, and community exorcisms.

Along with Guatemala and Belize, Panama is one of the most ethnically diverse nations of Central America. Panama has significant Afro-Caribbean, mestizo, Asian, and indigenous populations, although census data are collected only on self-identified indigenous peoples who make up approximately 10 percent of the population (Contraloría General de la República de Panamá 2000). The Kunas, with 61,707 members, are Panama's second-largest indigenous group.[16] The majority of Panama's Kunas live on the northern islands of San Blas that form the *comarca* of Kuna Yala, as well as in Panama City. A much smaller group of 3,305 Kunas lives in the Bayano region of eastern Panama.[17] Panama's Kuna Indians have been widely recognized as among Latin America's most active and empowered indigenous peoples, and their forms of internal governance and strategies of political mobilization have served as models for other Panamanian indigenous groups (Martinez Mauri 2003; Herrera 1972).

In the *comarca* of Madungandí, residents have struggled to maintain and reinforce control of territory and cultural integrity over the past 500 years through strategies of geographic withdrawal, armed resistance, and strategic alliances.[18] Following a successful uprising on San Blas against government efforts at forced assimilation, the Kuna population in the Bayano hired lawyers and lobbied the executive branch until the government authorized the Indigenous Region of Upper Bayano, a reserve the Kunas named Madungandí, or "River of Plantains," in 1935. In the decades that followed, Panama's distinct pattern of development—centered not on agro-exports but on global transportation and commerce in the metropolitan trans-isthmian strip—lessened elite pressure for control over indigenous labor and land and assisted Madungandí leaders in maintaining spaces of cultural and physical autonomy in the eastern lowland rain forests into the 1960s (Zimbalist 1991; Ropp 1982). More than absolute withdrawal, however, the strategy of Madungandí leaders through the 1980s was to selectively engage with Panama's broader economic structures, selling crops in Panama City and negotiating temporary work contracts for young men on United Fruit Company banana plantations along the north Atlantic Coast (IRHE 1978). In the 1960s the Kunas established the village of Ipetí along the planned Pan-American Highway route as a means to more firmly assert Kuna control over reserve boundaries in the face of likely non-indigenous migration.[19] A dozen families settled in Ipetí to cultivate plantains, corn, coffee, and a variety of fruit trees, including extensive avocado groves in the fertile lowlands of the upper Bayano.

In Guatemala, El Salvador, and Nicaragua, civilian elites and military officers employed repressive force to control rural labor forces, crush land invasions, and quell protests that arose in response to dislocations of the agro-export development model (Brockett 2005; Paige 1997). This state repression and the civil wars of the 1970s and 1980s led to the deaths of approximately 335,000 Central Americans of a total regional population of close to 30 million.[20] In contrast to the exclusionary and repressive military regimes of Nicaragua, El Salvador, and Guatemala, however, Panama's General Omar Torrijos, who took power in a 1968 coup, ruled through more limited repression combined with nationalist and populist discourse.[21] Torrijos sought to bring Indians voluntarily into the "nation" in physical and cultural terms by expanding state services into indigenous zones and developing personalistic and patronage ties to Panama's indigenous groups (Harding 2001; Wali 1989; Priestley 1986). Indigenous groups were given state recognition and encouraged to mobilize within the parameters of an authoritarian regime (Herrera 1972).

Torrijos's nationalist and developmentalist state policies directly impacted Madungandí in 1973, when the government obtained World Bank and Inter-American Development Bank (IDB) funding for the Bayano hydroelectric dam project (Wali 1989). Madungandí leaders apparently acceded to the project, which flooded around 80 percent of Kuna reserve land (Bartolomé and Barabas 1998).[22] In its Bayano resettlement plans, the Torrijos regime continued historical state patterns of differential treatment based on ethnic distinctions. The zone's 2,500 non-indigenous *interioranos*, or colonists, labeled as environmentally destructive because of their cattle ranching practices, were ordered to leave the zone (Wali 1989; IRHE 1978). In contrast, the Bayano's two indigenous groups—350 to 400 Embarás and 1,000 to 1,500 Kunas—whose cultural practices were deemed more environmentally sustainable by government officials, were allowed to remain (Wali 1989).[23]

The economic and spiritual losses the Kunas suffered as a result of the construction of the dam resonated in conversations over twenty-five years later.[24] When the river was dammed, it flooded Ipetí's most agriculturally productive land; and residents lost the labor they had invested in cultivating long-term fruit orchards, as well as future income streams. A survey conducted five years after the dam was completed found that planting of key fruit crops, plantains, avocados, oranges, and *pixbae* (fruit of the peach palm) had declined to 30 percent or less of pre-dam levels (Wali 1989:89). The presence of amoebas, diarrhea, and malaria increased in the Kuna population following dam construction, and some Ipetí residents blamed these health problems on the tree spirits' anger at the clearing (IRHE 1978). One community activist, Silvano, described the dam project as "a trick (*engaño*) played on indigenous people to conquer the lands, the most fertile lands that belonged to our grandparents." An Ipetí traditional authority, Rufino, concluded, "If it weren't for the dam, we would all live better today."

The environmental impact of the dam, however, has been more mixed. Direct negative impacts of the dam included the killing of large numbers of fish, contamination by herbicides used to control the abundant vegetation in the lake, and a huge displacement of fauna during the initial flooding (Wali 1989; IRHE 1978). In sociopolitical terms, however, the dam project linked conservation in the Bayano watershed directly to patterns of urban production and consumption. This expanded the perceived economic value of Bayano rain forests beyond local communities and encouraged a shift in policy toward conservation, at least within certain government agencies. For example, the Institute of Hydraulic Resources and Electricity (IRHE) no longer promoted the "conquest of the forest" but rather initiated measures to support the environmental integrity of the upper Bayano to prevent deforestation and accumulation of silt that would undermine the capacity of Bayano Lake and the dam (Joly 1982; IRHE 1978).

In evaluating the impact of the dam project and the extension of the Pan-American Highway along the border of Kuna territory, it is clear that the hydroelectric dam undermined Ipetí's base of economic support, although the community's continued access to land in the reserve provided greater subsistence security than, for example, was the case for landless workers in Nicaragua. In social and ideological terms, the experience of the hydroelectric dam project blends into a broader Ipetí critical narrative of loss of power, tranquility, and well-being through a process of externally imposed development and forced contact with "civilization."[25]

OSA PENINSULA

The Panama and Nicaragua experiences are also typical of the limited attention paid to issues involving the environment and sustainability in Central American development discourses and practices through the 1980s. A general neglect of environmental sustainability in Latin America can be linked to the region's early and rapid urbanization, destruction and devaluation of the region's indigenous knowledge, its historical reliance on rents and resource extraction, and, in Central America, intense political and social conflicts in the 1970s and 1980s that pulled attention and resources away from environmental issues (Goodman and Redclift 1991b). By the 1990s, a series of largely external dynamics—the shift toward a globalized discourse of environmentalism and increased funding from transnational institutions—brought sustainability to the forefront in Central America. Postdevelopment literature is critical of the dominant construction of developmental and ecological crises utilized to justify expanded bureaucratic interventions (Sachs 1999; Escobar 1995).

The recent focus on conflicting representations of environments, however, should not obscure the fact that profound environmental change has been under way in rural Central America even as discursive struggles continue over how such change is to be interpreted and represented. The narrow isthmus of Central America covers approximately half a million square kilometers and contains three major geographic-climatic zones: (1) the Atlantic lowlands, which receive from 2,000 to 6,000 mm of precipitation annually and where most intact tropical rain forests are found; (2) the central highlands; and (3) the Pacific lowlands, which, with a few exceptions such as the Osa peninsula of Costa Rica, have been largely deforested (Leonard 1987). Despite its small size, the region is a land bridge between North and South America and possesses an estimated 7 percent of the world's biodiversity (Comisión Centroamericano de Ambiente y Desarrollo cited in Proyecto Estado de la Nación 2003).

In the 1950s, approximately 60 percent of Central America was covered in primary and secondary forest.[26] In the early 1960s, deforestation accelerated rapidly in the region, reducing forest cover by one-third by 1990 (Utting cited in Kaimowitz 1997). While environmental monitoring in Central America is still incipient and estimates of deforestation rates in the region vary widely, it appears that Central America has had some of the highest deforestation rates in the world, with 341,000 hectares of forest lost annually in the 1990s (FAO 2003; Table 2.6).

Over the past four decades, pastureland has expanded rapidly, from 7.9 million to 13.4 million hectares, or 26 percent of Central America's total land, at the expense of tropical rain forests and agricultural land (Table 2.7; Utting 1996:29).

Table 2.6. Central America: National Forest Cover and Annual Deforestation, 1990, 2000

Country	Country's Forested Land (%) 1990	2000*	Average Annual Deforestation (ha) 1990–2000
Costa Rica*	33	39	16,000
El Salvador	12	6	7,000
Guatemala	35	26	54,000
Honduras*	42	48	59,000
Nicaragua	30	27	117,000
Panama	42	39	52,000
Region	36	35	341,000

Sources: 1990 estimates from Utting 1997:11; 2000 and 1990–1999 data from FAO 2003: 91, 93.
Note: *Data on increased forest size in Costa Rica and Honduras likely reflect methodological discrepancies in forest cover estimates.

Table 2.7. Central America: Changes in Land Use, 1972–1987

Land Use	1972 hectares (thousands)	% of total land area	1987 hectares (thousands)	% of total land area
Permanent cropland	6,107	12	6,807	13
Permanent pasture	7,860	15	13,428	26
Forest and woodland	23,478	46	17,916	35
Other	11,758	23	11,777	23
Total land area	50,977	100*	50,951	100*

Source: Adapted from Faber 1993:140.
Note: *Percentages are subject to rounding errors.

Logging in Central America rarely involves clear-cutting of forests but rather features the extraction of individual highly valued trees, such as cedar, oak, and mahogany. The penetration roads created by logging companies, however, often attract migrants who seek access to state lands. They clear the forests to establish land claims and engage in farming, ranching, or land speculation (Maldidier 1996; Heckadon Moreno and McKay 1982).[27] While general agreement exists on this migration-deforestation dynamic along Central America's agricultural frontiers, the underlying factors that push this cycle continue to be debated. Dominant institutions tend to place responsibility for deforestation on environmentally destructive poor migrants and state policies, such as government colonization programs and legal regimes, that subsidize and encourage deforestation (World Bank 2003d, 2001b; Deininger and Binswanger 1999). In contrast, early critical perspectives focused on the "hamburger connection," the external U.S. demand for low-quality beef that drove the rapid expansion of cattle ranching and deforestation (Nations and Komer 1987; Myers 1981), and the role of U.S. military and political interventions (Faber 1992a, 1992b). More recent research has questioned the view of Central American environmental degradation as primarily a consequence of U.S. geopolitical machinations and dependence on international markets. It identifies additional regional and national factors such as internal demand for beef (Edelman 1995), government financing of roads and infrastructure (Kaimowitz 1997), a deeply embedded "cattle culture" (Heckadon Moreno 1982), and the breakdown of traditional systems of resource management, land tenure systems, and the distribution of costs and benefits in deforestation (Utting 1996).

The recent experiences of the third case study community, Puerto Jiménez, Costa Rica, reflect the most recent facet of dominant development discourse in Central America: globalized environmentalism as mediated through state institutions and implemented in specific localities. While export crops, particularly coffee and bananas, have played a central role in Costa Rican economic development, factors such as democratic governance, a small population, and abundant land led to a relatively egalitarian distribution of income and a strong social welfare state in the postwar period (Edelman 1999; Rodríguez, Castro, and Rowland Espinosa 1998; Wilson 1998). Puerto Jiménez on the Osa peninsula presents the lowest levels of absolute poverty, the highest educational levels, and the most extensive government services of the three case studies (see Map 2.3, Table 2.8). The total population of the district of Puerto Jiménez is 6,102 (INEC 2000). The town offers basic services—a health clinic, several grade schools, a high school, and a bank branch—as well as a strong ecotourism infrastructure, including dozens of small hotels (*cabinas*) and half a dozen restaurants.

Extensive pastures and large-scale rice production dominate the western coast of the peninsula. The other 80 percent of the peninsula's land is under protected status (PDR 1995). This includes the 41,789-hectare Corcovado National Park and the 62,703-hectare Golfo Dulce Forest Reserve, where a substantial portion of the land is still in private hands.

The Osa peninsula was a remote, sparsely settled region until migrants began to move onto the peninsula in the late 1930s to pan for gold.[28] During this period, the U.S. United Fruit Company obtained control of large extensions of land on the peninsula. Peninsula land was not suitable for banana production, however, and in 1957 a large U.S. lumber company, Osa Forest Products (OFP), acquired approximately 47,000 hectares of land. OFP invested little in this property, leaving around 80 percent of the peninsula covered in rain forest (Rosero-Bixby, Maldonado-Ulloa, and Bonilla-Carrión 2002; Van den Hombergh 1999). In the 1960s, a series of

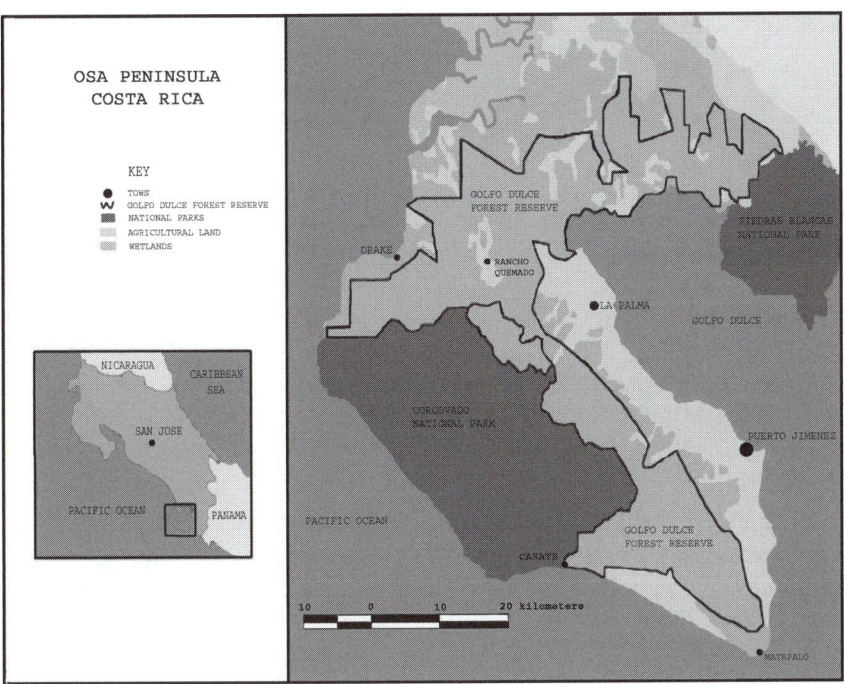

2.3. Osa Peninsula, Costa Rica

push and pull factors linked to Costa Rica's broader development model further intensified migration to the peninsula—they included state-sponsored extension of roads into southern Costa Rica, pressures of land concentration in northern and southeastern Costa Rica, and laws favorable to squatters.[29] As in other agricultural frontier zones of Central America, the forested and unutilized lands of the peninsula served as a social safety valve and environmental subsidy to the dominant model of development (Watson et al. 1998). In the early 1970s, squatters laid claim to approximately 8,000 hectares of OFP land and clashed, at times violently, with OFP personnel and the Costa Rican rural guard (Vaughan 1979:181).

During this same period, Costa Rica had taken the lead in Central America in the areas of environmental discourse and development of a national park system (see Steinberg 2001; Evans 1999; Watson et al. 1998; Wallace 1992). A small but highly influential group of Costa Rican scientists-conservationists successfully lobbied President Daniel Oduber to expropriate the OFP's land to create the Corcovado National Park in 1975.[30] International conservation NGOs provided funds to support the establishment of the park and the resettlement of families located within park boundaries, while the Costa Rican government was to provide financial compen-

Table 2.8. Basic Indicators: Puerto Jiménez, Costa Rica, 2000

Households: 1,628*
Total population: 6,102*
Mean annual household income: $3,120[†]
Population living at or below poverty line: 33%[†]
Total landholdings: N/A

Basic services:
  elementary school, yes
  potable water, yes
  electricity, yes
  access to health care, yes

Source: COBRUDES 1997; INEC 2000.
Notes: * District of Puerto Jiménez.
[†] Brunca region.

sation for the land lost (Wallace 1992; Vaughan 1979:135). Osa squatters, who had pressured the government to distribute the OFP land to them, opposed the creation of the national park as a top-down and undemocratic action.[31] They received support from the government Land Colonization Institute (ITCO) and the Marxist Vanguard Party, part of what Carriere (1991) labels the national "social reformism" policy nexus of the time. However, geographically isolated, with limited material resources and little access to the upper levels of the Costa Rican government, the squatters were unable to prevail over the transnational environmental coalition.

Studies by Barquero Barrantes (1988) and Christen (cited in Van den Hombergh 1999) contend that these peasants and ranchers aggressively cleared the forest. They support a perspective that park creation and exclusion of the squatters and, later, gold miners was necessary to prevent further environmental deterioration of the peninsula's rain forests. This discourse of environmental destruction by the poor on the Osa peninsula is challenged, however, by local counternarratives of OFP logging activities. Longtime peninsula resident Gaspar recalled, "It was huge quantities of wood that [OFP] exploited. There was so much wood cut that you could walk [across the water] from Puerto Escondido to Rincón. The gulf was covered with wood, thousands of trees [were] floating in the water." Such accounts incorporate elements of nationalism and exaggeration to contrast the "greed" and "waste" of the transnational company with more sustainable, local "subsistence" activities. As will be seen, these representations of historical events on the peninsula also underlie more contemporary forms of critical consciousness and frames of struggle over which groups benefit and lose in environmental protectionism.

While Costa Rica took the lead in implementing policies of environmental sustainability, by the end of the 1990s Central America as a whole

Table 2.9. Central America: Protected Areas, 2002

Country	Protected Areas (millions of hectares)	% of Territory
Costa Rica	1.300	25.0
El Salvador	0.007	0.3
Guatemala	3.100	29.0
Honduras	2.200	20.0
Nicaragua	2.200	17.0
Panama	2.900	26.0
Region	12.900	25.0

Source: Proyecto Estado de la Nación 2003:202.

had experienced a geographic and legal expansion of state power through the declaration of protected areas. The amount of land under some form of protected status in Central America expanded from 1.5 million hectares in the 1970s to 12.9 million hectares in 2000, or 25 percent of Central America's land mass (see Table 2.9). The Central American System of Protected Areas includes 554 protected areas, which encompass 58 percent of the region's remaining forest cover (Proyecto Estado de la Nación 2003:202; Girot 1998:24). In addition, with external funding and support, by 2000 all Central American nations had created environmental ministries or secretaries, passed national environmental protection laws, and in general established stricter environmental standards and compliance monitoring standards (USAID 2001).

Social conflict on the Osa peninsula did not end, however, with the creation of the Corcovado National Park. In response to the departure of United Fruit Company and the loss of jobs in nearby banana zones, as well as rising international gold prices, hundreds of would-be gold miners resisted state environmental policy by clandestinely entering the park in the mid-1980s.[32] President Luis Alberto Monge ordered a contingent of Rural and Civil Guards into Corcovado Park to remove miners and their families by force. In late 1986, miners organized a protest, and men, women, and children walked several hundred kilometers to San José, where they camped out in parks and makeshift shelters. After many delays, the government offered the displaced compensation in the form of cash payments of 250,000 *colones* (approximately $5,000) or Institute of Agrarian Development parcels of land outside the park (PDR 1995:34).

The postdevelopment literature is critical of top-down environmentalism, which fails to address underlying inequalities that propel deforestation and represents an expansion and deepening of state and elite control over land and natural resources that traditionally served as local commons and a type of subsistence safety net (Sachs 1999; Escobar 1995). Almost three decades later, local Ministry of Environment and Energy officials emphasized in interviews that the park's creation successfully facilitated the conservation of one of Central America's last remaining Pacific Coast rain forests, a view shared by many area environmental activists. In interviews, however, former landowners and gold miners listed economic, political, and cultural grievances that centered on the process through which the park was created, as well as the distribution of the costs and benefits of environmental conservation. On Osa, the Costa Rican state hastened the end of the agricultural frontier model of subsistence and upward mobility subsidized by the exploitation of natural resources on the peninsula. Local residents, who had struggled for possession of OFP land for farming, cattle ranching, and gold mining, were now excluded from accessing and utilizing natural resources on 80 percent of the peninsula (PDR 1995). Global environmental claims were privileged over local claims to land and natural resource use, and Osa's ranchers, agriculturalists, and gold miners paid a direct and at least temporary cost in loss of income and disruption of livelihood.[33] Bartolomé, whose family was removed from the park, stated, "They [the government] created the park behind our backs. They never asked us when they declared the park. The decree [to create the park] was not accepted [by the local population]. The campesino lost the liberty he had to hunt, pan for gold, and exploit the wood. The space for all of this was reduced."

Lucrecia, a gold miner, recalled: "[Before the creation of the national park] we lived well; we found a lot of gold; we had money to spend. Then in 1986 the [government] dislodging came. They allowed only one suitcase per person. I had to abandon all of my belongings: my chickens, clothing, dishes. It was very sad." As this narrative suggests, the gold miners emphasized the forceful nature of the expulsion and increased tensions between the state and the population. They contrasted family subsistence—here a list of belongings—with the stated environmental goals of the state. Several gold miners also expressed fears that environmental conservation had virtually destroyed the gold miners' unique way of life. Government officials, in contrast, argued that state compensation was more than adequate and that in the long term, with the ecotourism boom of the 1990s discussed in Chapter 3, the national park has improved the quality of life on the peninsula.

The gold miner invasions of Corcovado National Park also highlighted the weakness of a top-down "policing" approach to conservation that attempts through vigilance and force to prevent local populations, seen as environmentally destructive, from entering protected areas or accessing natural resources. The remote, difficult terrain of protected areas like Corcovado, combined with the government's generally limited funding and enforcement capacity, meant that controls often existed only on paper, and local populations like the gold miners entered parks at will. The protests by Osa residents, along with shifts in the discourse of sustainability at the global level, influenced government officials to reconsider early park policy, in which funds were channeled toward land acquisition and conservation (Zúñiga Villegas 1998; Barquero Barrantes 1988).

In the mid-1980s the Costa Rican government sought international funding for sustainable development projects targeted at communities in ecologically at-risk or fragile zones, designed to help alleviate poverty and simultaneously promote environmental conservation (Brandon and Wells 1992). These projects, as incorporated into dominant visions of sustainability, do not necessarily bring social or economic equity but rather seek to mitigate poverty and provide income-generating alternatives, to the degree necessary so communities will desist from engaging in environmentally damaging activities. Partial data available for Panama, Costa Rica, and Nicaragua suggest that since 1990 there has been a large increase in external funding available for project interventions designed to promote sustainability (CONADES 1998; MICE 1996a, 1996b; FACS and CEPAD 1993). The case studies that follow incorporate three such sets of activities—ecotourism, nontraditional exports, and collective indigenous land rights—and explore whether in practice such synergetic positive outcomes occur.

CONCLUSION

This chapter has introduced the case study communities' post–World War II patterns of development, drawing out patterns of regional convergence and national and local divergences and evaluating the impact of such processes on the empowerment of communities as agents of sustainability. Globalized processes of agro-export expansion and activist state roles in modernization in the Nicaragua and Panama case studies have contributed to growth at the macro level. From the localized perspectives of the poor, however, these processes also undermined subsistence security, cultural integrity and way of life, and local environments. "Development" in the form of a hydroelectric dam project and cotton production has been a disruptive process of outside origin and external imposition. In all three case studies, the costs of development have been disproportionately borne by groups relatively powerless because of their poverty, ethnicity, and social stigma.

Development in these local experiences has been both an imminent process of funded and planned IFI and state interventions and an immanent process of market dynamics (Hickey and Mohan 2004b). While Central American states have historically been relatively weak and dependent vis-à-vis external political and economic agents, we should not assume that these states are simply "conveyor belts" of more powerful external interests. Rather, they play a mediating role between global discourses and policies and implementation at the national and local levels. State violence in the Chinandega region of Nicaragua contrasts with the more populist (although still coercive) tactics of the Torrijos regime in Panama. In Costa Rica, a series of nationally specific factors led governments to promote environmental protectionism in advance of the more global shift in discourse.

Finally, although these experiences of development to varying degrees undermined the material base of support of the case study communities, in ideological terms they engendered resistance more than quiescence. In the Chinandega zone, the expansion of cotton haciendas, social and political exclusion, and violent repression of squatters laid the basis for a class-based critical consciousness. The Costa Rican state implemented a top-down environmentalism that generated a livelihood type of resistance and inadvertently created an economic and social space in which a more localized and radical environmentalism would be nurtured. In Panama, state patterns of corporatist incorporation of indigenous peoples further reinforced historical patterns of ethnically framed mobilization and claims making.

CHAPTER 3

"All the Land Belongs to the Foreigners"

Ecotourism and Sustainability

This is the first of three chapters that explore specific policies and practices—ecotourism, nontraditional exports, and collective indigenous land rights—promoted by international financial institutions (IFIs) and nongovernmental organizations (NGOs) as pathways to sustainable development. The first two activities, addressed in the Costa Rica and Nicaragua case studies, respectively, are market-driven practices tied to a broader project of economic globalization. Institutional supporters contend that ideally these activities generate economic growth and employment while largely avoiding environmental destruction and other negative consequences associated with traditional development activities of mass tourism and agro-exports (Stonich 1998). To explore these claims, linked to dominant sustainability discourse, the present chapter and Chapter 5 examine the economic, social, and environmental impacts of these activities from a local perspective.

COSTA RICA'S ECOTOURISM BOOM

In the late 1980s, the Osa peninsula of southwestern Costa Rica was a remote, off the beaten track travel destination, with very limited infrastructure and services—five small hotels (*cabinas*) and five restaurants—and a way of life centered on traditional activities of agriculture, cattle ranching, and gold panning (Leininger Mehroff and Vindas Carballo 1988). A decade later, small planes transporting ecotourists buzzed overhead, backpackers filled dozens of new *cabinas,* and local taxis and expatriate SUVs clogged the main streets of the peninsula's ecotourism hub, Puerto Jiménez. The number of annual peninsula visitors exploded, from several thousand in 1990 to over 20,000 in 2000 (Van den Hombergh 1999).

These changes on the Osa peninsula reflect Costa Rica's recent emergence as Latin America's leading ecotourism destination.[1] Ceballos-Lascuráin first defined ecotourism as "traveling to relatively undisturbed or uncontaminated natural areas with the specific objective of studying, admiring, and enjoying the scenery and its wild plants and animals, as well as any existing cultural manifestations" (cited in Fennell 1999:30). The more traditional development activity of mass tourism is associated with packaged trips involving large groups and largely controlled by transnational corporations. In contrast, ecotourism is characterized as consisting of flexible, small-scale, responsible activities in natural environments carried out by individuals or small groups (Mowforth and Munt 2003).

Mass tourism in Costa Rica—featuring transnational hotel chains and luxury facilities—has been concentrated in the northwestern Pacific beach zones of Puntarenas and Guanacaste. To date, however, relative geographic isolation has inhibited large-scale tourism investments on the Osa peninsula, making it a best-case scenario for examining the potential of ecotourism as a sustainable activity.[2] Institutional proponents suggest that ecotourism is an ideal sustainable economic activity, as it may provide employment and income for local peoples, build environmental awareness, generate direct financial benefits for conservation, revitalize local cultures, and strengthen human rights and democratic movements (Fennell 1999; Honey 1999).[3] Ideally, ecotourists, with their commitment to the environment and social justice, should contribute to sustainability as culturally sensitive, minimal-impact tourists who model and impart to local peoples positive environmental values in relationships that move beyond subject-object dichotomies to create spaces of egalitarian interaction and self-development (Cheong and Miller 2000).[4]

Similar to broader critiques of dominant sustainable development, critical perspectives question ecotourism from both political economy and ideological perspectives. The former suggests that whatever its more laudable social and environmental intentions, ecotourism, like mass tourism, is still driven by the dynamics of capital accumulation and does not challenge in any profound way global and national systems of power and unequal accumulation (Mowforth and Munt 2003; Duffy 2002). Rather, ecotourism is seen as a transnational activity compatible with and even advancing processes of corporate-dominated economic globalization (Robinson 2003). Critics suggest as well that ecotourism, as with other sustainable development activities, is inherently political in that it incorporates struggles not only over access to land, natural resources, and economic benefits but also over representations of the environment and quality of life (Mowforth and Munt 2003; Vivanco 2002; Cheong and Miller 2000; Hall 1994). Because ecotourists seek out geographical and cultural spaces relatively distant from processes of market expansion and ideological projects of modernization, some analysts argue that their impact is particularly pernicious and disruptive of local cultures (Mowforth and Munt 2003; Duffy 2002).

ECONOMIC IMPACTS

While the government's expansion of protected areas to eventually incorporate 25 percent of national territory laid the groundwork, Costa Rica's ecotourism boom was largely a private-sector initiative (Proyecto Estado de la Nación 2003:202; Cordero and van Duynen Montijn 2002). On the Osa peninsula, individual North Americans and European investors led the initiative to purchase land with ecotourism potential in the late 1980s.[5] These individuals possessed key economic and cultural advantages that enabled them to first identify ecotourism business opportunities and then to buy up land on the peninsula. First, they had greater access to capital to purchase land and invest in ecotourism infrastructure. In contrast, under the neoliberal reforms that began in the mid-1980s and emphasize market criteria over social criteria, Costa Ricans have had greater difficulty obtaining bank loans (Edelman 1999). In addition, foreign investors possessed specific cultural knowledge of postindustrial societies, had a greater range of international experience, and participated in fluid, transnational social networking, enabling them to recognize the peninsula's ecotourism potential much sooner than Costa Ricans, still embedded in more localized and limited networks, did. Small farmer Hortensio expressed the frustration of many Costa Rican peninsula residents who have felt excluded from participation in ecotourism activities: "There is no one here in La Palma who has the means to start a tourism project; even the simplest of projects cost millions [of *colones*]."

Based on these initial investment patterns, a three-tiered model of participation in ecotourism has resulted on Osa. On the top tier are small to medium-sized, largely foreign-owned eco-lodges with up to several dozen salaried employees. These eco-lodges, located on private reserves with rain-forest and beach access, on the edges of Corcovado National Park, and in Drake Bay, offer an average of sixteen rooms each whose prices range from fifty to several hundred dollars a night (Ruíz 2002). They attract wealthier ecotourists. While local informants estimate that as many as a quarter of the eco-lodges run into financial difficulties, they also offer the greatest opportunities for profit. The peninsula's second tier of ecotourism enterprises includes thirty-three *cabinas,* small hotels with an average of seven rooms each located in the town of Puerto Jiménez, which cater largely to low-budget travelers and backpackers (Ruíz 2002; COBRUDES 1997). The *cabina* owners, generally more affluent residents of the town before ecotourism, charge ten to twenty dollars a night for lodging. They employ family labor, along with two to three salaried, often part-time, workers.[6] In addition to *cabinas,* local Costa Ricans also operate taxi, fishing, aquatic, and horseback services for ecotourists. The third tier of participation in ecotourism is that of less well-off Costa Ricans who are employed as cooks, maids, handymen, caretakers, guides, and similar laborers, generally by the foreign-owned enterprises.

Informants from community organizations and government agencies in Puerto Jiménez estimated that in this epicenter of ecotourism activity, 20 percent of the economically active population works directly in ecotourism, while another 60 percent receives indirect economic benefits. Ruíz (2002) estimated that for the Osa peninsula as a whole, ecotourism generated 589 direct jobs and 696 indirect jobs in 1999 (317). Costa Ricans who are self-employed in ecotourism, those who work as salaried employees, and those whose businesses are indirectly impacted by ecotourism widely evaluated ecotourism as having a positive economic impact on the peninsula.[7] Similar to residents of Costa Rica's other ecotourism zones—Ostional, Monteverde, and Quepos—Osa residents identified the generation of new employment opportunities as the most important economic benefit of ecotourism (Weinberg, Bellows, and Ekster 2002; Cordero and van Duynen Montijn 2002; Campbell 1999). Wage labor in traditional mass tourism has been characterized by low pay, long hours, and the unstable, seasonal nature of the work—conditions disadvantageous to or even exploitative of local workers (Stronza 2001; Brohman 1996). On the Osa peninsula and elsewhere in Costa Rica, however, ecotourism wages, approximately 2,400 *colones* ($8) per day in 2000, have been generally on a par with or higher than wages in sectors such as agriculture (Cordero and van Duynen Montijn 2002:86).[8]

While traditional gender norms have limited women's participation in the paid labor force in rural Costa Rica, ecotourism has provided women with new opportunities to work in *cabinas,* restaurants, and other small businesses seen as "natural" extensions of women's role of nurturing and caring for others (Apostolopoulos, Sonmez, and Timothy 2001).[9] In interviews, women credited their participation in ecotourism with providing them with income they could more directly control, although gender stratification persists as better-paying positions—nature guides, fishing and scuba diving expedition leaders, for example—are filled largely by men.[10]

In addition to stratification by nationality, the economic benefits of ecotourism are geographically concentrated in Puerto Jiménez, which serves as a transportation and services hub, and in the communities of Matapalo, Carate, and Drake Bay on the east coast—zones with large areas of private, intact rain forest and access to beaches and Corcovado National Park. In contrast, other areas of the peninsula, such as the community of La Palma, where much of the land has been deforested for rice and cattle production, and communities far from the beach or without passable roads have minimal ecotourism activity.[11]

CONTROL OF LAND

Proponents stress that a key element that makes ecotourism qualitatively different from traditional development activities is the opportunity it offers for local power and control (Scheyvens 1999). On the Osa peninsula, however, an important degree of economic control has shifted to foreigners who, in a pattern that extends across Costa Rica, own substantial portions of the peninsula's coastal, ocean-view, and forested land in private reserves (COBRUDES 1997).[12] One estimate suggests, for example, that 66 percent of the peninsula's beachfront concessions are controlled by non–Costa Ricans, primarily North Americans and Germans who have purchased the land for recreation and ecotourism ventures (Fernández Morillo 2002a:364).[13] These nationality and class-stratified patterns of land ownership are a source of some social tension on the peninsula. A La Palma small businesswoman, Inés, explained, "They [the foreigners] exploit us. From Puerto Jiménez to Carate [beach] all the land belongs to foreigners. There is only a little bit of wage labor for us." When one travels the dirt and gravel road down the coast Inés referred to, cattle pastures line the road for the first several kilometers. Then the road becomes steeper, and the rain forest appears on all sides. It is an unusually beautiful zone where one can hear the pounding of distant surf and catch occasional glimpses of mist-covered beaches through the trees. The road, however, is also lined with numerous signs stating "Private Property" in English and Spanish, warning local people not to enter.

The loss of local access to land and natural resources has also been accelerated by ecotourism-fueled land speculation on the peninsula. According to Puerto Jiménez real estate agents, during the 1990s the value of coastal, ocean-view, and forested land on the peninsula doubled every year. By the early 2000s, peninsula oceanfront property was selling for as much as $25,000 per hectare, and purchase of land for ecotourism projects or agriculture had become prohibitively expensive for many Costa Ricans. Ecotourism influences balances of power and wealth accumulation not only between foreign investors and local residents but also within the very heart of communities (Duffy 2002; Stonich 2000). On the Osa peninsula, wealthier Costa Ricans—those who own forested or beachfront land, housing that can be converted into *cabinas,* restaurants, fishing boats, or pickup trucks, and those who have access to investment capital—have been most able to take advantage of the economic opportunities offered by ecotourism.[14]

I have stressed the need to locate and evaluate sustainable development initiatives not in a frozen tableau of traditional communities but rather within the broader context of immanent development. On the Osa peninsula, prior to ecotourism large producers dominated cattle ranching and rice cultivation. Sixty-two percent of agricultural land was in the hands of 11 percent of the population, and six ranchers controlled over 17,000 hectares of peninsula land (COBRUDES 1997). In other words, ecotourism represents a continuation of these patterns of stratified landholding and unequal social and economic power, albeit with a new set of actors involved—foreign ecotourism investors—rather than a rupturing of an egalitarian society. Furthermore, when ecotourism began to expand on the peninsula, gold mining was already in decline because of new environmental restrictions and falling world market prices.[15] Likewise, cattle and rice production on the peninsula has stagnated since the mid-1980s, in part because of government policies of trade liberalization. Ecotourism on Osa, therefore, has not so much directly disrupted more traditional local- and nationally oriented economic activities as offered additional income-generating opportunities.

Despite a discourse of support for small-scale ecotourism as a sustainable development practice dating from the 1990s, the Costa Rican state appears to have played a limited role in mitigating the patterns of stratification in ecotourism on the Osa peninsula. Such unequal outcomes, in fact, have been facilitated to a degree by the Costa Rican state's weak enforcement of regulations to limit foreign control of coastal land and tourism incentive laws, whose tax benefits and subsidies have been disproportionately captured by large-scale and international tourism enterprises (Honey 1999).[16] A member of an NGO that supports ecotourism on Osa explained, "For the businessmen, the large projects, the big hotels, there is a very clear policy of government support, but for people like us there's no support and little chance of competing with the big enterprises." Jacinto, struggling to establish an ecotourism business, is one of a number of ecotourism participants who have called upon the government to play a more active role in supporting small, local ecotourism businesses. Jacinto stated, "The government is to blame. They should control the foreigners, give work to the ex-miners. Foreigners carry out tourism projects; they make big investments and all the profits go to them. And all we can do is sit here watching them pass by and do nothing [to change the situation]."

ENVIRONMENTAL IMPACTS

Local government and NGO officials, as well as ecotourism operators, widely credit the park creation and the expansion of largely foreign-owned private ecotourism reserves with bringing deforestation on the peninsula almost to a halt and in some instances actually facilitating forest regeneration.[17] Many key environmental problems identified on the peninsula—logging in the Golfo Dulce Forest Reserve, poaching in the national park, agrochemical runoff into the gulf, and solid waste disposal in the towns—are linked to more traditional extraction and agricultural activities (MIDEPLAN 2003; Van den Hombergh 1999; COBRUDES 1997; Maldonado Ulloa 1997). Indirectly, ecotourism has helped shift local participation away from such environmentally damaging activities as rice cultivation and cattle ranching. It has also provided a material underpinning for collective mobilization on environmental issues discussed later.

Several studies of the Osa peninsula have identified no serious negative environmental impacts to date from ecotourism lodges and related services (Rosero-Bixby, Maldonado-Ulloa, and Bonilla-Carrión 2002; COBRUDES 1997). Although only one Osa eco-lodge, Lapa Rios, has received a government Certificate of Sustainable Tourism, local informants have reported that most eco-lodges leave as much rain forest intact as possible on their properties, build in styles that blend in with the natural environment, and employ technologies such as solar panel heating and environmentally friendly waste control measures (Lapa Rios 2002). Furst and Hein's (2002b) research on the environmental impacts of ecotourism on Osa, however, is more pessimistic, arguing that the water use, sewage, and solid waste linked to the peninsula's ecotourism are not environmentally sustainable. Minca and Linda (2000) note as well that less well-funded Costa Rican–owned ecotourism ventures employ more environmentally damaging techniques of waste disposal than foreign-owned eco-lodges on the peninsula.

On Costa Rica's northwestern coast, the mass tourism projects involving transnational hotel chains and subsidized by the government have been criticized for causing environmental damage (*Tico Times* 2003; Inman 2002). The experience of Costa Rica's most popular national park, Manuel Antonio, suggests that without mitigating measures, ecotourism may also lead to environmental damage similar to that caused by mass tourism. The park receives around 250,000 ecotourism visitors a year and has experienced overcrowding; a proliferation of hotels, bars, and tourist concessions; damage to plants and animals; and pollution (Honey 1999; *Tico Times* 1999a, 1999b).

SOCIOCULTURAL IMPACTS

The experience of the Osa peninsula also suggests the need to move beyond abstract generalizations of the sociocultural impacts of ecotourism and take into account specific local contexts that mediate the ecotourism experience.[18] Overall, Puerto Jiménez residents' assessments of the sociocultural impact of ecotourism were mixed and highlighted the complexities of these processes. Increased drug use and prostitution, as well as cultural disruption, emerged as the most important areas of concern in Puerto Jiménez.[19] Town residents interviewed believed ecotourists and foreign residents have encouraged recreational drug use among local young people. They also alleged that some foreigners have used ecotourism as a cover for international drug trafficking activities.[20] Other informants suggested that with the constant presence of foreign visitors and residents in Puerto Jiménez and the air of glamour and excitement they have brought to this once quiet rural town, local young people now want to imitate the foreigners' lifestyles.

In modeling or imposing new norms and values on the peninsula, ecotourists have a number of advantages—generally higher levels of wealth, education, and status than local residents and participation in broader transnational institutional and social networks (*Tico Times* 2002; Cheong and Miller 2000). This unequal discursive power is not centered on state or bureaucratic agents but rather on relatively privileged foreigners who bring specific, external ways of life and representations of the environment and its uses. In the worst-case scenario, the integrity of place-based ways of life is lost as local people seek to imitate and please ecotourists. Skeptics also ague that however strongly it is packaged as a sustainable form of development, ecotourism is at bottom green capitalism. As such, it is inextricably linked to an ideology that may be disempowering. This ideology, on an individual and collective level, critics suggest, inculcates values of competition, individualism, material accumulation, consumption, and commodification that may atomize communities, limit collective action, and restrain local imaginings of qualitatively different forms of economic and social development (Mowforth and Munt 2003; Duffy 2002).

On the Osa peninsula, informants have suggested that ecotourism has intensified a longer-term dynamic of cultural modernization by shifting earlier values of frugality and commitment to family and social relations to a greater emphasis on consumption, efficiency, and foreign lifestyles. These implicit and explicit cultural requisites embedded in ecotourism as a market-based activity, while resonating with postindustrial societies and the deepening of economic globalization, represent cultural change and even loss for local residents. Ecotourism is not simply an economic alternative, but for certain subcultural groups on the peninsula it signifies a transformation of valued ways of life. Gold miners, for example, have lost the relatively autonomous lifestyle of panning for gold to a more modern form of work, having to answer to a boss and work a fixed schedule. Likewise, during the high season, certain ecotourism workers such as cooks may be required to work fifteen-hour days or longer, disrupting family and social life in a way more traditional economic activities on the peninsula have not done.

It is also important, however, not to overlook local peoples' agency to contest and appropriate dominant discourses and practices. The Osa experience suggests that while significant inequalities exist, in some instances ecotourism has facilitated more sustained and more egalitarian interactions between local residents. A number of Costa Rican ecotourism operators and employees interviewed, for example, expressed self-confidence in their interactions with ecotourists and a willingness to verbally confront them about perceived inappropriate or demeaning behavior. In addition, these Costa Ricans see some expatriates and ecotourists as contributors to positive social change at the local level. Ecotourists have offered their time and funding for medical services, environmental education seminars, programs for single mothers, and other community projects on the peninsula.

As discussed earlier, a key element of empowerment is a material base for communities. Ecotourism, even with its patterns of stratification, has drawn together and provided a material base of support for a critical mass of politically active Costa Ricans, whose localized environmental discourses will be explored in Chapter 4. In the early 1990s these Puerto Jiménez residents, the majority of whom are participants in ecotourism businesses, collectively mobilized against the plans of a transnational wood product company, Stone Container, to build a wood chip plant on the peninsula, citing both environmental and nationalistic concerns (see Van den Hombergh 1999). Through alliances with national and international NGOs, media and political lobbying campaigns, demonstrations, and highway blockages, the activists were able to halt the project.

Local environmental activism on the peninsula has also served as a counterweight to at times weak and poorly funded state enforcement of environmental laws and regulations. A 1996 Forestry Law allowed logging within the Golfo Dulce Forest Reserve under sustainable management plans to be approved by the Ministry of Environment and Energy (MINAE).[21] Soon after this law was passed, Osa activists protested the fact that hundreds of trees per week were being logged in violation of the law and with the complicity of corrupt local MINAE offices (La Nación 1998, 1997a; *Tico Times* 1997a, 1997b). As with the Stone campaign, local activists sought out the news media to present their claims. They carried out protests that included blocking the highway and a visit by Greenpeace's Rainbow Warrior, and they succeeded in greatly reducing logging on the peninsula by 2000 (La Nación 2001, 2000a, 2000b).

CONCLUSION

In evaluating the degree to which ecotourism is a market activity that may contribute to sustainable development, the Osa peninsula represents in many senses a best-case scenario, with an absence of transnational corporations and a historically active and mobilized local population. Even so, the results have been mixed. On the one hand, ecotourism has brought important economic benefits to zones such as Puerto Jiménez, most notably employment opportunities, with limited negative environmental impact to date. It has also provided a material base of support that has enabled some peninsula residents to develop alternative ways of life that in part eschew the dominant economic and cultural trends of expanding capitalism of ever-increasing efficiency, productivity, and accumulation.

On the negative side, however, Osa's ecotourism boom has further eroded local control of and access to land and natural resources while advancing state and foreign influence on the peninsula. The peninsula's tiered ecotourism sector also suggests that even in zones transnational corporations have yet to penetrate, smaller-scale patterns of stratification and exclusion are still likely to emerge. Hierarchies of nationality, social class, and gender have been reproduced through unequal initial access to land, capital, and cultural knowledge; unequal insertion into social and institutional networks; restrictive gender norms; and the relative absence of redistributive, leveling state policies. In the 1980s exclusion was physical as gold miners were removed from Corcovado National Park in the name of environmental conservation. The 1990s saw a shift to a less dramatic but still powerful process of market exclusion as key groups of poorer Costa Ricans faced obstacles to equal participation in the most profitable ecotourism activities.

Chapter 4

"Nature That Gives Them Life"

Grassroots Sustainability on the Osa Peninsula

I have argued that sustainable development is an inherently contested concept and that particular interpretations and practices of sustainability have often been implemented in a top-down manner in Central America. In contrast, this is the first of three chapters to explore specific visions of sustainability as articulated and practiced from the bottom up and the ways those discourses converge with and diverge from dominant discourse. This chapter also focuses on the multiple strands of dominant sustainable development policies—development interactions, neoliberal reforms, and environmental protection—evaluating the ways these interactions influence community empowerment as agents of sustainability. While this chapter considers collective identity formation and ways community groups may articulate and act to defend common interests, I attempt not to perpetuate an uncritical rural populism or to assume a unitary set of interests among all community members. Rather, I seek to identify inequalities, tensions, and potential cleavages within communities and consider which voices and perspectives emerge to the forefront and why.

In exploring Osa peninsula residents' visions of sustainability, several caveats should be kept in mind. First, only in a limited number of instances do these data result from direct questioning about the concept of sustainable development. The phrase "sustainable development" (*desarrollo sostenible*) forms a part of technical and institutional discourse, most commonly employed by middle-class professionals, government officials, and nongovernmental organization (NGO) technicians. Osa residents with more limited formal education and localized social networks are often unfamiliar with the term or find it difficult and abstract. The analysis that follows, therefore, draws on more concrete discussions of key economic, social, and environmental issues in the communities. In building a comparative analysis of grassroots and institutional discourses of sustainability, I am not simply identifying preexisting categories of thought. I am inevitably rearranging, omitting, and imposing order on complex discourses to construct external typologies. This discussion is not meant to imply that there is a single or unitary vision of sustainability. Rather, I have drawn together perspectives with similar elements, some more directly and clearly articulated and others implicit, expressed in both collective and individual day-to-day practices. The interviews incorporated two key sectors on the peninsula: ecotourism operators and environmental activists in the town of Puerto Jiménez and a smaller sampling of agriculturalists and gold miners from the community of La Palma, located at the edge of the Golfo Dulce Forest Reserve. (See the Appendix for further details.)

LOCALIZED ENVIRONMENTALISM

Many of those who migrated to the Osa peninsula in the twentieth century brought with them an instrumentalist perspective of the natural world. Nature in this narrative was a space of hardship and even danger, primarily serving the material subsistence needs of the human population.[1] The Osa peninsula's ecotourism boom led to both an economic reconfiguration on the peninsula and a social, cultural, and ideological transformation. On the one hand, the ecotourists and expatriates arrived on the peninsula seeking an escape from the mundane and stressful lifestyles of postindustrial society through contract with the natural world. This sector has tended to view nature as a space of adventure, risk, aesthetic enjoyment, and leisure activity while representing local practices and ways of life as environmentally destructive (Mowforth and Munt 2003). In some instances, ecotourists bring ecocentric orientations, a belief in the intrinsic value of nature.

Some of the critical ecotourism literature has argued that external representations of the environment are imposed upon relatively powerless local populations.[2] I suggest that on the Osa peninsula, however, local residents have not been passive receptors of external environmental discourses and a unidirectional exercise of power. In fact, what has emerged is a greater plurality and complexity of meanings given to the environment.³ On the one hand, strong pockets of instrumentalist representations of the environment persist, particularly in communities still dependent on agriculture and cattle ranching. Simultaneously, ecotourism has facilitated the formation of new, localized socio-environmental discourses and forms of collective mobilization. Ecotourism has provided the basis for a self-selection process through which environmentally conscious Costa Ricans from other regions have relocated to the peninsula and utilized ecotourism as a means to materially support a lifestyle composed of close contact with the natural world and activism on environmental issues. In other instances, longer-term peninsula residents have moved gradually toward this new environmentalism through interactions with ecotourists, environmental education, and a more pragmatic recognition of ecotourism's economic benefits.⁴ The individuals who produce this localized environmental discourse tend to be concentrated in the Puerto Jiménez area, have been active in both ecotourism and the peninsula's major environmental campaigns, and are generally middle class by Costa Rican standards. Women also have a strong presence in this group.

This localized environmental discourse suggests that human beings in a universal sense—across differences of class, race, gender, and nationality—share a fundamental ethical and spiritual relationship with the natural world and that ultimately it is impossible to separate the well-being of humanity from that of nature. Leonardo, an environmental activist who works with a local NGO, defined sustainability as "a commitment to the human species . . . a philosophy of life. It's quality of life, a commitment to the earth, love for the generations to come. Sustainable development will guarantee us life but not riches. . . . With intuition, by smell, people believe in nature. Nature is everyone's stock. It's a collective good, the most important good humanity possesses."

Elena, an ecotourism operator and community activist, argued that even the campesino migrants who came to the peninsula and cleared the forests for pasture could not negate their ties to the natural world: "People have an innate appreciation of beauty. They appreciate the ocean, seeing the dolphins leap. As human beings, we cannot deny the connection between ourselves and nature. Those who first came and cut down the forests, it hurt them. The campesino says, 'I was destructive.' We have to recognize the power of natural resources over human beings. The majority love nature that gives them life."

This environmental discourse challenges precepts of dominant sustainability which purport that increases in material wealth can be universally equated with improved quality of life and that economic growth should always be maximized. Leonardo argued that the dominant economic system "treats nature like one more good to be bought and sold. It's a culture to make money however you can, and this logic says that the forest has to produce something—if not tourists, then lumber or pastures. This kind of mercantilism is opposed to the logic of true sustainable development."

In practical terms, these and other local residents have opposed large-scale tourism projects promoted by the Costa Rican Tourism Institute, forgoing potential economic benefits in favor of the quality of life supported by small-scale tourism projects (*Tico Times* 2000). Quality of life is reframed in this perspective as daily contact with the natural environments of beaches and rain forests, time for leisure, and relative material simplicity. In other words, a mirror image of the stressful daily routines in the "cement prisons" of artificial urban environments. This localized environmental discourse differs from some key assumptions of the dominant discourses of sustainability, but it also diverges from more strongly ecocentric perspectives held by some ecotourists. Specifically, this localized environmental discourse views conservation of nature as inseparable from social reform and social justice. These Costa Ricans negotiate complex intermediary positions, recognizing that they have been influenced by and share many of the environmental values and beliefs of the ecotourists and expatriates. Yet as *Ticos* their perspectives are grounded in nationalism and social justice concerns and in long-term experiences of place. They are embedded in networks of family and friends and local ways of life that challenge external "global" environmentalism in which protected areas are closed off from local populations. Specifically, this group questions both foreign control of large amounts of land on the peninsula and the dominant role foreigners have played in certain environmental conservation efforts on the peninsula.[5]

Leonardo, a cooperative leader, approves of the conservation measures promoted by expatriates but added, "I wouldn't like ever to see a country that isn't ours. The foreigners have millions of dollars and buy the land only for recreation (*para pasear*)." One Costa Rican environmental activist highlighted these tensions as she described a debate with a European colleague:

> [T]he difference between the two of us is that I live inside of this country, and I can't stop thinking about the people who live here. It is not enough just to put up demonstration parcels and buy up land. . . . The impact of the conservation measures on the local population has been very hard. They are told you can't use certain nets at the mouths of the rivers to fish and don't touch the animals. People are here with their arms crossed [doing nothing]. . . . We would arrive at the houses of the campesinos and see their humble faces, and we would go to the kitchen and maybe they would have a little rice, a little lard, two or three plantains, and you know that's all the food they have. Women have just a little bit of soap to wash a week's worth of clothes. It's very hard to see that.

In addition, as a counternarrative to external accounts of environmentally destructive local populations, this discourse draws attention to transnational companies, Osa Forest Products (OFP), and international mining companies that have caused direct environmental damage on the peninsula (Van den Hombergh 1999). Individuals with a localized environmentalism orientation generally recognize the subsistence needs that drive agriculturalists in the Golfo Dulce Forest Reserve to sell trees to loggers, but much like government officials, they highlight unequal market processes in which the bulk of the profits go to lumber companies from outside the zone (see Maldonado Ulloa 1997).

This frame, which combines environmental, nationalist, and populist struggles—Costa Ricans versus foreign investors and transnational corporations—was an effective means to build a coalition in opposition to the Stone Container wood chip plant in the 1990s.[6] In contrast, activists found it more difficult to build support for subsequent anti-logging activities, which highlighted the internal tensions of populist mobilization on the peninsula because local agriculturalists have been the ones active in logging. Activist Tania explained, "To go against the campesino is very difficult. We don't want to strike a blow against the campesinos. We are against the lumber companies, the wealthy people." In this instance, Tania attempted to maintain intact the rural populist orientation of her discourse, including in it the small and medium landowners of the Golfo Dulce Forest Reserve and signaling that her opponents are the "wealthy." For similar reasons, local environmental activists have reported a reluctance to raise issues of pesticide contamination linked to rice production, given the powerful local interests involved (Van den Hombergh 1999).

LIVELIHOOD DISCOURSE

In contrast to this localized environmentalism, some Osa peninsula residents have an instrumentalist perspective toward the environment that prioritizes material subsistence and well-being, as well as way of life.[7] Members of this group are concentrated in the Golfo Dulce Forest Reserve and zones that have largely been excluded from the benefits of ecotourism, are employed in farming and gold mining, and range from poor to moderately well-off. The theme that emerged most strongly in interviews was not economic growth at the macroeconomic level highlighted in dominant institutional discourses of sustainability but rather personal economic well-being, the ability to meet individual and family material needs. The tone of interviews with participants in ecotourism activities and environmental activists was relatively optimistic in terms of the peninsula's ecotourism boom and the partial successes of environmental campaigns. In contrast, the tone of interviews with livelihood supporters was often pessimistic, with a great deal of frustration directed at the Costa Rican state. In many senses this is also a defensive discourse. Miners and agriculturalists, aware that their actions have been represented as environmentally destructive, emphasized the "greed" and "waste" of international mining companies and Osa Forest Products, in contrast to their more benign "subsistence" activities. This discourse is nationalistic, framing agricultural activities in particular as central to Costa Rican cultural identity and economic well-being. Stating "we are all Costa Ricans," these peninsula residents appealed to the imagined collective of national identity and an implicit set of rights and state obligations embedded in particular in the post–World War II expansion of the social welfare state (Edelman 1999; Wilson 1998).[8]

This instrumental livelihood discourse also challenges a key precept of dominant sustainability discourse, which purports that resources are best allocated through the supply-and-demand rationality of markets. In contrast, this perspective implies a more permanent moral and ethical claim to resources to meet basic needs that is outside of, and indeed "above," market forces. Livelihood-oriented residents argue that while they are not necessarily anti-environment or anti-development, what must take priority is meeting the basic needs of the local population, commonly defined by respondents as food, shelter, medical care, and education for their children. Jacinto, a former gold miner and unemployed nature guide, explained, "The [national] park is good, but we need a means of subsistence, work. All of us are in agreement with conservation. It's very beautiful to conserve trees, to have clean rivers. It's all very romantic, very beautiful; but how are we going to eat?"

Another former gold miner in La Palma also emphasized hunger: "People here are environmentally conscious, but people have to eat. And if all they have is trees, what are they going to eat?" Several government officials interviewed, as well as some environmental activists, however, questioned landowners' claims that logging was a matter of family subsistence. It appears that in practice, these "basic needs" claims are made not only by the poor but also by more affluent Costa Rican agricultural producers who recognize that subsistence linked to nationalism is a more effective frame for advancing their claims than the profit motive.

This livelihood perspective essentially frames sustainability not as a "win-win-win" proposition but rather as a set of zero-sum, material trade-offs among environmental protectionism, commercial profit, and local subsistence needs in which the local population has generally emerged as the loser. Tomás, a cattle rancher and cooperative leader, argued that the creation of the national park and the forest reserve "was a hard blow that took away many people's means of subsistence." He also criticized the fact that much of the external funding has gone for environmental projects: "Everything is conservation . . . they [the environmentalists] don't consider at all the farmer who lives off the land. It's only about protecting the forests. They are extremists, and there is no help for farmers. Environmental conservation has arrived [from outside Costa Rica] to impose lots of different laws."

The view that "everything is conservation" is an exaggeration, given that a number of agricultural and income-generating projects have been funded on the peninsula, but it reinforces the claim that environmentalism has made invisible and excluded the needs of the population. Ulises, a rancher who is also active in local politics, stated: "More laws and [environmental] education don't convince me. Environmental programs and posters are for schoolchildren. What is most important are sustainable management projects so that the farmer can live from the farm, eat, send his children to school, diversify. Well-designed programs that guarantee a market, real assistance for rural areas. Not just talk, we want action."

Postdevelopment scholars suggest that state and institutional interventions in the name of dominant sustainable development are not merely ineffective but actually form part of a more insidious project of cultural homogenization and expansion of power by northern elites to create markets for mass-produced global products (Goldman 2005, 2001, 1998a; Sachs 1999, 1993; Rahnema and Bawtree 1997; Escobar 1995). Such dynamics of cultural homogenization can be seen among the peninsula's subgroup of former and current gold miners, who have experienced dominant sustainability as a cultural disruption in which their locally grounded way of life has been constrained in the name of national and global environmentalism.

Representations and the normative value of the gold miners' way of life, however, are deeply contested on the Osa peninsula. Widespread negative stereotypes of this subculture, repeated by activists and NGO and government personnel interviewed, emphasized miners' "shady pasts," individualism, and high level of alcohol consumption. Ministry of Environment and Energy (MINAE) officials, for example, characterized the former gold miners as interested in "easy money" and lacking in the cultural orientation and long-term perspective necessary to engage in more sustainable income-generating activities. Gold miners interviewed acknowledged some of the criticisms but offered a more complex portrait of the subculture that emphasized autonomy, mutual support systems, and respect for nature. Néstor, who panned gold for twenty years, stated, "If you arrive sometimes without food, without money, you go by a friend's site and he asks, 'Have you eaten?' and makes food for both of you. And then he invites you [to] 'work with me for a while.' As miners we shared a lot." Gold miners also challenged studies that have argued that they are environmentally destructive (see González Giraud 1992; Brenes et al. 1988). Studies by Donovan (1994), Barquero Barrantes (1988), and Vargas Ulate (n.d.) provide evidence that in the 1970s and 1980s transnational mining companies damaged the peninsula's riverbeds with greater intensity than did the artisan gold miners, with the tacit permission of the Costa Rican government.

STATE ENVIRONMENTALISM

I have suggested that dominant sustainability as a multistranded discourse holds implications for the range of functions and policy options available to Central American states. The role of the state is expanded in environmental protection, reduced in economic interventions under neoliberalism, and reshaped in social policy to carry out targeted assistance programs (World Bank 2006a, 2003d, 2000). The government of Costa Rica has enjoyed high levels of legitimacy linked to the nation's post-1948 democratic forms of governance, use of negotiation over force in resolving social conflicts, and a social safety net (Edelman 1999; Rodríguez, Castro, and Rowland Espinosa 1998; Wilson 1998; Seligson and Booth 1995).[9] Since the 1980s, with external support, the Costa Rican government has expanded the size and functions of its environmental agencies and strengthened its legal and regulatory environmental frameworks through such legislation as the 1996 Forestry Law.[10] Reflecting this trend, funding for the Corcovado National Park administration has increased since the park's founding in the mid-1970s. In 1987 the park had one administrator, two forest inspectors, and five forest guards. Fifteen years later the park administration had expanded and over twenty rangers patrolled the park, although poaching within the park has recently emerged as a serious problem (*Tico Times* 2004; Barquero Barrantes 1988:64).[11] Programs have also been launched to improve relationships between park authorities and the local population, such as the 1995 Osa Conservation Area program, funded through the Global Environmental Facility and the World Bank, which created an advisory committee made up of representatives from the government, the private sector, and civil society to manage funds for local sustainable development projects (Barquero Barrantes 1988; MINAE and SINAC n.d.).

In light of the ecotourism boom and the park's relative success in conserving the peninsula's rain forest, government and NGO informants suggested that by the 1990s, local residents widely accepted the presence of Corcovado National Park. Conflict continues, however, in communities such as La Palma over the present and future status of the forest reserve, MINAE regulation of logging activities, and Agrarian Development Institute (IDA) prohibitions on the buying and selling of land.[12] In essence, as the Costa Rican state has expanded its regulatory control over peninsula land and natural resources, the locus of land tenure conflict has shifted from a struggle between local squatters and a transnational company to one between the local population and the state. Osa's ecotourism boom, which has sharply increased the value of land on the peninsula, has further intensified this conflict. Landholders in the Golfo Dulce Forest Reserve interviewed concurred with the dominant sustainability perspective, that they should be granted full legal title to their landholdings so they can invest in the land or sell it to foreign investors for a profit (Deininger and Binswanger 1999). For their part, officials working for IDA, a government institution where leftists have historically had a strong influence, have emphasized from a social justice perspective that government controls are designed precisely to inhibit growing foreign control of peninsula land and the exacerbation of social and economic inequalities.[13]

In interviews, few Osa residents questioned the scope of state authority in regulating access to and use of land and natural resources under the rubric of environmentalism. Rather, Osa residents, from both the environmentalist and the livelihood perspective, contended that the Costa Rican state has not served as a counterweight to market inequalities or as a neutral arbiter of class-based conflicts. Instead, they believe the state has favored the wealthy and the well connected in environmental enforcement efforts, incentives, and subsidies (see Van den Hombergh 1999). Inés, a small businesswoman and activist, stated: "There are no incentives for the small farmers. But the big companies, yes, they're allowed to exploit the wood and MINAE lets them. . . . Those people who have political power are the same ones who have economic power. Honest people don't get involved in politics, or they don't last long [if they do get involved]." A La Palma small farmer argued: "People should be allowed to cut down trees. MINAE has a policy of no wood, not even to complete a house (*cerrar la casa*). Then a millionaire goes [after wood] and they [the government] will let him do whatever he wants. The campesino is a poor guy holding on by his fingernails, and dozens of [the millionaire's] trucks leave full of wood."

MINAE officials and some environmental activists, however, argued that local residents often deceptively frame their claims to natural resources as meeting subsistence needs, providing "food for their children" and shelter, when in fact logging is commercial and profit seeking.[14] My field observations suggest that it is not necessarily always the poorest individuals but at times the more affluent who are engaged in logging activities. Another key issue that emerged in interviews with residents of both Puerto Jiménez and La Palma was corruption. A large number of environmental activists and agriculturalists raised this issue on their own initiative in reference to specific government agencies, as well as NGOs and local cooperatives. Comments of this type included:

> The environmental service payments go only to those with [land] titles or the powerful people who have money to pay a lawyer or bribe officials to get a title. (local NGO technician)
>
> The government is too susceptible to bribes (*choricero*). We don't feel tranquil. (La Palma agriculturalist)
>
> There was corruption in past governments, but now it is more shameless (*descarado*). (local government official)

It was beyond the scope of this study to investigate specific allegations of corruption, and it is important to keep in mind that some such commentaries are not the product of firsthand experience. Rather, some of the comments may be hearsay and rumors easily accepted by a local population already skeptical of the government.[15] Regardless of their veracity, such allegations undermine the credibility of government environmental rules enforcement and may be utilized by the local population as a means to "justify" their own illegal activities, such as logging in the forest reserve.[16]

NEOLIBERAL REFORMS

From the 1950s to the 1970s, government presence greatly expanded in rural areas through the extension of social security benefits to a majority of the population and the expansion of health, telephone, water, and electrical services (Edelman 1999). Costa Rican agriculturalists in particular benefited from state-subsidized loans (largely for cattle production) and from the presence of the National Production Council, which purchased grains from farmers at guaranteed prices, stored surpluses, and set subsidized consumer prices (Edelman 1999). In the early 1980s, facing high inflation, government deficits, and external debt, the Costa Rican government initiated its first structural adjustment program, and over the next several decades neoliberal reforms advanced slowly, the subject of much political controversy.

The World Bank contends that neoliberal reforms in Costa Rica have been necessary to control fiscal deficits and inflation and to revitalize the export sector (World Bank 2000).[17] The World Bank (2000) points to Costa Rica's relatively strong economic growth in the 1990s and the successful establishment of a microchip plant in the late 1990s as evidence of neoliberal policy success. Although some agricultural producers supported free trade in general by the 1990s, the implementation of neoliberal policies in Costa Rica has been highly contested, as highlighted by the 2000 "combo" protest (Seligson 2001; Raventos 1997; Román 1994; Edelman 1991).[18] For Costa Rica's rural sector, neoliberal reforms have signified an end to guaranteed purchase prices, greater restrictions and higher real interest rates on credit, and a lowering of tariffs and nonmonetary trade barriers for agricultural products (Edelman 1999).

On the Osa peninsula, local government officials, NGO technicians, ecotourism operators, and agriculturalists interviewed were widely critical of neoliberal reforms. They argued that policies popularly referred to as "free trade" or "globalization" have been externally imposed on Costa Rica by international financial institutions (IFIs) and the United States and contributed to the stagnation of cattle and rice production on the peninsula in the 1990s (see Van den Hombergh 1999). Community activist Cordelia argued: "The government imposes globalization and small farmers suffer the most. The small ranchers and rice growers can't sell their crops for a good price. In Costa Rica our quality of life, higher per capita income, and social benefits all increase the cost of our goods, and it becomes cheaper to import goods from abroad than to produce [them] here." Tomás, a rancher and community leader, stated: "International policies pressure whatever [Costa Rican] government is in power to follow those same policies. In order to receive loans, Costa Rica has to follow these orders. Globalization is a total failure. We plant corn in March and harvest it in August. In September it goes on sale, but then a Mexican company floods the market with U.S. corn."

A number of farmers interviewed also suggested that bank loans are difficult to obtain and that high interest rates erode profits. Martín, a farmer, concluded, "Why bother to take out a loan? What are you going to use to pay it back?" A local government official, Lucas, was also critical of free trade policies, stated, "The investors come from Japan, North America, Europe, and they choke us. They don't let us grow slowly in our own way. They choke us economically, like the policies of global commerce choke the small farmer."

Studies by Ruben (2001), Reed (1996), Gibson (1996), and Goodman and Redclift (1991a) document cases in Central and Latin America in which neoliberal policy measures have led to disincentives for sustainable land and natural resource use. Many Osa agriculturalists and environmental activists interviewed echoed the argument that neoliberal reforms have pushed some peninsula residents toward environmentally damaging logging activities and made it difficult to achieve sustainability on the peninsula. Environmental activist Leonardo was pessimistic in his assessment of peninsula conservation measures: "Here we're doing small things, but the world economy doesn't change. The big companies contaminate ten times more than we protect here. Before, they [the developed countries] wanted primary materials from us. Now they quiet their consciences by paying for a little oxygen." Along similar lines, activist Tania stated, "The policies of the United States are choking the developing countries. They make it difficult to have sustainable development in our own way, to conserve our biodiversity.... You can fight against a specific company, a specific policy, but to fight against everything is very difficult."

PROCESSES OF EMPOWERMENT

This book has suggested that community empowerment—understood here as processes and pathways that reinforce the power, meaning, and cultural and environmental integrity of local settings while contributing to broader social and structural transformations—lies at the heart of sustainability. One thread of the critical livelihood literature has suggested that the sources of community empowerment are largely internal—cultural traditions, identification with place, solidarities nurtured in the spaces of everyday life—and are therefore weakened through contact with and penetration of external ideologies, ways of being, and market processes linked to globalization (Sachs 1999; Friedmann and Rangan 1993). Osa agriculturalists in particular have perceived the implementation of neoliberal reforms as a loss of control and power, as they are forced to compete with powerful economic actors in wider global markets within the context of limited state support. A more multistranded examination of local engagement with exogenous forces, however, suggests more complex processes that both undermine and support community mobilization in favor of self-defined sustainability.

I have suggested that two elements of community empowerment to be explored are the material basis of collective action and the development of a critical ideology. On the Osa peninsula, transnational processes of ecotourism, while unequal in their impacts and advancing foreign control of land, have drawn a self-selected critical mass of environmentally oriented individuals to the peninsula and provided them with a material base of support for their activism. Similarly, longer-term residents whose income is now linked to ecotourism reported that they have greater interest in and support for environmental issues.[19] Likewise, the arrival of ecotourists and expatriates, with their particular forms of environmental discourse and perceptions of nature, has fomented the localized environmentalism discussed earlier, which mixes a universalized environmental view of the connection between humankind and nature with nationalism and embedded local livelihoods. Puerto Jiménez is the peninsula's focal point of both ecotourism and environmental activism, in contrast to zones such as La Palma, a community with little participation in ecotourism and a center of opposition to environmental campaigns.

Contemporary mobilization on the peninsula also draws upon a longer-term localized culture of resistance dating from the 1970s nationalist struggles against Osa Forest Products (OFP). Environmental activist Elena argued, "The essence was the same as before: a struggle against a transnational corporation, corrupt politicians, lack of respect of the constitution, of the law. Opportunists who want to take advantage of the poorest [residents]." The movement's success in pressuring the government to expropriate OFP land and the physical risks involved increased a sense of the efficacy of collective action and the self-confidence to act in public spheres among some Osa residents.[20] These past struggles also provide a motivational frame for contemporary struggles, in that residents feel control of the land was "earned" through past struggle and should not be ceded to foreign investors or state environmental agencies.

Community interactions with external NGOs, in turn, have had a more mixed impact on community empowerment. In the 1990s, external funding for sustainable development projects in Central America increased substantially and helped propel a sharp growth in the number of NGOs.[21] Central America's NGO sectors are heterogeneous, with important national variations in size, organizational and administrative capacity, and political orientation (Fundación Arias 1997b, 1993). NGO technicians interviewed noted that Costa Rica has the region's strongest network of environmental NGOs, but its social development NGO sector is small and relatively weak. NGOs in general continue to depend heavily on external funding. Costa Rica's largest and best-funded NGOs generally share many of the values and assumptions of the dominant discourse of sustainability and have personnel who move easily between government and NGO positions (Young 1994). NGOs that promote more profound economic and social transformations that resonate with critical discourses of sustainability tend to have the most difficulty obtaining funds, and they rely heavily on volunteer labor.

One such NGO, the Costa Rican Ecological Association (AECO), played a key role in supporting Osa residents in their campaign against the proposed Stone Container wood chip plant (Van den Hombergh 1999). AECO has taken a critical approach to sustainability, arguing that Costa Rica's neoliberal model of economic growth has augmented poverty and environmental damage (AECO n.d.). Activists interviewed who worked with AECO during the Stone campaign praised the relationships NGO personnel built with residents and the ways AECO encouraged local activists to overcome their fears and lack of knowledge and move into new spheres of collective action. In some instances, interactions with NGOs such as AECO also appear to have facilitated a type of consciousness raising, enabling some local residents to move beyond a local "project" focus and conceptualize sustainable development in broader, more systemic terms.

In contrast to other, more traditional male-dominated mobilizations of rural Central America, much of the leadership and drive behind Osa's 1990s environmental campaigns came from women, and those campaigns have indirectly promoted female empowerment.[22] Community informants traced women's activism back to the 1970s and 1980s land struggles, when men targeted by the government for arrest went into hiding or were jailed. For practical reasons, women stepped forward into public spheres of activism, traditionally considered the exclusive space of men. Female environmental activists also framed their participation in collective action in largely essentialist terms, suggesting that women by nature have a deeper connection to the natural world and hold a more holistic and long-term vision of human well-being (Mies and Shiva 1993).[23] Activist Tania stated, "It's a woman's nature to be a mother, and that motivates us to protect others. We women are more responsible, more committed [than men]. It's part of our nature. Men are interested in other things. A father will never give the same affection and attention as a mother. You see this in children. Girls will sweep and clean the house, and boys quickly leave this [the house] behind."

A number of activists, both male and female, also recognized that the environmental campaigns opened up space more broadly for women's participation in public spaces and collective action. Elena stated,

> We are recognized as "women in pants," capable of doing anything. No one says, "Ay, she's just a woman." . . . The women stood up when the men were quiet, they were the brave and risk takers, in the house, on the street, at work, they would go to dangerous places. Women never missed a meeting or said "I'm too tired." Women were the first to volunteer to do a task. Women were called to defend the land, the gulf, the children, all [the] people.

OBSTACLES TO EMPOWERMENT

Even as ecotourism and environmentalism have advanced processes of empowerment for some peninsula residents, gender-specific obstacles continue. First, traditional gender norms of rural Costa Rica—particularly the *machista* precept of gendered space, "men in the street, women in the house," and the concept of male "jealousy" (*celos*), efforts to control women's movements outside the home to prevent potential sexual contact with other men—have limited women's activism. Women whose husbands or *compañeros* do not approve of their political activities have been forced to employ subterfuge, such as working on campaign activities late in the evening or lying about attending meetings, so as not to be accused of neglecting traditional female responsibilities in the home. Another gender-specific form of social control on the peninsula has been gossip critical of female activists, accusing them of promiscuity with men and lesbianism (Van den Hombergh 1999).

In addition to these gender-specific issues, NGO-administered projects designed to promote sustainable development have not always achieved their stated objectives and in some instances appear to have contributed to cynicism and demobilization. The BOSCOSA project, funded by USAID, was developed in part as a response to the mid-1980s conflict between park authorities and gold miners.[24] Components of the BOSCOSA program included protection of natural resources, resolution of land tenancy issues through individual titling, promotion of agriculture and sustainable forestry, ecotourism, environmental education, research, and mining—all implemented through grassroots organizations and local participation (Donovan 1994; Fundación Neotrópica 1991). Program evaluations note that BOSCOSA was successful in improving forestry practices on 6,439 hectares of land (Carbarle et al. cited in Donovan 1994). Van den Hombergh's (1999) survey found, however, that participants felt the projects were poorly designed and that personnel were unable to win residents' trust. Soon after the BOSCOSA project, the European Community launched a multimillion-dollar project in the resettlement communities to promote nontraditional export crops such as cassava, yam (ñame), and fruit of the peach palm (pixbae). Several different accounts exist as to why the project did not achieve its stated goals, but government and NGO informants agree that marketing goals were not met (see Lewin et al. 1993).[25]

A great majority of Osa residents interviewed believe that to date, development projects on the peninsula have done little to advance sustainability in either dominant or alternative forms, and they expressed frustration at and mistrust of projects and specific NGOs. La Palma farmer Hortensio stated, "They [the NGOs] capture all the money for themselves. It's all good for them. They pay no taxes, buy their cars. They use the money donated by other countries for their own personal benefit."[26] Tomás, a rancher and cooperative leader, stated, "The government and NGOs don't plan projects well. They spend their time doing experiments on poor farmers." In contrast to this mistrust of local and national NGOs, some residents gave more distant, transnational actors the benefit of the doubt as to their good intentions. Nature guide Boris explained, "The developed countries with problems with carbon dioxide and the ozone cap, they are giving lots of money to Costa Rica, [to] countries with rain forests, to give people subsidies. But the money never reaches its destination, and the European donors don't even realize this." This mistrust of sustainable development projects and NGOs on the peninsula may mean that some residents will be more reluctant to participate in organizations and collective activities in the future.

Ideally, grassroots organizing on the Osa peninsula serves as a type of incubator of empowerment and democratic practices, a space of face-to-face interactions where participants are able to gain knowledge, experience, and self-confidence in collective decision making and action. The Costa Rica experience, however, suggests that even to the degree that such incipient, democratic, and empowered spaces can be nurtured at the local level, they will also likely face constant pressures of encroachment from political parties and the political culture of the state. Ethnographic studies by Meyer (1999) and de Vries (1997) have identified patterns of political patronage, clientelism, and dependency in state–civil society relationships in rural Costa Rica. Along these lines, forest reserve landowner Gaspar is suspicious of calls for government-community negotiations on land issues:

> People are illiterate, they don't understand things. The government manipulates them, offers them ice cream as if they were children so they will stop crying. But what we have to do is organize ourselves ahead of time so we can defend ourselves against so many anomalies that have happened here. . . . During the campaigns all the politicians arrive here with big favors. They go around hugging the campesinos. The campesinos are their favorites, and there are lots of pats on the back. But when they are in power, they forget everything.

Osa activists suggested that grassroots mobilization on the peninsula is also undermined by a lack of true autonomy of organizations. They cited instances in which local political figures have attempted to infiltrate community organizations and utilize them for political party support and personal ambitions. Ulises, himself active in local politics, also argued that local organizations must break ties of dependency and clientelism:

> There are people who undermine our organizational efforts. They don't want us to get ahead. They make our work difficult, and we have to spend a lot of time explaining to people why they should organize. . . . Community organizations have to be autonomous. They have to define their own way of thinking and working. They aren't independent, and it's bad to depend on the institutions, that kind of paternalism like a father and child.

These critiques contain an implicit characterization of Costa Rican formal politics and political culture not as a space of service but rather as nurturing self-interest, manipulation, and opportunism, in contrast to the ethical and even spiritual principles claimed by environmental activists. Yet even as grassroots organizations seek to shield their spaces of mobilization from dominant political culture, they have not stopped making claims to the state. On the contrary, Osa residents continue to seek out engagement and attempt to manage the risks of cooptation and dependency to try to obtain resources and legal and regulatory support from the state.

CONCLUSION

This chapter has explored the contrasting content and claims of discourses of sustainability that have emerged on the Osa peninsula. The localized environmental perspective, concentrated in Puerto Jiménez and among ecotourism operators, places primary value on conservation of ecosystems and the quality of life that comes with frequent contact with the natural world. This perspective offers a more radical critique of the assumptions and values of dominant sustainability discourse, questioning its primary focus on economic accumulation and identifying underlying contradictions of free-market policies and maximization of economic growth. A combination of local and global factors—a historical and localized culture of resistance, alliances with national and international NGOs, and material support resulting from ecotourism—has enabled ecotourism operators and environmental activists to take collective action in favor of their vision of sustainable development. In contrast, other peninsula residents engaged in agriculture, ranching, and gold mining hold a livelihood vision of sustainability that places as its core value not economic growth on a national scale but rather meeting family subsistence needs.

The Osa experience also illustrates that the multistranded package of policies of dominant sustainability may impact local communities in complex and even contradictory ways, both empowering and disempowering. The withdrawal of the state in economic terms and the simultaneous expansion of the state's role in environmental protection have undermined to a degree traditional ways of life and increased tensions with key population sectors on the Osa peninsula. On the other hand, state expansion of the park system laid the basis for the ecotourism boom, with its economic benefits and support for localized environmentalism. In addition, while I have framed sustainable development as a transnational discourse supported by IFIs, its policies are still overseen and implemented by states. In this case study, it appears that the "politics" of sustainability are also still focused on the state more than on transnational institutions. The state remains a target of community activism, and its agents in turn seek to influence and channel more autonomous grassroots organizations. Finally, the Osa experience draws our attention to the ways the formation of interests and claims and "community" mobilization are mediated by an individual's location, particularly in terms of geographic zone, occupation, class, and gender.

Chapter 5

"Right Behind Him Are the Campesinos with Axes"

Developing the Estero Real

This chapter shifts focus to Nicaragua and the community of Miraflores, located on the edge of the Estero Real, a 46,000-hectare mangrove ecosystem that offers a refuge and food for a variety of estuarine species (IDR and CATIE 1999). It explores the implications for sustainability of the transformation of the Estero Real from a locally controlled space of subsistence to a site subject to state environmental control and commercial activities. In particular, I consider the economic, social, and environmental impacts of estuary shrimp production and the ways these processes have advanced or undermined the capacity of local communities to act as empowered agents of sustainability.

OVERVIEW OF THE ESTUARY

Like the Osa peninsula and the Bayano region of Panama, for many years the Estero Real, whose "saltwater" lands are not suitable for agriculture, was a remote, sparsely settled zone. With the cotton boom of the 1950s and 1960s, the region's poor experienced economic and social displacement, and some turned to the Estero Real as a type of subsistence refuge (Paniagua and Aguilar 1996). Miraflores community members who lived in the zone during that era supplemented their diets and income by capturing fish, shrimp, "lobsters" (*Ucides occidentalis*), and iguana in the estuary. A Danish International Development Agency (DANIDA) survey found that 28 percent of communities in or near the Estero Real relied on the estuary's flora and fauna to provide them with natural resources and 36 to 48 percent of their total household income (cited in Paniagua and Aguilar 1996). Until the 1990s, commercial activities in the Estero Real were small-scale, as local people extracted wood to make charcoal and banana tree stakes, extracted mangrove bark to make tannin, and captured shrimp that grew in naturally formed pools of water. State control and oversight of the estuary in this era was limited, and the Estero Real remained a type of commons, largely regulated by local custom. While economic and social inequalities permeated northwestern Nicaragua during the Somoza era, the Estero Real represented a space of relatively equal access for families willing to face the isolation and physical hardships of extracting natural resources from the estuary.

As part of policy makers' broader regional shift toward environmental sustainability, the Nicaraguan environmental agency—the Institute of Natural Resources (IRENA)—declared the Estero Real a natural reserve in 1983, thus restricting local use of land and natural resources. However, IRENA failed to develop a management plan or policy framework for use of the estuary (IDR and CATIE 1999).[1] A decade later, the Ministry of Natural Resources (MARENA) further prohibited the cutting of any mangrove trees in good condition (Rocha and Barahona 1999).[2] A legal and policy framework now exists to oversee activities within the estuary, and the Nicaraguan government has initiated externally funded conservation programs for the Estero Real. Parallel to this extension of state regulations over once open-access land and natural resources, the government has also supported the expansion and deepening of market forces in the estuary through the promotion of nontraditional exports.

THE SHRIMP BOOM

After the 1979 revolution, patterns of land concentration and social marginalization were partly reversed as the Sandinista National Liberation Front (FSLN) initiated a large-scale agrarian reform program and grassroots rural organizing (see Enriquez 1991). Cotton production declined drastically by the 1990s; and the Nicaraguan government, international financial institutions (IFIs), and international donors began to promote nontraditional exports in the Chinandega region—production of shrimp in the Estero Real and peanuts, sesame, and soybeans on agricultural land (World Bank 1995). Similar to ecotourism, nontraditional exports have been incorporated into the dominant vision of sustainable development as a globally oriented, market-driven pathway to sustainability (Murray 1994; Achong 1993; Barham et al. 1992). Proponents of nontraditional exports such as shrimp suggest that they may find favorable marketing niches and provide vital foreign exchange earnings.[3] In Chile and Guatemala, nontraditional exports have been linked to increased gross domestic product and household income growth (Barham et al. 1992). The United States Agency for International Development (USAID 2002) contends that shrimp production in the Estero Real has the potential to create economic wealth and alleviate local poverty while not damaging the estuary's ecosystem. Critics, on the other hand, argue that nontraditional export earnings are not sustainable over the long term; that benefits accrue largely to transnational companies, not the poor; and that nontraditional products intensify environmental contamination (Thrupp 1997; Barham et al. 1992).

Nicaraguan cultured shrimp production expanded from 2.3 million pounds per year in 1994 to 8.9 million pounds in 1998, becoming Nicaragua's most important nontraditional export (Cato, Otwell, and Saborío Coze 2005:17–18). Three-fourths of the land suitable for shrimp production in Nicaragua, around 29,000 hectares, is located in the Estero Real (Paniagua and Aguilar 1996). This growth of shrimp farming in the Estero Real caused a shift in control of land and production away from the local population and toward national and transnational companies. In the late 1980s, half a dozen local cooperatives carried out extensive low-technology shrimp production, blocking off natural pools and filling them with wild shrimp larvae (IDR and CATIE 1999). A decade later, however, eighty-five Nicaraguan and foreign shrimp companies had gained control of 80 percent of the concessionary zone, and three transnational companies dominated processing and sales (Cato, Otwell, and Saborío Coze 2005; Rocha and Barahona 1999; Paniagua and Aguilar 1996).

Nicaraguan state agencies have also played a critical role in facilitating access to land, resources, and funding for shrimp production.[4] The designation of the Estero Real as a protected area has served to insert the state, specifically the state fishing agency (Fishery Administration [ADPESCA]), as a key mediator in the distribution and control of natural resources, as it exercised its authority to issue twenty-year land concessions for shrimp production. Observers suggest that the agency's role has not been one of a neutral arbitrator, as imagined in IFI discourse, but rather that its complicated requirements for granting land concessions have favored large companies with political connections, legal resources, and the ability to pay fees to expedite bureaucratic processes.[5] The Nicaraguan government has also offered shrimp producers tax incentives and Certificates of Tax Benefits (Certificados de Beneficio Tributarios) (Rocha and Barahona 1999), while the Japanese government, the European Union, and USAID have provided financial and technical assistance for sustainable shrimp production projects in the Estero Real (USAID 2002; Rocha and Barahona 1999).[6]

Economic Impacts

Institutional assessments of the economic impact of shrimp on the communities surrounding the Estero Real are mixed. On a national level, the World Bank (2006a, 2004b, 2003b) has linked Nicaragua's 50.3 to 45.8 percent drop in rural poverty in the 1990s to that period's robust growth in the agricultural export sector.[7] A centerpiece of the Nicaragua Poverty Reduction Strategy is further promotion of agricultural exports such as shrimp. Several studies of the Estero Real suggest that the principal economic benefit of the shrimp boom has been the creation of 950 direct jobs, as well as 3 indirect jobs, per hectare of shrimp harvested in the municipality of Puerto Morazán (USAID 2002; Paniagua and Aguilar 1996).[8] Cato and colleagues (2005) conclude that employment in the shrimp sector has improved the quality of life of cooperative members; decreased basic food insecurities; increased access to education, health, and entertainment; and offered women opportunities to work in larvae collection and shrimp cleaning and deheading. Rocha and Barahona (1999), in contrast, conclude more pessimistically that "the important financial benefits of this activity [shrimp harvesting] have been obtained at the expense of the ecosystem and the misery of the residents of the municipality" (9). They point out that many of the jobs on the semi-intensive shrimp farms have been professional and technical positions, beyond the reach of local people with low levels of formal education. Local residents interviewed were also divided in their opinions. For some, shrimp production represents an opportunity to insert themselves into global markets in a way that would bring economic advancement for their families. Other residents expressed frustration not with shrimp farming per se as a new economic activity but rather because they have felt excluded from the process and its potential profits.

Since the 1990s, hundreds of area residents have joined shrimp cooperatives in hopes of directly benefiting from the shrimp boom. Local nongovernmental organization (NGO), government, and community informants echo the conclusions of studies by Flores and colleagues (1997) and Alemán and colleagues (1996), however, that shrimp production profits have gone largely to private companies. Many of the shrimp cooperatives have been plagued by technical and administrative difficulties, low productivity, and debt (Cato, Otwell, and Saborío Coze 2005). Unable to access formal bank credit and lacking capital to cover even basic operational costs, cooperatives often depend on commercial processing companies, which provide loans at 5 percent interest a month or more and require that the cooperatives purchase their packages of technical assistance and goods (Rocha and Barahona 1999). While a majority of men interviewed in Miraflores and Río Hondo expressed optimism about potential income from shrimp production, none of the dozen Miraflores men who have worked in shrimp cooperatives at some point over the past decade reported economic success in his ventures. In the worst case, one Miraflores resident sold the family's land and animals to purchase membership in a shrimp cooperative, only to lose all the money, as the cooperative failed to make a profit.[9] A broader study of shrimp production across the Gulf of Fonseca found that small-scale shrimp producers faced common problems of limited access to credit and capital and unfavorable insertion into markets (Stonich, Bort, and Ovares 1999).

Social and Environmental Impacts

In social terms, the expansion of shrimp farms onto thousands of hectares of land in the Estero Real has meant a reduction of the access the local population once had to the estuary's land and natural resources (Rocha and Barahona 1999). Lida, a long-term resident of the zone and one of the poorest women in Miraflores, described this physical exclusion: "We would go there [to the Estero Real] to look for our subsistence, to fish, to look for lobsters, and now we can't go. Only if they [the shrimp companies] give us permission can we go. Only they can eat; us no." Another Miraflores community member, Abelardo, stated, "The big businessmen have done a large amount of damage. They cut everything down and don't allow people to go to catch their lobsters, their fish. People aren't even allowed to pass through. It would be good if the land could pass to the state or be collectively owned. That [local] people [could] be allowed to enter and look for what they need."

One study found that 14,421 hectares of mangrove forest were lost from 1976 to 1986, a loss that increased to 19,816 ha in the period 1986–1997 (PROGOLFO n.d.). The deforestation associated with shrimp production has also reduced mangrove habitat and subsequently the availability of fauna and flora used by local populations, forcing local artisan fishermen, for example, to travel greater distances to the mouth of the Estero Real (Paniagua and Aguilar 1996). In environmental terms, although the Estero Real has been under legally protected status for almost two decades, in practice government implementation of environmental protection measures in the estuary has been contradictory and largely ineffective.[10] In the 1990s, a lack of funding undermined MARENA's enforcement capabilities (Knutson 2001). According to local MARENA personnel, the ministry had only three full-time technicians working in the department of Chinandega in the early 2000s, one of whom had responsibility for overseeing all 46,000 hectares of the Estero Real. In 1998, MARENA's regulatory control over the Estero Real was further weakened when responsibility for oversight of the mangrove forest was shifted to the National Forestry Institute—an agency that forms part of the Ministry of Agriculture and

Forestry (MAG-FOR)—and ADPESCA began to process shrimp concessions in the Estero Real.

As in the Costa Rican case study, local and regional government officials highlighted tensions and contradictions between the relatively new agencies such as MARENA, working under the mandate of global environmentalism, and more traditional economic growth–oriented government agencies. Local MARENA and municipal government personnel have characterized ADPESCA as a centralized, secretive agency that fails to take environmental impact into account in its distribution of land concessions (see PROGOLFO n.d.). Miraflores residents also commented on the lack of coherence in government management policies for the estuary. Ignacio concluded, "There is a big contradiction. On the one hand, they [the government] say they want to protect the forests. On the other hand, they give the companies complete freedom to take over the beaches to establish shrimp farms."

In dominant sustainable development discourse, the direct and indirect roles of transnational corporations and wealthy individuals in environmental destruction are rarely considered (Peet and Watts 1996b). Yet in the Estero Real, MARENA official stated that the greatest environmental damage is caused by the large shrimp companies, whose semi-intensive production techniques destroy mangrove forests and natural lagoons and contaminate water with fertilizers, concentrated feed, and shrimp waste products (Mendoza 1999; Rocha and Barahona 1999). A number of local residents noted that where shrimp farms are present, there is no mangrove forest, only barren beaches.

FIREWOOD EXTRACTION

In addition to shrimp farming, commercial extraction of firewood from the Estero Real intensified during the 1990s.[11] Red mangrove trees (*Rhizophora mangle*) are cut down in the Estero Real for household consumption in the towns of Tonalá and Puerto Morazán and to sell in the nearby urban centers of El Viejo and Chinandega city. Miraflores community members have developed strategies, discussed in Chapter 7, that have enabled them to avoid active participation in this deforestation. In contrast, in Río Hondo, the number of community members engaged in the wood trade increased from a dozen in the 1980s to around ninety-two woodcutters (*leñeros*) in the mid-1990s, who were cutting an estimated 10 hectares of mangrove forest a month (Paniagua and Aguilar 1996). Río Hondo residents framed their deepening involvement in the firewood trade and the deforestation of the Estero Real in terms of poverty and meeting the basic need for food. They noted that as part of the land reform of the 1980s, the community received only 127 hectares for thirty-two families, a portion of which is unsuitable for agriculture. The children of the original land reform beneficiaries in particular, who are unable to inherit or purchase land, must rely on wage labor.

Local government officials, NGO representatives, and local residents also widely cited lack of employment as a key factor behind the increased firewood trade.[12] In the Estero Real zone as a whole, a study by Paniagua and Aguilar (1996) linked high rates of unemployment among twenty- to thirty-nine-year-olds to nontraditional exports, soybean and peanut production, which have reduced demand for agricultural labor.[13] According to a local National Union of Farmers and Ranchers official, for example, a 70-hectare cotton hacienda would typically hire 5 permanent employees and 100 or more people for the harvest. In contrast, a soybean farm of similar size requires 5 permanent employees and only 15 people for the harvest, which is largely mechanized (Rocha and Barahona 1999). Lack of salaried employment was an important concern for many Miraflores residents like Dora: "Here the problem is that soybean production doesn't create work. It doesn't need people, just tractors. There is no work. Here we're all ruined. A lot of families are living a disaster, parents without work and so many children. It wasn't like this before [under the FSLN]. Before, we lived differently."

In addition, rural wages have stagnated in Nicaragua in recent years, a product of the large supply of unskilled labor in rural areas and the lack of non-agricultural opportunities (World Bank 2003b, 2003c). Echoing the arguments of Osa agriculturalists, Río Hondo residents suggested that households unable to meet subsistence needs have no alternative but to turn to environmentally damaging activities. Carlos, a firewood trader from Río Hondo, explained, "There is still a lot of wood left [in the Estero Real]." A moment later he added, "Look, we know that should give the mangrove trees a break (*una tregua*), but we can't give the mangrove trees a break. We adults can stand to go without food for three or four days, but the children no." A local MARENA official expressed a similar perspective: "They [Río Hondo residents] want to conserve resources. The problem is that there is no economic alternative that allows people to develop an activity that's not shrimp production or wood cutting."

Cultural factors have also influenced the firewood trade. Unlike Miraflores residents, who have relied primarily on agricultural activities and, more recently, migration, many Río Hondo residents participate in a subculture of resource extraction and have gained detailed knowledge of the Estero Real. In times of deepening economic pressure, they may be more likely to choose intensification of resource extraction as a survival strategy. Typically, in the economic chain of the firewood trade, the fewest earnings go to individuals who directly extract the mangrove from the forests. The *leñeros* bring the wood back from the Estero Real by small boat to a collection point in Río Hondo, where the owners of ox carts pay 170 *cordobas* per 1,000 pieces of wood and transport it to the city of El Viejo, where they sell it for 320 *cordobas* per 1,000 pieces (Rocha and Barahona 1999). Although the bulk of the profits goes to intermediaries, a DANIDA-Manglares (n.d.) study found that firewood extraction paid slightly more than agricultural wage labor at 10 to 15 *cordobas,* or just over a dollar, a day. After paying the costs of transportation and chain saw rental, *leñeros'* average net earnings equal 400 *cordobas* ($38) per month.

Patterns of stratification also exist within the firewood trade, however. While for many, firewood extraction is part of a survival strategy, I observed that several Río Hondo households that extract firewood are also intermediaries in the trade and are among the better-off members in the community. These residents choose to frame their activities in terms of subsistence for strategic reasons. In realty, they appear to be using natural resource extraction and the opening left by weak state environmental enforcement to advance out of poverty and toward accumulation.

While the cutting of live mangrove trees has been illegal since the 1990s, the law has been largely ineffective, and I witnessed on a daily basis ox carts full of mangrove wood heading from Río Hondo into Tonalá. The *leñeros* reported that if they give twenty-five to fifty pieces of firewood to the police, they are allowed to pass the checkpoint at the exit of Tonalá with their wood. For a fee, the mayor's office in Tonalá will also give them a permit for wood transport that is valid until they enter the neighboring municipality of El Viejo. MARENA officials also suggested that they have little or no control over the illegal wood trade in the Estero Real, and the one technician responsible for the entire Estero Real zone has little time for interaction with the local population. Rare efforts by the police to more strictly control firewood extraction have been met with protests and highway blockages by the *leñeros* (Olivas 2006a, 2006b). In addition to their livelihood discourse, which places the basic needs of family above environmental regulations, Río Hondo *leñeros* highlighted the perceived contradiction that shrimp companies that deforest the estuary receive government support while poor *leñeros* face possible government confiscation of their firewood, fines, and even time in jail. A study by Mendoza (1999) in the neighboring department of León documents a widespread perception that when environmental enforcement does occur in the mangrove zone, the law is applied unevenly, targeting the poor and turning a blind eye to the damaging activities of the wealthy and well connected.

SUSTAINABLE DEVELOPMENT PROJECTS

Dominant sustainable development discourse has increasingly recognized the ineffectiveness of a purely policing approach to environmental protection and has shifted resources toward funding integrated conservation and development projects. From 1992 to 1997, DANIDA provided over $1 million for a sustainable development project in the Estero Real and neighboring communities known as DANIDA-Manglares (Rocha and Barahona 1999). The project's stated goals were to formulate and implement a mangrove forest management plan, promote diversification, reduce the demand for products with low economic value, develop a program of environmental education, and support government policies to maintain the integrity of the Estero Real ecosystem (Rocha and Barahona 1999:52). One of the key social strategies of the DANIDA project was the promotion of firewood cooperatives that would develop plans to extract firewood in a more rational manner and participate in mangrove reforestation. By the early 2000s, however, I found only one of these cooperatives still functioning on a small scale and providing members with little more than subsistence. *Leñeros* from Río Hondo, who do not participate in the cooperative, expressed frustration that they were unable to obtain DANIDA financing for shrimp and cattle projects. One *leñero* concluded,

> They [DANIDA project personnel] bought motorcycles, boats, cars. They spent 20 million [cordobas], but they didn't remove the pressure from the mangrove [trees]. A [forestry] engineer from Managua who earns $3,000 per month visits once a month, does a study that is worthless. He measures a tree and puts a ribbon around it. He walks around putting ribbons on trees, and right behind him are the campesinos with axes.

CONCLUSION

The experience of the Estero Real illustrates some potential contradictions of the dominant model of sustainable development in its economic, social, and environmental dimensions. On the one hand, the Nicaraguan state has extended its regulatory control over the once open commons of the Estero Real as part of a broader policy of environmental protection. In practice, however, state enforcement has been largely ineffective. This reflects the broader weakness of the Nicaraguan state in rural areas in terms of resources and personnel and the degree to which state agents are influenced by (or are themselves) powerful economic interests that seek to maximize economic gains at the cost of local environments. While postdevelopment writing often focuses on the interventionist role of the state, from the perspective of the poor who live near the Estero Real, they must struggle against intertwined state and powerful private interests that have impeded their access to the resources of the Estero Real.

In accordance with World Bank (2003b) and USAID (2002) claims, shrimp production as a new nontraditional export appears to have succeeded in absolute terms in creating employment opportunities and improving the material well-being of a percentage of local households. Yet shrimp production has also partly displaced previous, more locally controlled subsistence activities. Likewise, unequal political access and power, high capital costs, lack of land and productive resources, and limited education and training for the poor in Nicaragua have meant that the economic benefits of shrimp production have gone largely to companies and large-scale producers. Commercial shrimp production has also directly contributed to the environmental degradation of the Estero Real. In addition, a combination of economic pressures, cultural orientations, and economic ambitions in some cases accelerated the extraction of mangrove firewood by Río Hondo residents in the 1990s (Ruben 2001; Gibson 1996).

Chapter 6

"He Has Been Taught Not to Be Afraid"

Grassroots Sustainability in Miraflores

Much of the literature on alternative sustainability has focused on communities with deep ties to place. Patterns of accelerated national, regional, and transnational mobility in Central America, as well as increased state and market incursions into once remote zones, suggest, however, that such traditional communities are becoming the exception rather than the norm. Under these circumstances, we need to further explore the more fluid and complex ways communities as empowered agents of sustainability may be formed and reinforced. In the case of Miraflores, a government land reform program brought together groups of families who over the subsequent two decades constructed a sense of shared identity and capacity for collective action. This chapter provides a brief overview of the revolutionary history of the community and then examines residents' visions of sustainability, as well as the ways the policies of dominant sustainability—neoliberal reforms and sustainable development projects in particular—have influenced community empowerment.

THE REVOLUTIONARY YEARS

Following the 1979 revolution, the Sandinista National Liberation Front (FSLN) expropriated around 20 percent of Nicaragua's agricultural lands that had been owned by Somoza and his close associates, including the hacienda that became the community of Miraflores (Enriquez 1991; Kaimowitz 1988).[1] The founding families of Miraflores invaded the hacienda, and eventually Sandinista state officials offered to turn over the 162 hectares to the families on the condition that they farm it collectively. The founding residents agreed and established Miraflores as a Sandinista Agricultural Cooperative (CAS), under which male heads of household were recognized as *socios*, legal members of the cooperative. These *socios* were given collective title to the land and elected a board of directors (*junta directiva*) that administered the cooperative, assigning daily work and distributing profits equally among members.

The FSLN at first urged Miraflores and other CAS in the Chinandega region to grow cotton for export, but members resisted this pressure. Typical of other cooperatives in the zone, they cultivated corn, rice, beans, and plantains—subsistence crops that could also be sold in local and regional markets.[2] In addition, cooperative members received government loans to start a herd of cattle that eventually numbered 160. During the 1980s, the cooperative was moderately profitable, and relative economic equality existed among the households. Similar to other CAS, Miraflores benefited from a series of government subsidies, including generous credit at low to negative real interest rates and highly subsidized agricultural equipment, such as an irrigation system and two Soviet tractors (see Kaimowitz 1988). On the other hand, Nicaragua's growing economic crisis and the hyperinflation of the late 1980s, as well as the FSLN's economic stabilization measures of 1988, eroded many of these benefits. The FSLN was defeated in the 1990 elections, and the opposition governments that followed initiated important policy shifts in Nicaragua's development model, discussed later in this chapter.

ENVIRONMENTAL PERSPECTIVES

Turning to community visions of sustainability, none of the Nicaraguan community members interviewed expressed the strong environmental orientation detailed in the Costa Rica case study (see Chapter 4).[3] On the Osa peninsula, people on both sides of the debate often gave detailed and passionate responses to questions about environmental issues. The Nicaraguan community's responses to environmental questions, on the other hand, were more perfunctory and at times appeared to reflect environmental opinions that were less well developed or deeply held. In contrast to Osa ecotourism participants, who characterized daily interactions with the natural environment as a form of quality of life, Miraflores residents generally perceived their surrounding national environment as a space of physical and psychological discomfort and hardship and a force to be endured or controlled through human labor. Community residents emphasized not the tranquility of the mangrove forest but rather the Estero Real's swarms of mosquitoes, poisonous snakes, and heavy downpours during the six-month rainy season, which are seen as making people more vulnerable to illness. According to a *leñero* from Río Hondo, "We would go at 11 o'clock at night to the estuary (*yangua*) to cut down mangrove trees. It's not too bad in the dry season, but in the rainy season it's malaria, people wet and sick." Miraflores residents also rarely commented on the aesthetic qualities of forested areas, plants, or animals. In contrast, a cleared and "orderly" field or pasture was praised as a representation of the triumph of human labor and technology over the disorder and "laziness" associated with unmodified nature, of economic advancement over subsistence.[4]

When Miraflores was founded, roughly two-thirds of the families had been landless cotton harvest workers, while the other one-third of families, who self-identify as campesinos, were more experienced agriculturalists from the department's northern zone. This campesino group in particular values its autonomous rural way of life but views the natural world first and foremost from a utilitarian perspective, as a means to meet basic needs. When Miraflores was first established, residents agree that their environmental knowledge and awareness was minimal. They actively deforested their land, and I witnessed many instances of unsafe handling of pesticides, profligate pesticide applications, and regular incidents of pesticide poisoning.

In the subsequent fifteen years, however, participation in sustainable development projects and a gradual exposure to a more globalized discourse of environmentalism have led a number of Miraflores residents to gain environmental knowledge and participate in conservation measures. Miraflores residents recalled, for example, a series of workshops on the health risks of pesticides, conducted by the nongovernmental organization (NGO) CARE International, as an important factor in the sharp reduction of earlier extensive use of pesticides in favor of natural remedies such as neem (*Azadirachta indica*) and integrated pest management. In addition, in the early 2000s, approximately half of Miraflores families participated in a European Community–financed soil conservation project that involved construction of drainage channels, dikes, fences of live trees, and a tree nursery. Miraflores residents have also been critical of the deforestation of the Estero Real and do not participate in the firewood trade. They noted in interviews that forests provide shade for human beings and cattle, offer a home for wild animals, and reduce the winds that carry away soils in dust clouds.

Economic incentives have also influenced increased environmental awareness in Miraflores. Residents have decreased pesticide use as a cost-saving measure, and women have participated in soil conservation projects, both to receive food provisions from donors and to improve crop yields. In the zone's post–Hurricane Mitch construction boom, one community member made a profit of several thousand dollars selling his reforested laurel trees to NGOs for reconstruction projects. He explained, "The more trees there are, the more life there is. Reforestation is profitable." In addition, unlike Tonalá residents who must purchase firewood as their main source of cooking fuel, Miraflores citizens meet household firewood needs from their own land.

LIVELIHOOD PERSPECTIVES

While environmental awareness and conservation practices have increased in Miraflores since the early 1990s, residents' overall vision of sustainability still focuses most strongly on livelihood issues of household subsistence and access to land. Miraflores residents describe themselves as "poor," an all-encompassing identity that has carried a series of limitations and obstacles to overcome—hunger, hard labor during harvests, illness and death of children, and lack of educational opportunities.[5] Many community members have, for example, strong memories of the harsh conditions they faced as children working in the cotton fields. Typical comments on poverty by community members include:

> My parents never gave me the opportunity to study because they were poor. My father worked a lot, and that's why we didn't learn to read. My parents were poor, very poor. (Lorenzo)

> It's a situation to survive, only that; only to be able to eat because poverty squeezes us. (Raimundo)

> The little work the rich give [us] doesn't support (*abastece*) people. (Lida)

> The *terratenientes* don't want anything to do with small producers. They make our lives impossible. We live suffering. (Ignacio)

> We worked [in the cotton harvests] submerged under the laws made by the rich. (Diego)

In Miraflores discourse, this concept of "poor" has as its foil the "rich," or large landowners (*terratenientes*), whose interests are seen to conflict with those of the poor. The dominant perspective of sustainability characterizes class formation as a fluid and relatively open product of neutral market processes. Miraflores residents, in contrast, are more apt to perceive polarized wealth accumulation in Nicaragua not as ethically or socially neutral but rather as linked to authoritarian government, exploitation of the poor, and, more recently, corruption. From their central identify of "poor," Miraflores residents make class-based and social justice claims for subsistence rights, which they believe take precedence over free markets or global environmentalisms.

PROCESSES OF EMPOWERMENT

Miraflores is not the type of deeply rooted, traditional, or indigenous community often identified in the critical literature as the linchpin of sustainable development. Yet the experience of Miraflores suggests ways in which a shared identity, a critical ideology, and a capacity for collective action may develop through more complex and multifaceted interactions with external actors, in this instance the FSLN and, later, development NGOs. When the Sandinistas took power in 1979, they promoted a wide range of grassroots organizations that included unions, farmers' organizations, youth groups, and neighborhood associations (Luciak 1995; Serra 1993). Miraflores men participated actively in the National Union of Farmers and Ranchers (UNAG), as well as in the collective management of the cooperative.[6] Following the 1990 elections, these grassroots organizations declined and the number of NGOs surged dramatically, from fewer than 20 in the early 1990s to over 200 by 2000 (Meyer 1999; CAPRI 1999, 1990).[7] A decade of armed conflict deeply divided Nicaragua's population along ideological grounds, and by the mid-1990s a large portion of Nicaragua's NGO sector had taken a critical stance toward the Alemán government in particular and neoliberal policies in general (see Kampwirth 2004; Biekart 1999; Coordinadora Civil 1999).[8]

Sustainable Development Projects

In the Tonalá zone, the presence of NGOs expanded rapidly in the 1990s, even as the state was withdrawing. In contrast to the sometimes negative assessments of sustainable development projects on the Osa peninsula, Miraflores residents, without exception, expressed positive opinions of the NGOs and of projects carried out with the community (listed in Table 6.1).

From the perspective of community members, NGO-administered projects have not, per the postdevelopment critique, undermined the control, authenticity, or voice of the community but instead have advanced its empowerment. Although not all projects have achieved their objectives, Miraflores residents reported that NGOs have provided the community with substantial material and moral support, information, and access to social networks. A housing project sponsored by the U.S. NGO Habitat for Humanity was Miraflores's first major development project. Community members recalled that conscious of their poverty, lack of formal education, and low status in Nicaraguan society, they initially felt

Table 6.1. Major Development Projects: Miraflores, Nicaragua, 1984–2003

NGO/Government Agency	Project Activities	Dates
UNAG (National Union of Farmers and Ranchers)	Technical training, advocacy on government rural policies, land titling, loans	1984–present
Habitat for Humanity/CEPAD (U.S./Nicaraguan NGO)	Housing project, food donations, technical training, reforestation	1986–1992*
CARE International (large U.S. NGO)	Sustainable agriculture, reduction of pesticide use, revolving credit fund	1989–1994*
Nuevo Amanecer (Catholic Church project)	Sewing and health training projects for women, credit fund	mid-1990s*
SELVA (Nicaraguan environmental NGO)	Grants for reforestation	mid-1990s*
Technoserve (U.S. NGO funded by USAID)	Land titling, sustainable agriculture, nontraditional exports	1998–1999
Pro-Tierra (government program)	Short-term loans, sustainable agriculture, reforestation, soil conservation, wetlands	1998–2001
Save the Children (large U.S. NGO)	Food for work, posthurricane road construction	1999–2000
Plan International (international foster parents' plan)	Community infrastructure, latrines and wells, teacher salaries, health training, children's programs	1998–present
Cooperative League of the U.S.A. (U.S. NGO funded by USAID)	Sustainable agriculture, non-traditional exports	2000–2001

Note: *Dates are approximate.
Source: Fieldwork data.

intimidated and fearful in interactions with North American and college-educated Nicaraguan project personnel. Through their work with Habitat, however, men gained new experience at participating in committees and collective decision making, as well as increased self-confidence. Community leaders, encouraged by these positive experiences, actively sought further project opportunities in the following years.

In a competitive environment in which local demand for aid has exceeded project funds, NGOs have favored Miraflores because community members attend meetings, develop contacts, and generally act collectively to present an outward image of an organized, energetic community able to successfully carry out projects and promote institutional NGO success. As one Miraflores community leader explained, "We don't show our dirty laundry to outsiders." When Plan International, a European "foster parents" NGO, came to Tonalá in the late 1990s, for example, Miraflores sent a representative to every meeting and was eventually selected by the NGO as a "model community." For several years Plan International poured a large amount of funding into the basic infrastructure of Miraflores—constructing wells, latrines, sidewalks, a schoolhouse, a day care center, and three health posts—held health and education seminars, and established two revolving credit funds.

My observations of NGO personnel visits to the community over the years suggest that community members are almost always outwardly accommodating, but they are also selective in terms of what information or technical assistance they accept as true and what NGO-suggested techniques they eventually put into practice. In part as a result of these experiences, male Miraflores residents have expressed a sense of self-confidence and efficacy. One community member, Félix, stated, "Here [in Miraflores] we all rule. It's a democracy because we all know what's going on." Ignacio explained, "The Nicaraguan man [sic] can now stand up in front of a group and speak . . . because he has been taught not to be afraid of speaking, to stand up for his rights, to understand that he has the right to be heard. This is what they [the FSLN and the NGOs] taught us, along with organizational unity, administration, and accounting."

NGOs often promote the formation of community-based committees as an instrumental measure to facilitate project administration. Yet the Miraflores experience suggests that when combined with critical discourse, this may also be a source of longer-term empowerment of the poor. Miraflores residents have been able to transfer skills learned in project settings to other public arenas, such as interactions with the government or confronting challenges to their land titles. Also, as discussed earlier, their contact with critical discourse both under the FSLN and with NGOs has nurtured a critical conceptual framework by which they evaluate their social reality.

Land Struggles

As the process of empowerment has advanced for at least some Miraflores residents, the forms and content of collective community mobilization have also adapted to shifts in broader national political opportunity structures. Under the Somoza regime, community members were divided between an "active accommodation" and land invasions that directly confronted landowners and a repressive state. When the FSLN took power in the 1980s, residents appropriated its class- and nationalist-based discourses and attempted to probe and exploit the ideological and personalistic openings offered by the revolutionary regime. Although community members are unfamiliar with terms such as "social capital" and "social networks," in practice they have deliberately cultivated friendships and relationships of reciprocity with government officials and NGO technicians. In the mid-

1980s, for example, the cooperative's efforts to obtain a collective land title were blocked by a relative of the former landowner who held a position in the Ministry for Agrarian Development and Reform (MIDINRA) and refused to process the paperwork. Miraflores leaders, however, persisted in visiting government offices month after month. Eventually a lawyer, to whom the community had given sacks of plantains in the past, agreed to take their case pro bono and was able to convince MIDINRA officials to give the cooperative its collective land title. Reinaldo, a leader in such social networking, explained in 1989, "You can get things done with the FSLN, but to ask for something takes a lot of effort. If one person in the *frente* [FLSN] says no, we just go and see someone else until we get someone who agrees with us."

In the more recent postrevolutionary era, community activism has focused on legal and bureaucratic processes to obtain land titles. Following the FSLN's 1990 electoral defeat, the Chamorro government initiated a process of reviewing claims by former owners whose land had been expropriated in the 1980s. With World Bank support, postrevolutionary governments promoted the parcelization of the Sandinista cooperatives as well as privatization of state farms (World Bank 2003c). While World Bank–sponsored studies have shown that the poorest households in rural Nicaragua are those with little or no land, land reform had fallen out of favor with national and multilateral policy makers by the 1990s and thus has generally been excluded from the dominant conceptualization of sustainability (Davis and Stampini 2003). The World Bank has instead supported individual land titling projects in Nicaragua and the rest of Central America as a precondition for economic growth (Deininger and Chamorro 2002). The World Bank perspective contends that secure individual property rights increase the value of land, provide incentives for owners to invest in the land rather than exploit it for unsustainable short-term profit, and serve as collateral to obtain agricultural credit (Deininger and Chamorro 2002; World Bank 2003c, 1997, 1995).

Following the 1990 elections, Miraflores residents decided by majority vote to divide their collective landholdings of 162 hectares into individual parcels of 8 hectares, but they did not file for individual land titles because of the legal expenses involved. Over a decade later, opinions in Miraflores were still deeply divided as to whether it is better to work the land collectively or individually. All of the campesino families who originally owned land in northern Chinandega, as well as some former cotton worker households, strongly favored the individual model. In the 1980s they often expressed frustration that under the collective model of the time, their economic advancement was blocked by neighbors who lacked administrative and farming skills and did not do their fair share of work. Nuria, whose husband was considered one of the harder-working community members, stated, for example, "[Collective] wasn't the best because there were people who worked more and people who worked less and when they [were] paid, they divided everything equally. And the *socios* who worked more didn't like that." As individual farmers, these families have increased their wealth primarily by expanding their land and cattle holdings and encouraging their children to pursue formal education and professional careers.

Just under half of the community residents, however, continued to prefer the collective model because they believe it was more efficient in that all the land of the cooperative was farmed and it provided a subsistence safety net for community members. Dora explained:

> As a collective it was better. People worked united, and when they had profits they shared them with everyone. But my husband was already elderly, and they said he couldn't work as hard as the rest, and for that reason they said it was better [as an] individual [system]. . . . There are people with good hearts, but others no. With bad hearts they said they weren't going to continue to support him if he couldn't work.

Under individual farming, the relative equality of the 1980s has given way to economic inequality within the community. Abelardo, one of the residents who has prospered as an individual farmer, stated:

> I like working collectively because the work gets done more quickly. It gives more help to the people who have less, who can't contribute as much. But now the land has been divided into equal parcels, and we work as individuals with each person harvesting what they sow. But what I see is that the people who work are seeing the fruit of that labor. Others who don't think things through are producing little.

Community debates over the meaning of land parcelization resonated over a decade later, suggesting that this was not simply an economic or a technical decision. Rather it holds deep personal, social, and even ethical implications. In the end, Miraflores, similar to the vast majority of Nicaragua's cooperatives, favored the individual model, but residents recognized that this choice has involved both gains and losses (Merlet and Pommier 2000).

While community members were divided on the initial decision to divide collective landholdings, in subsequent years a key collective community priority has been to maintain control of the land and obtain individual land titles for their parcels. In the 1990s, landholdings in Nicaragua were characterized by violent land invasions, multiple land claims, contradictory legal frameworks, complex and overlapping bureaucratic structures, and in some cases outright chaos (World Bank 2003c; Baumeister 1999).[9] Although it is difficult to obtain accurate data on landholding trends, case studies from other regions of Nicaragua suggest variable patterns of land reconcentration (see Fernández Quisbert 1997; Matus 1994). The Chinandega UNAG office estimated that wealthy individuals have taken out loans to purchase or rent approximately 70,000 to 105,000 hectares of high-quality land in Chinandega, while approximately thirty former cooperatives have faced strong internal land conflicts. A study by Barahona Najlis and Mendoza (1999) also identified a pattern of land reconcentration in the province. In 2003, patterns of land stratification were clear, as 1 percent of landowners controlled 36 percent of Chinandega land (INEC 2004:5).

It is not difficult to identify the steep obstacles Nicaragua's rural poor have faced in these new bureaucratic and legal arenas of land rights. In advancing land claims, literacy and formal education are needed to deal with complex texts and technical jargon. Yet approximately half of Miraflores adults are functionally illiterate and vulnerable to the manipulation of lawyers and other intermediaries.[10] Similarly, transactions are filled with open and hidden expenses—transportation to and from urban centers, lost wages, lawyer's fees, and sometimes bribes as the only means to move the process forward—that are prohibitive for the poorest rural residents. In 1994, Miraflores received a letter from the family of the original landowner who claimed the community owed the bank 400,000 *cordobas* (approximately $57,000) and ordered residents to vacate the land immediately. Male community members quickly sent back a message clarifying that they did not owe the bank any money and claiming (falsely) that they had hired a lawyer to defend their land rights. Once the former owner's family realized that Miraflores residents would not be easily intimidated or manipulated into abandoning their land, they withdrew their legal action against the community.[11] In contrast to Miraflores, Río Hondo, established on 90 hectares of a cotton hacienda once owned by one of Nicaragua's wealthiest families, has been embroiled in a decade-long legal conflict over its land, in part because a key signature was left off the 1980s collective title. A number of case studies illustrate that Nicaragua's poor have spent considerable time and expense defending their land claims in legal cases "of dubious nature" (Merlet and Pommier 2000).

DISEMPOWERMENT

Miraflores is a relatively empowered community, able, when necessary, to mobilize to defend important interests such as land. Several factors, however—interactions with the state, neoliberalism policies, and growing inequality—have undermined community empowerment. Post-1990 Nicaraguan governments have negotiated agreements, most recently known as Poverty Reduction Strategies, with international financial institutions to implement neoliberal policy reforms and qualify for debt relief (World

Bank 2006b, 2001c).[12] World Bank analysis links Nicaragua's current high rate of poverty in part to the Sandinista government's 1980s interventionist economic policies, which contributed to hyperinflation and a decline in gross domestic product (GDP) (World Bank 2001c).[13] Post-1990 neoliberal policy measures supported by the World Bank include reduction of the "oversized" state sector, privatization of state-owned enterprises and power and telecommunications services, and the closure of state-owned banks (World Bank 2002). While recognizing that these structural reforms have entailed a cost for Nicaragua's population, the World Bank credits the policies with renewing economic growth from 1993 onward and reducing rural poverty (World Bank 2001c).

In contrast to the World Bank's negative assessment of Sandinista policies of the 1980s, Miraflores residents have given strong political support to the FSLN, with as many as 80 percent of community members reporting having voted for the party in the 1990, 1996, and 2001 elections. The pro-Sandinista political views of Miraflores citizens reflect relatively high levels of support for the FSLN in the municipality of Puerto Morazán, where the party has won every local election since 1990 (CSE 2000). Such strong support for the Sandinistas, however, is not typical of rural Nicaragua, where in the mountainous interior in particular, support for the FSLN remained low in the 1990s (see Horton 1999). Residents explained that they favor the FSLN primarily because they believe the revolutionary government actively intervened on behalf of poor residents such as themselves, in particular through land reform and generous credit policies. Ignacio explained, "We the producers, we the workers, we felt like we were taken by the hand with the Sandinista government because they arranged the land, technical assistance, credit, and markets where we could sell our products. There was no pressure to pay back the bank. Instead the Sandinistas walked hand in hand with us."

Some community members have been critical of Daniel Ortega's efforts to consolidate control over the FSLN, as well as of the party's 2000 pact with the Liberals (see Close and Deonandan 2004). A substantial number of community members, however, continue to identify with revolutionary values, and this ideological filter likely influences to a degree their more critical and distrustful position toward post-1990 government policies.

Neoliberal Reforms

Scholars and Nicaraguan NGOs have criticized Nicaragua's neoliberal reforms as having a particularly negative impact on the most vulnerable: women and the poor (Close 2004; Babb 2001; Coordinadora Civil 1999). Similarly, Miraflores and Río Hondo residents identified the withdrawal of past state services and subsidies under neoliberalism as the most important factor that has negatively impacted sustainability in the zone, undermining the subsistence security of the poor and pushing local people toward deforestation in the Estero Real. As a cooperative in the 1980s, Miraflores received a variety of economic benefits from the Sandinista government—generous bank credit at interest rates below the inflation rate and subsidized farm machinery—and sold most of its crops to a government agency at set prices.

Under the neoliberal reforms of the 1990s, as state banks were privatized, interest rates rose and requirements for obtaining loans became stricter, leading to a sharp contraction in credit available to small and mid-sized farmers (Enriquez 2000; Baumeister 1999; Jonakin 1996). Miraflores has not taken out bank credit, either collectively or individually, since 1991, in part because private banks would not accept the collective land title as a loan guarantee.[14] Other Miraflores residents who might qualify for loans using their cattle as collateral commented that they are afraid to take out loans because unlike the FSLN, which on several occasions universally forgave agricultural debt, private banks are more likely to foreclose for nonrepayment of loans.[15] Miraflores resident Santiago explained, "What those people [the private bankers] want is to increase the capital they charge. And if the due date arrives and you don't pay, they take your house and everything you have and you're left with absolutely nothing." Along similar lines, his neighbor Ignacio stated,

> If they [banks] lend you 2,000 pesos [*cordobas*] you have to put up cattle or property. If you don't pay they take it away from you, and you're left worse off without your property or cattle. And what will you do out on the street? . . . We need money to cultivate the land because otherwise it's useless that we have land. We want to cultivate, but we need fertilizer, insecticide, labor, a lot of things that we can't get anywhere. So we don't do anything.

Miraflores community members had relied on NGO loans of less than $1,000 with low interest rates. Because of problems with repayment, however, approximately one-third of families in Miraflores have been unable to obtain even NGO loans, and some have left their land idle as a result.[16] In the early 1990s, the government crop purchasing agency was dissolved. Miraflores residents expressed frustration at the low prices they have subsequently received for their crops under free markets, suggesting that intermediaries, not small farmers, are benefiting. Raimundo stated, "What use is it to sow and then sell cheaply? It's a waste of time. The person who buys and sells is the one who earns money. A few months ago my son grew green peppers and they gave him five pesos [*cordobas*] for two and a half boxes of green peppers. With five pesos what can you buy?"

Although Miraflores is relatively close to urban markets, poorer residents are in a disadvantageous position relative to buyers because their absolute poverty has trapped them in a cycle of ongoing debt. These households are under great pressure to pay off as quickly as possible agricultural loans, wages promised to day workers hired on credit, and their accumulated debts with Tonalá shopkeepers. Once crops are harvested, therefore, these families rarely have the time or the money to ship crops to urban centers and instead sell them to the first buyer they encounter in Miraflores or Tonalá. Intermediaries in the Chinandega province also share information and coordinate to offer low prices during seasonal gluts of crops.[17] Only a few of the better-off families in Miraflores are able to store their crops until prices rise.

Governance

Closely linked to this community critique of neoliberal economic policies is a normative vision of the state that contrasts markedly with the World Bank concept of good governance. By the mid-2000s, the World Bank had expanded its discourse of development to incorporate governance, understood as a limited but "transparent" state, able to establish stable rules of the game and adequately regulate the private sector (World Bank 2006a). Such good governance is seen as key to growth and private-sector development (World Bank 2004b). Miraflores residents, however, envision not a state limited to the administration of targeted and transitional safety net programs but rather a government that will intervene in more profound ways to address the perceived inequalities and disadvantages of the poor in competing in national and global markets.

Second, the World Bank (2006a) portrays a relatively optimistic situation in which citizens will be able to hold states accountable (for example, by controlling corruption). Miraflores residents, on the other hand, emphasized their relative lack of power, even under formal democracy, vis-à-vis a largely nonresponsive state. They characterized the 1980s Sandinista government as strongly democratic, suggesting that through their participation in rural organizations such as the UNAG, their voices and opinions were heard and taken into account by the government for the first time.[18] They contended that Nicaraguan democracy has not moved forward or deepened in a linear manner but instead has lost ground in important ways. Scholars have linked Nicaragua's early 2000s concentration of power in the executive and political party pacts to "discomposing democracy" (Close 2004). In addition, Miraflores and Río Hondo residents emphasized the ways wealth and political power are still deeply intertwined, even under democracy. They framed this critical perspective in class-based terms, arguing that postrevolutionary governments favor the "rich" or the "capitalists" over the "poor" like themselves. Carlos, a *leñero* from Río Hondo, stated,

> In the time of the FSLN there was credit for the campesino. Now it's only for the capitalists. It's a government of the rich. Before, it took eight days to get a loan. Now a poor man goes to the bank, and the [bank officials] won't even turn around to look at him. . . . A rich person can be foreclosed [upon] and still get more loans. Here a poor man owes 1,000 [*cordobas*] and they cut him off. Soon they [the government] will just erase us from the map.

Santiago of Miraflores explained, "Now the government doesn't send anyone to see how we are. Thanks to the organizations [NGOs] we are doing alright. It's the organizations that are helping us with projects, but the government, no." Sonia, one of the poorest residents of Miraflores, stated, "In the United States the government looks after the poor. Here, no."

In addition, they suggested that state benefits are distributed on the basis not of need but rather of political party loyalties. Abelardo stated, "The government has put the poor off to one side. They're not interested in the poor. Here we have two political parties, and all [Alemán] looks out for are his own people." Along with political patronage and marginalization, respondents claimed that politicians attempt to undermine the grassroots organizational gains of the 1980s and foment partisan divisions among the poor. Ignacio argued,

> The government is on the side of the large farmers, the terratenientes, and they don't want anything to do with small farmers who organized [in the 1980s]. The government has made our lives impossible. We live suffering, without technical assistance, without credit. . . . Politicians grab people and create hatred that this one doesn't want anything to do with the other because of his political beliefs [*color*].

Raimundo, a Miraflores resident who attempted to run for mayor of Tonalá in 1998, stated, "The government doesn't help us at all. In fact, the government wants to destroy the NGOs. The government doesn't want us to participate. They don't want us to organize."

Intra-community Inequality

An additional factor that has undermined organization in Miraflores has been deepening economic inequality in the postrevolutionary period. Approximately one-third of the second generation of residents has left the community, largely seeking economic opportunities in urban centers and in Costa Rica and El Salvador. Of the remaining twenty-three Miraflores households that formed part of the original cooperative, five reported that they are better off economically than a decade earlier.[19] Four of five of these families had owned land in the pre-revolutionary period, identify strongly with campesino and rural culture, and have advanced economically through agricultural and ranching activities. These five families have purchased land from other cooperative members and now own 10 to 18 hectares of land and twenty-five to fifty cattle each.

Another ten families saw neither an improvement to nor a worsening of their economic circumstances in the 1990s. They kept at least some of their original 8 hectares of land and most of their cattle, but other than some items purchased in the early 1990s, they can point to little sustained improvement in their economic status. This group of families tends to be less committed to the campesino identity and has followed more diverse economic strategies that include both farm and nonfarm activities and increasingly frequent temporary migration to Costa Rica and El Salvador.[20] Eight Miraflores families reported that in 2006 they were economically worse off than they had been a decade earlier. Studies from other regions of Nicaragua indicate that in the postrevolutionary period, small farmers in Nicaragua have sold formerly cooperative land because of debt, internal conflicts, lack of credit, and low productivity (Merlet and Pommier 2000; Fernández Quisbert 1997; Matus 1994). Miraflores families who have sold all or part of their original land and cattle suffer chronic or seasonal difficulties meeting basic subsistence needs. Such families may at times eat only one meal a day, are continually in debt to stores in Tonalá and to their neighbors, and have difficulty purchasing basic items such as medicine, clothing, shoes, and school supplies.

In addition, the impact of the transition to individual farming has varied by gender. Women in Miraflores have an average of two years of formal education, compared with four years for men, and are largely restricted by gender norms in the types of income-generating activities in which they can participate. Miraflores's original collective land title listed only male heads of household.[21] In the 1990s, with the de facto division of land, intrahousehold economic conflict increased as some men informally sold part or all of their land and took the profits against the wishes of their common-law wives (*compañeras*).[22] In one case, a male community member left his common-law wife of ten years for another woman and through physical intimidation gained de facto control of the land, animals, and house he had shared with that wife in Miraflores.

Other community members who have been vulnerable to the post-1990 development model are the elderly and the handicapped, who are unable to engage in prolonged agricultural labor. Several of these households, which were subsidized by other families in the collective model of the 1980s, now survive largely through assistance from extended family members. It is important to note, however, that while community members were critical of the macro-economic policy changes of the post-revolutionary period, they also linked growing inequality to individual and household cultural characteristics and personal choices. The better-off men distinguished between those who are "true campesinos," knowledgeable and dedicated to farming, and those who are not. Ignacio, who identifies strongly with campesino culture, stated,

> The first year [after the land was divided up] everyone produced crops, everyone did well. Then after three years we began to see inefficiency because it's easier to obtain money than to administer it. When they [poorer families in Miraflores] earned money they bought nice shoes, nice clothes, and went to restaurants, this and that. But they should have thought, "We should buy fertilizer. We need to keep fighting to plant crops next year." We campesinos with experience did that. We bought everything we needed to plant, and we are the people who are doing better now because if we have a personal economic crisis we can sell a cow and resolve this crisis. In contrast, the others don't know what to do. They have no way to get ahead.

Community members also attributed household poverty to male alcoholism. My observations suggest that in half a dozen families, male alcohol abuse has contributed not only to intrafamily conflict and domestic violence but also to economic hardship, as men miss days of work and spend money on alcohol rather than on food and basic family needs.

Neoliberalism, while presented as an economic and technical project, also carries important social and political implications; and in Miraflores, growing economic inequality has contributed to the weakening of community social ties. During the 1980s, the primary schism in Miraflores was between two large extended family blocs that often voted against each other in meetings. In the 1990s, however, wealth differences emerged as an important divide. Those families who have done relatively well economically since the community shifted to individual farming are the same families who in the past have played an important leadership role by building social networks and seeking out projects and opportunities for the community. They believe less well-off community members have reacted to their economic success with jealousy and suspicion rather than appreciating their efforts to defend collective community interests.[23] Less well-off households, in turn, distrustful of the better-off families, have been reluctant to join them in implementing projects. One of Miraflores's poorest residents, Mauricio, explained, "If we were all the same it wouldn't matter, but there are some who are clever (*vivos*). They are social climbers (*arribistas*); everything is for them. We can't work with people like that."

The cooperative and project activities of the 1980s involved all male community members, and in the 1990s a few NGOs, most notably Plan

International, included all adult women in project benefits and activities. A pattern emerged in the 1990s, however, in which the better-off households participated the most in community development projects. In contrast, Miraflores's eight poorest families participated in few project activities. These households were at times unable to afford even the small expenses involved in participation in development projects, such as bus fare or missing a day's work. Women also face a series of gender-specific obstacles that include a lack of child care options, household responsibilities, and social norms that discourage them from spending long periods of time away from home in collective activities, particular in mixed-gender settings. Several Miraflores women, who have had fewer opportunities than men to interact in formal meetings, reported, for example, that they feel intimidated and uncomfortable in such settings. Finally, both the poorest residents and women with low levels of participation tended to express skepticism as to the benefits of participation and collective action in general.

CONCLUSION

The experience of Miraflores offers an interesting case study of how in an "artificially" created community, land reform, exposure to a critical revolutionary discourse in the 1980s, and ongoing participation in sustainable development projects in the 1990s have facilitated community empowerment. Like their Osa peninsula counterparts, Miraflores residents' discourse of sustainability challenges dominant constructs in important ways. The community's historical ties to both squatter movements and Nicaragua's revolutionary government of the 1980s, combined with deep economic and social tensions in this zone of Nicaragua, have fomented a critical, class-based discourse among residents. Land reform formed the material basis of empowerment in the community; participation in development projects has been a source of further economic support and an opportunity to build alliances with NGOs. Although environmental protection measures have not greatly impacted Miraflores, post-1990 neoliberal reforms have contributed to economic inequality in the community.

The Miraflores experience suggests as well that neoliberal policies may not only bring distributional impacts but that they also have consequences for social organization. In Miraflores, a shift from collective to individual farming has allowed some families to advance economically beyond subsistence while at the same time weakening community ties of trust. Community members are now more likely to view their interests as distinct and even in conflict, thereby discouraging collective action. Even with these challenges, however, Miraflores continues to nurture a strong alternative voice that insists on the continued relevance of class struggle and collectivity, that questions the processes of economic globalization, and that makes demands on the state beyond what is conceptualized under dominant sustainability.

CHAPTER
7

"Before, There Were Only Kunas"

The Struggle for the Comarca

The previous case studies explored ecotourism and nontraditional exports as market-based sets of practices incorporated in the dominant model as pathways to sustainability. This chapter considers a third set of policies linked to both dominant and alternative perspectives of sustainability: support for collective indigenous land rights. It explores the particular strategies Ipetí leaders have employed to gain legal recognition for *comarca* (semi-autonomous indigenous territory) status and to have non-indigenous settlers who occupied land inside the *comarca* removed. I focus in particular on one critical element of this process: Kuna leaders' ability to draw on the new discourse of sustainability to advance their land claims.

MIGRATION TO THE BAYANO

Ipetí traditional authorities and activists have insisted since the mid-1980s that the most important issue the community faces has been its struggle for de facto and de jure recognition of Kuna land rights.[1] The arrival of thousands of non-indigenous migrants to the Bayano region has further intensified the urgency of this issue for residents. With funds from private and multilateral lending institutions, the Panamanian government extended the dirt and gravel Pan-American Highway to the eastern boundary of

Madungandí in the 1970s. Road construction in Central America has historically attracted migrants and accelerated deforestation, and the Bayano zone was no exception as non-indigenous, *interiorano* colonists quickly outnumbered the Kunas three to one (Consorcio Louis Berger International Inc. and Delca Consultores S.A 1998c; de Groot and Ruben 1997; Leonard 1987).[2] Heckadon Moreno (1982) argues that the expansion of large cattle ranches in Panama's central and western provinces, combined with population growth and environmental deterioration, pushed rural residents toward zones such as Bayano, where national lands were still available for occupation.[3] The military government's nationalist, developmentalist policies of the 1970s and 1980s also encouraged colonists to "conquer" forested land (Leonard 1987; Joly 1982). Table 7.1 highlights the rapid expansion of both pasture and agricultural land in the Bayano region from 1970 to 1997.

While forested land in the Bayano declined from 357,854 hectares in 1970 to 241,980 hectares in 1997, pasture increased almost 55,000 hectares and agricultural land expanded by nearly 30,000 hectares during the same period (Table 7.1).[4] In the late 1990s the Bayano region was composed of 49 percent primary forest, 19 percent intervened forest, and 13 percent pasture (Consorcio Louis Berger International Inc. and Delca Consultores S.A. 1998a:RE-6). The *interiorano* colonists initially formed small communities such as Wacuco, Loma Bonita, and Curtí on the southern border of Madungandí. Following the 1989 U.S. invasion and the overthrow of the Noriega regime, approximately 100 families took advantage of the collapse of government authority to move onto Kuna land close to the community of Ipetí. Some of these individuals were newly arrived migrants, but a number of them already occupied land on the southern border of Madungandí and took advantage of the post-invasion breakdown in state authority to extend their landholdings into the reserve (*La Prensa* 1992c).

In response to this external pressure of increased *interiorano* migration and invasions of Kuna land, the Madungandí leadership, and Ipetí residents in particular, established two priorities for collective action over the next two decades: government removal of the colonists, by force if necessary, and state recognition of Madungandí as a *comarca*. Ipetí traditional leader Rufino stated, "The greatest necessity we have is the invasion of the *colonos* [colonists]. They have invaded the lands that we were working. They've taken our plantain tree orchards, aquaculture, and fences." Ipetí leaders suggested that the enhanced autonomy and added legal security of formal *comarca* status, as well as maintenance of territorial integrity, are critical in several ways—as a base of material support for the community and as a segregated space that allows for the continued expression of distinct Kuna cultural and religious practices and beliefs.

Table 7.1. Bayano Land Use, 1980–1997 (hectares)

Land Use	1970	1980	1990	1997
Agriculture	2,981	7,420	26,108	32,548
Pasture	5,803	15,670	48,423	60,365
Forest	357,854	342,854	260,362	241,980

Source: Consorcio Louis Berger International Inc. and Delca Consultores S.A. 1998a: A/9-4.

In mobilizing to defend its land rights from these external pressures, Ipetí has relied on a traditional community governance structure that has been modified in recent decades in response to a need for greater inter-community coordination (Bartolomé and Barabas 1998). One or two traditional community leaders, or *sailas*, oversee the administration of a complex set of internal norms and regulations.[5] Ipetí men also choose at least one cacique, a *comarca*-level leader who represents the community in Madungandí General Congresses and takes charge of relations with the Panamanian government and other external institutions. *Sailas* and caciques are elderly males chosen by the men of the community on the basis of their speaking ability and knowledge of Kuna traditions, and they are aided in their tasks by half a dozen bilingual *comisionados*, or secretaries (Tejeira 1972).

It was this latter group of secretaries who utilized traditional Kuna techniques of oral persuasion to convince Ipetí traditional authorities to adopt new, stronger protest tactics against the *interiorano* presence in the reserve and assumed a leadership role in the land protests.[6] These men have spent extensive periods outside the community, gaining greater knowledge of dominant, non-indigenous Panamanian culture and institutions. Yet rather than distance themselves from their indigenous origins and culture, they have chosen to remain connected to Ipetí community life and have served as key intermediaries in community struggles to defend Kuna land and autonomy. Privately, some of them have questioned whether their elderly traditional leaders, who have little knowledge of Spanish and little formal education, are capable of confronting the contemporary national and global challenges the community faces. Yet recognizing the strong moral and religious hold these traditional authorities have over community residents, they prefer to work within traditional governance structures. One such activist, Narciso, explained, "Ipetí was the most active community in the *comarca* struggle. It's recognized that we called the strike, closed the highway, and burned the houses (*ranchos*). In other communities they lack people to lead. But here, when we see problems, we want to solve them one way or another (*por lo bueno o por lo malo*)."

LAND PROTESTS

In the 1990s, Ipetí residents launched a series of protests, employing direct action, intimidation and violence, and indigenous symbolism in these actions. On the morning of April 28, 1993, for example, dozens of Ipetí men, carrying bows and arrows and shotguns, gathered on the Pan-American Highway.[7] The men blocked the highway with tree trunks and overturned vehicles, demanding that the government remove the *interioranos* occupying Kuna land and grant Madungandí full *comarcas* status. Police and government officials rushed to the scene, and the protestors forcibly detained the governor of the province of Panama and the mayor of the nearby town of Chepo. Police fired shotgun pellets at the protestors. Only after the government agreed to form an ad hoc commission and negotiate Kuna demands did the protestors release the government officials and unblock the highway. The typical response by the government, however, was to agree to negotiate and to form committees in an effort to demobilize the immediate protest but then to fail to follow through on addressing the underlying conflict. While no one was injured in the 1993 Ipetí protests, in a similar action in August 1996, thirty Ipetí protestors armed with shotguns and rifles wounded five police officers (Quintero de León 1996). During this period, Madungandí leaders also intensified their lobbying campaign with the National Assembly to gain *comarca* status. The draft of the law to create the *comarca* of Madungandí, however, remained stuck in National Assembly legislative committees (*La Prensa* 1993a).

In addition to highway protests and lobbying efforts, Ipetí residents have also developed inter- and intra-ethnic alliances to aid in their struggle for land rights.[8] A pan-indigenist movement emerged in Panama in the 1970s, inspired in part by the emerging transnational indigenous rights movement of that time and supported by the Torrijos regime, which sought to build corporatist ties to indigenous peoples (Herrera 2002). Over the next several decades, Panama's indigenous groups issued declarations on a series of issues of common interest, calling for the legalization of *comarcas* and a halt to colonist invasions of indigenous lands (*La Prensa* 1993c). Madungandí leaders have also built intra-ethnic networks of support with Kuna professionals originally from Kuna Yala, and these lawyers and politicians have employed their influence as advisers to the indigenous committee of the National Assembly to advance Madungandí's issues. In addition, caciques from Madungandí have attempted to transform their intra-ethnic community cohesion into a corporatist political bargaining chip, offering politicians a bloc of community votes in exchange for support of land rights. In 1993, leaders threatened not to vote in the 1994 elections if the *comarca* law did not pass, and this threat, along with the negative publicity resulting from the Ipetí highway protests, succeeded in moving the proposed *comarca* law to full debate in the National Assembly committee.

SUSTAINABILITY AND LAND CLAIMS

When the *comarca* law moved to full debate in the Panamanian National Assembly, Ipetí residents counted on an important additional advantage in their struggle for land rights: the new discourse of sustainability linking environmental conservation and support for indigenous land rights. In the 1970s, international financial institution (IFI) policies called for the dismantlement of communal landholdings in favor of private landownership (Deininger and Binswanger 1999). In contrast, two decades later IFIs had shifted their policies, in theory at least, to give indigenous groups greater voice and participation in project design and implementation and to support indigenous collective landholdings on several grounds (Plant and Hvalkof 2001; World Bank 1999a). This shift in discourse has been in part a product of a resurgence of indigenous mobilization from below (Warren and Jackson 2003).[9] In addition, from an economic perspective, IFIs now argue that under certain conditions, collective forms of land control may be more cost-effective while still allowing participation in markets (Deininger and Binswanger 1999). As part of their broader discourse of sustainability, IFIs have also acknowledged that indigenous control of land has in many places been strongly correlated with conservation of natural resources (Davis 2002; Plant and Hvalkof 2001; Deininger and Binswanger 1999).[10]

Keck and Sikkink (1998) have suggested that such shifts in discourse at the transnational level provide a positive boomerang effect in which indigenous groups are able to bypass unresponsive states and instead seek the support of transnational institutions, which then pressure the states. In this sense, the transnational forum is additive, not displacing more localized forms of indigenous discourse and mobilization but rather serving as an additional space for mobilization and a source of resources (Stiles 2000). Globalization from above, therefore, can be appropriated and strategically utilized in a type of globalization from below that seeks to defend more localized ways of life.

The policy shift by IFIs in support of indigenous land rights also has important limitations, however. I argue, in fact, that IFI support for collective land rights in Panama has been framed as a compartmentalized type of "indigenous exceptionalism." Dominant institutions have represented Panama's indigenous peoples as culturally bounded and separate, seeking only minimal levels of material subsistence through frozen or slowly changing community practices in harmony with the natural environment. Therefore, this new institutional recognition of the collective over the individual, of social meaning over profits in indigenous communities is framed as a limited "exception" that does not fundamentally challenge the (almost) universality of markets, consumption, individualism, and private property rights that undergirds the broader dominant discourse. State and IFI recognition of Kuna models of governance is perceived as isolated and nontransferable to other populations. It is halted in its advance and in its challenge to dominant economic and cultural models by reified barriers of cultural difference.

Despite these important limitations, this shift in dominant institutional support has aided Ipetí residents in consolidating land rights in several ways. First, the World Bank and the Inter-American Development Bank (IDB) pressured the executive branch in the mid-1990s to support indigenous land rights, holding out as an incentive funding for programs such as the Darien Sustainable Development Program, discussed in Chapter 8.[11] These efforts combined with Kuna lobbying in the National Assembly contributed to the approval of Madungandí's *comarca* status in 1996. In response to these shifts from above, Ipetí leaders have also shifted their discourse from below. They have framed their claims for *comarca* status on the basis of a historical presence in eastern Panama dating to the pre-Conquest era.[12] Ipetí residents also draw on a social justice frame that emphasizes a series of past injustices—from the Spanish Conquest to the hydroelectric dam project—through which land was forcibly taken from the Kunas and the size of their territory reduced. One Ipetí resident active in the community's NGO stated that the Kunas are often accused of not wanting or even of blocking development. The truth, he suggested, is that Ipetí residents have historically made great sacrifices in terms of lost land and income, in favor of larger national development projects.

The new global discourse of sustainability has provided a powerful additional frame for claims making that links localized land rights to global environmental interests. This new discourse highlights the role of the Kunas as environmental caretakers, in contrast to the "destructive" practices of the colonists. Traditional Kuna cultural beliefs and practices, such as low-input fruit tree cultivation and rejection of cattle, are no longer represented as "backward" or "unproductive" but rather are reconceptualized as "sustainable" and "environmentally friendly." Ipetí residents contrast the lands of the *comarca*, with its tens of thousands of hectares of intact primary rain forest, to the central and western provinces of Panama, which have been heavily deforested. Horacio, a representative of the *comarca*'s official NGO, Orkum, stated in 1992, "They [the *colonos*] have taken our best lands. They have cornered us on the high lands. The colonizers devastate and destroy their territories and now they've come to take away ours. . . . We are the best guardians of the forests because we use the land for our subsistence and not for commerce like many of them do" (quoted in *La Prensa* 1992a).

Ipetí activist Antonio also highlighted the common interests between the government, which wants to prevent deforestation and prolong the useful life of the hydroelectric dam, and the Kunas: "We have a commitment with the government to protect the lake [Bayano], and that's why we don't allow invasions of the area. If not, they [the *colonos*] would turn it into pasture." Another Ipetí secretary, Edgardo, stated, "The Wacuco *colonos* should be removed. It's not possible to negotiate anything with them. The General Congress has always said this. Some institutions [of the government] want us to give up some of our land. They say that we have too much land. But it's not only for us. We conserve the land for everyone."

In essence, the Kunas have taken a local and limited ethnic claim to land and natural resources and merged it with the global claims of environmentalism, overlapping the well-being of Kuna society with the well-being of everyone.

OPPOSITION TO THE COMARCA

This newly adopted Kuna discourse of sustainability has been contested, however, by the colonists and some government officials.[13] In contrast to the Kunas' frame of sustainability, the colonists interviewed in the communities of Wacuco, Curtí, and Loma Bonita framed their land claims in terms of social justice and nationalism arguments similar to those presented in the Nicaraguan and Costa Rican case studies. They argued that they need land both because "we are Panamanians" and to meet basic needs. The *interiorano* settlers emphasized that they depend on the land to meet individual and family needs of food, housing, health care, and education for their children and argued that the Panamanian constitution guarantees them this basic right to subsistence. Some *interioranos*, however, were uncomfortable with the Kunas' expressions of difference and framed the *comarcas* as geographically and culturally "breaking" or "delinking" the nation in a way that challenges the ideal construct of unitary and homogeneous national identity. They questioned Ipetí residents' nationalist loyalties, a tension echoed on the national level between nationalist leftist groups and the Kunas. Kuna Yala residents in particular developed ties to the U.S. military dating from the 1930s. In the 1990s many Kunas were still employed on U.S. military bases and were reluctant to support Panamanian nationalist campaigns to end the U.S. military presence.[14] *Interioranos* interviewed were also critical of state and IFI multiculturalism policies that appear to challenge the concept of citizenship as entailing equality and contended that the government and NGOs have unfairly "favored" the Kunas in recent years. Poor colonists have also been allied in action and discourse with the wealthier members of their ethnic communities through ties of province of origin, extended families, and clientelism (Consorcio Louis Berger International Inc. and Delca Consultores S.A. 1998a; Wali 1993).

The *interioranos* also offered an implicit critique of commercial uses of natural resources and impugned Ipetí residents for seeking control of land and resources for profit rather than for subsistence or conservation. They questioned the sincerity of the Kunas' commitment to environmentalism, suggesting that the Madungandí communities seek logging contracts, a topic discussed further in Chapter 8. In addition, their discourse echoes more generalized fears of a mobilized indigenous population presumably not content with exceptionalism but moving toward broader and more transformative claims that would fundamentally shift the balance of power between the indigenous and the non-indigenous. Luís, a colonist leader, expressed such a fear in 1996: "Now that they are being given the *comarca*, the indigenous want to take over our lands to marginalize us" (quoted in *La Prensa* 1996a). Along similar lines, a resident of Loma Bonita stated in an interview, "The *indios* [Indians-pejorative] want to control all of the land from Chepo to Colombia."

In private conversations, several government officials linked to the Bayano zone also expressed concern that granting *comarca* status to Madungandí has not satisfied indigenous groups but rather has encouraged further indigenous land demands in Panama. One internal government report prepared in the late 1990s, for example, characterized residents of Ipetí in particular as "radical" and "belligerent" in their threats to block the IDB-financed highway project. The report concluded, "It is evident that the indigenous have gone extending their borders all across (*todo lo largo y ancho*) the country. . . . It is important to note if we concede the comarca demarcation of Madungandí then all the other indigenous groups will demand that they also be given the same privileges."

In July 1999, three years after the Madungandí *comarca* was legalized, I observed a debate in the National Assembly over the creation of another Kuna *comarca*, Wargandí, which reflected many of the same issues at the center of the Madungandí legalization process. The Wargandí *comarca* includes 200,000 hectares of land in the province of Darién and shares an eastern border with Madungandí. During the debate, the strongest open opposition to the *comarca* came from a legislator from Darién, Haydee Lai.[15] Lai expressed concerns that approval of the *comarca* would greatly limit agricultural frontier land available for settlement by the impoverished mestizo and Afro-Darienita populations.[16] Further issues were raised in opposition to the *comarca*—200,000 hectares of rain forest was "too much land" for a relatively small group of 2,000 Kunas to control, and some feared the *comarca* would "divide the nation." Just as the debate appeared to be moving definitively against *comarca* recognition, however, the Kunas and their supporters initiated a skillful shift in discourse, from one involving threats to the nation to one highlighting sustainability and the environment. "The rain forests [of eastern Panama] are the lungs of the world!" one legislator proclaimed. "The world supports them [the Kunas] because they are the defenders of nature," argued another, adding, "the world is watching us." Soon afterward, the National Assembly voted in favor of the new Kuna *comarca* of Wargandí.

Overall, Panama's indigenous peoples have been among the most successful in Latin America in winning legal recognition for their land rights and autonomy. Panama's largest indigenous group, the Ngöbe-Buglé, launched a series of protests in the mid-1990s and won legalization of a 694,000-hectare *comarca* in 1997 (Herrera 1998; Wickstrom 2003).[17] In 1983 the Embará-Wounaan, Panama's third-largest indigenous group, won legal recognition of a 406,040-hectare *comarca* in the sparsely settled province of Darién (Herrera 1998).

COMARCA AUTONOMY

The Madungandí charter approved in 1996 recognizes *sailas*, caciques, and General Congresses as the legitimate and final authority within the *comarca*.[18] Although the charter grants the Kunas substantial autonomy, it also states that all inhabitants of the *comarca* are subject to the Constitution of Panama and the laws of the republic (Gaceta Oficial 1996). For example, traditional Kuna marriage ceremonies will be recognized by the state, but in case of conflict, the Panamanian Legal Code of the Family will prevail. I have suggested that interactions between Ipetí and the state shifted in intensity and content from the 1970s onward as the state agencies moved in as purveyors of infrastructure and development projects, extractors of natural resources, and would-be mobilizers of the indigenous. Madungandí's 1996 organic charter further shifted this relationship, as it gave formalized recognition to distinct Kuna forms of governance and the authority of traditional leaders within the *comarca*.[19] *Comarca* authorities, while not seeking separate state status, have also asserted their right to limit or exclude state presence within the physical boundaries of their territory. Leaders of the Madungandí community of Aguas Claras, for example, have openly confronted the government on public health policies in recent years and required that the government negotiate the entrance of health workers into the community.[20]

Even as they have asserted their right to collectively manage a space of geographical and cultural difference, however, Ipetí leaders have also continued to engage with the Panamanian state. Specifically, they have continued to pressure the Panamanian government to use its material and coercive resources to have the colonists removed from inside the *comarca*.

CONFLICTS WITH COLONISTS

The *comarca* charter stipulates that colonists already living within the reserve could remain there but would be given no formal title to the land and would not be allowed to expand, sell, transfer, or give away their farms. If the owner died or the land was abandoned, the land would revert back to the *comarca*. Conflicts continued to simmer over the next decade, however, between Ipetí residents and the approximately fifty families remaining within *comarca* boundaries, with periodic outbreaks of protest and violence (Roldan Ortega 1998). Ipetí activists like Narciso contended that colonists have not abided by past agreements: "We respected the *colonos*, allowed them to stay. But they didn't comply. They expanded, rented land. The government should remove them. We [Kunas] could use physical force to remove them one by one. We have enough strength, enough people to do it, but we want to respect the agreement."

Ipetí activists have acted directly against the *interioranos* occupying *comarca* land on at least four occasions. In one incident in April 2005, for example, a group of armed Ipetí residents confronted colonists whom they claimed had extended their landholdings in the *comarca*. They tied up one male head of household, hitting his face with a stick, and burned down three colonist houses (González Pinilla 2005). To date, the Panamanian government has taken limited action to resolve these conflicts. As in the 1990s, the government has essentially carried out short-term and temporary measures to demobilize Ipetí residents without addressing the underlying conflicts. The government also reinforces the perspective of land conflicts as a local inter-ethnic struggle rather than, for example, an issue of unequal patterns of landholding on a national scale.

The restoration of democracy has led to intense competition between Panamanian political parties, rooted less in ideological differences than in struggles for control of state resources, power, and individual prestige (Correa, Adames M., and Leis 2001; Perez 2000). In this hyper-competitive political context, government officials may avoid taking a more active role for fear of losing the electoral support of either the Kunas or the colonists. In addition, this localized, low-level violence since the mid-1980s has not negatively impacted the interests of Panama's political or economic elites, whose accumulation is centered in the trade and services sector. The burning of settler houses and crops and physical intimidation by Ipetí activists, however, have created bitterness in *interiorano* communities and deepened the zone's ethnic divisions.

CONCLUSION

The Ipetí experience illustrates an instance in which the adoption of a sustainability discourse by IFIs has provided tangible benefits to the community. Ipetí activists have appropriated external representations of the indigenous as a slow-changing, environmentally sensitive people to influence IFIs to pressure reluctant Panamanian government officials. Ipetí leaders have also added the frame of sustainability to their prior claims of historical presence and social justice to gain advantage over the colonists' nationalist and social justice claims. Other successful Ipetí strategies have included ethnic solidarity, formation of alliances, and direct protest actions, most commonly blocking the Pan-American Highway.

The Ipetí experience also highlights some of the complexities of community engagement with development discourses and practices. As will be discussed in greater detail in Chapter 8, Ipetí residents are deeply ambivalent about the arrival of "civilization" to the Bayano. Yet their response has not been to attempt to withdraw altogether from dominant institutions and practices but rather to attempt to engage with development processes and institutions and shape outcomes to their own interests. In this sense, Ipetí residents who are bilingual, have formal education, and have spent extended periods outside the community have served as important intermediaries in the struggle for land rights and cultural integrity.

CHAPTER
8

"There Are No Poor People Here"

Grassroots Sustainability in Ipetí

F ollowing the model of the previous two case studies, this chapter explores the visions of sustainability held by Ipetí residents, focusing in particular on community livelihood concepts of poverty, as well as ethnically distinct cultural values and concepts of the environment. It next considers the implications for environmental sustainability of both Ipetí control of land and community participation in logging. This chapter also explores the impact of sustainable development projects and neoliberal reforms on community empowerment. Finally, it examines immanent processes of development, broader pressures of modernization, and patterns of gender inequality that may constrain the community's capacity to act collectively as an agent of sustainability.

Overall, Ipetí residents' attitude toward development or "civilization" is complex and at times ambivalent.[1] Residents identified both potential benefits of and problems with external development processes and struggled to define a process of change on their own terms that would allow for cultural and political autonomy while addressing community material and physical well-being. Rather than speaking of development in the abstract, Ipetí residents most often referred to its concrete manifestations—the public school, the hydroelectric dam, and the Pan-American Highway paving project. Silvano, one of a dozen Ipetí residents who had attended high school, stated, "Study [formal education] has brought both problems and well-being. It has supported the *comarca* because if we don't study we won't be able to fight on behalf of the caciques, speak up to the government officials. But it has also changed the young people. They don't want to work, they just want to play all the time."[2]

Ipetí cacique Benigno echoed these concerns. On the one hand, he appreciates the fact that the road project has made his frequent trips to Panama City to advance Kuna land rights and conduct *comarca* business faster and more comfortable. On the other hand, he is deeply concerned about the changes civilization has brought: "Before, there weren't sports. We lived better. Boys did advanced studies to become religious chanters (*cantules*), to dedicate themselves to the spirits. Now they don't want to learn Kuna traditions, they just throw stones, wander the streets (*andan en la calle*)."[3]

BASIC NEEDS AND POVERTY IN IPETÍ

The problem of material poverty was a strong and persistent theme in the discourse of small farmers from Nicaragua and Costa Rica. Data from the 2000 Panamanian census show an average Ipetí household income of $231 a month.[4] Although official government statistics classify Ipetí residents as poor, they do not necessarily consider themselves poor as long as their basic subsistence needs are met, and some question the need for economic development projects. An Ipetí community authority, Rufino, stated,

> We as indigenous people feel there are no poor people here. This is to say, while it's true we don't have much in terms of money (*estado económico*), we have 100 percent of what we need to eat and drink. . . . Inside of the community right now we don't have any real necessities. . . . The greatest concern we have is that the government remove the *colonos*. If the government removes the colonos, then we will see about health and education.

Another traditional authority, Begnino, stated, "When I grew up we didn't have poverty. We all lived in a healthy way. We worked in agricultural production. . . . In Panama City you have to buy everything, even fish. If you don't have money (*recursos*) you don't eat."[5]

Community elders and traditional authorities characterized their lack of economic development and accumulation of material wealth not as a form of deprivation or marginalization but rather as secondary to the social and spiritual richness of community life in that era. In these narratives the relative isolation of the pre-1960s period was beneficial to the Kunas and their need for the integrity of separate space to nurture cultural difference. Elderly resident Jorge asserted, "Before, no one lived here on the river. It was an empty area, without *colonos*. We lived peacefully without anyone to cause us problems."

Other Ipetí residents, in particular the younger intermediaries identified earlier, who have spent greater periods of time in the dominant consumption-focused culture of urban Panama, suggested that traditional authorities need to devote more attention to health and educational problems in the community, such as malnourished children, high morbidity, and low literacy levels. They support a type of development for Ipetí that would signify a material advance beyond subsistence and have actively sought project opportunities with the government and nongovernmental organizations (NGOs).[6] Community activist Silvano stated, "Economically, on the *comarca* level, in terms of food we're doing fine. But to better develop the *comarca* we need financial support. We can't do big projects ourselves. We need financing." These individuals emphasized, however, that any development projects must be under community control and be compatible with Kuna culture.

Ipetí traditional authorities presented a generally positive picture of the community's ability to meet its basic needs, and the community has strong networks of mutual support and mechanisms to help equalize wealth among households. In recent years, however, informants suggested that incipient patterns of inequality have emerged that have weakened the ability of some households to meet basic needs. Informants linked this incipient inequality to inter-household variation in the amounts of land farmed and crops harvested. Under the terms of the *comarca* charter and according to Kuna custom, all land in the *comarca* is under the control of the communities and cannot be sold or rented to non-Kunas (*waga*). Individuals or groups of men organized in traditional work associations gain possession of land by partially or completely clearing rain forests, and land can be passed down as inheritance (Brizuela 1972). Informants reported that older men own the most fertile lands and the parcels closest to the community, and many younger men must travel long distances down the Ipetí River to find unoccupied land to cultivate.

While as late as the 1950s little money was used in the community, by the early 2000s Ipetí daily life had become increasingly dependent on cash, particularly for school expenses and to purchase processed foods.[7] Men increasingly participate in logging and agricultural wage labor as means to gain access to cash (Consorcio Louis Berger International Inc. and Delca Consultores S.A. 1998a). Some households have also accumulated a degree of wealth through government and NGO employment, remittances, and small commercial ventures. Traditional Kuna norms call for sharing subsistence crops within and between households, an egalitarian system that has provided a degree of food security to women and children in particular. In contrast, cash income from wage labor is largely controlled by men, some of whom, rather than redistributing the income within the household, may spend it on individual consumption (Moeller 1997).[8]

CULTURAL IDENTITY

While opinions are divided in Ipetí as to the degree to which material poverty is a problem in the community, issues of defense of ethnic identity resonate strongly.[9] Ipetí residents and their colonist neighbors characterized this collective identity as solid, even essentialized. They emphasized a series of readily apparent markers—language, clothing, food, physical appearance, religion, residential segregation, and political structures—that distinguish the Kunas from their *interiorano* and Embará neighbors. In addition, Ipetí authorities have developed community norms and strategies to reinforce and revive distinct cultural traditions.[10] Residents are required, for example, to participate in communal activities that include building and repairing houses and communal buildings, demarcating *comarca* boundaries, and preparing food and drink for community celebrations such as puberty ceremonies. Community authorities have also forbidden items believed to undermine Kuna culture such as electricity, television sets, and cinder block houses—measures that also reinforce community egalitarianism by limiting conspicuous consumption inside Ipetí boundaries.

As Ipetí is located on an ethnic borderland, Kuna identity has been reshaped and rearticulated through interactions with dominant Panamanian culture as well. Following independence in 1903, Panama's elites envisioned the new nation as a transnational outpost linked economically and culturally to Europe, its status and prestige validated by whiteness beyond the borders of the nation-state (Szok 2001). By the 1940s a second elite nationalist project had emerged linking national identity to the Hispanic and embodied in the dress, music, and traditions of the *interioranos* even as Indians, blacks, and Asians continued to be largely "unimagined" in elite nationalist discourse (Szok 2001; Ropp 2000). After he took power in a military coup in 1968, General Omar Torrijos initiated a corporatist form of multiculturalism with the promotion of controlled mobilization of indigenous peoples (Herrera 2002; Gjording 1991). By the 1990s, the dominant discourse of the Panamanian government and media tended to no longer be openly racist and instead incorporated multiculturalism into a broader concept of national identity.[11] Racial-ethnic hierarchies and discrimination persist to the present day, however (United Nations Development Program 2002; Ropp 2000; Priestley 1986; Conniff 1985).

Ipetí residents are well aware of dominant cultural representations of their culture as "backward" and "ignorant" and have developed counternarratives of Kuna cultural strengths. Cultural conflicts are particularly intense in the area of health, and Ipetí residents counter non-indigenous disparagement of traditional Kuna healing techniques and medicines with stories of the effectiveness of those medicines.[12] In other instances, discourses of Kuna identity emerge in opposition to those promulgated by their colonist neighbors. To be Kuna, for example, is not to be stingy or sexually promiscuous, common resident representations of the colonists (see Moeller 1997). Likewise, Ipetí residents stress the subsistence nature of their land claims, the fact that the *comarca* is necessary for their physical and cultural survival. In contrast, they refer to the colonists as "large landowners" and opportunistic "speculators" who jump from property to property seeking quick profits, not subsistence. One *comarca* authority stated, "The fact that we live in [a] democracy gave them [the colonists] the idea that they could take everything they want[ed]."[13]

ENVIRONMENTAL PERSPECTIVES

While environmental concerns and values are strongly present in Kuna discourse, they are generally not expressed in ecocentric terms, that is to say, as valuing nature for nature's sake. Rather, Ipetí residents interviewed suggested that Kuna health and well-being are closely tied to, indeed inseparable from, the health and well-being of the natural world. Historically, residents have utilized natural resources much more comprehensively than Miraflores or Puerto Jiménez residents have. Fish are a staple in the Ipetí diet, and while hunting has depleted wildlife near the community, men travel to less populated areas of the *comarca* to hunt deer, iguana, and monkeys.[14] Ipetí residents use the *uaka* palm in the construction of houses and communal buildings, such as the meeting house (*onmaket neka*) and the chicha house (*inna neka*), and they cook in the traditional style, using three large tree trunks.

In addition to these material needs, Ipetí residents reported that the forest protects and shelters them and suggested that the forest is key for future generations. Botanical healers (*inatulet*) and women collect medicinal plants from the rain forest to treat a variety of illnesses.[15] Traditional Kuna beliefs hold that not only human beings but also plants, animals, stones, and rivers possess souls (see Merry 1998; Ventocilla, Herrera, and Núñez 1995). During the highway project, Kuna Ipetí residents joined with their *interiorano* neighbors to oppose a proposal to dredge stone out of the Ipetí River, concerned that dredging would injure and kill the rock spirits upriver from the community and negatively affect community health. Ipetí households employ traditional "garden" farming techniques, with little or no use of chemicals or machinery.[16] Kuna tradition also requires that when Ipetí residents clear land for crops, they set aside a forest sanctuary (*kalumar*) in which large trees, where spirits are said to string their clotheslines, may not be cut down (Ventocilla et al. 1996). Given the critical role of the rain forest in the material and cultural life of Ipetí, cacique Benigno expressed concern:

> In that [earlier] time the animals were nearby. Because with the environment, with the nature around them, the animals were able to feed on the edge of the river. At that time there were no *colonos,* only Kuna. The river wasn't contaminated. We drank from the source of the river, and the trees along the river provided natural medicines for us. The change came with the highway. The colonos came, and everywhere it was pastures and cattle. That's why the [wild] animals left.

Jorge, who was a boy when Ipetí was founded, stated, "The *colonos* arrived with the highway and frightened away the animals. Things were better before because there was food. There were *machos del monte* (wild boars), tapirs, macaws. The *colonos* frightened them away with their hunting dogs. Now the only animals left are a few iguanas." Another community member, Amalia, who works with medicinal plants, explained that in recent years the medicinal plants are becoming scarcer and losing their medicinal effects: "The earth is being mixed with mechanized things. Diesel, the contamination of the highway, chemicals, and gasoline spread through the water systems. These plants no longer have the same effect, and that's why the *sailas* say we shouldn't damage the earth."

In their narratives, Ipetí leaders and residents emphasized the role external non-indigenous agents have played in environmental destruction in the Bayano zone.[17] They hold their *interiorano* and Embará neighbors responsible for the agrochemical contamination of the Ipetí River—so central to the Kuna way of life—and denounce colonist deforestation and hunting. On the other hand, population growth, the increased monetarization of community life, and cultural contact with the colonists have led Ipetí residents to intensify some traditional practices and adopt new activities that are environmentally damaging. Ipetí residents' contamination of the river with human waste and trash has increased as the community has grown (Moeller 1997). At the *comarca* level, Kuna communities located on Lake Bayano have intensified their own fishing and allowed non-Kunas to carry out commercial fishing for a fee, to the point that one NGO technician familiar with the lake now fears certain fish populations are in danger of extinction.

LOGGING IN THE COMARCA

The most sensitive and divisive environmental issue the Ipetí and the *comarca* of Madungandí face, however, is that of logging within the *comarca*. Logging in the Bayano region began in the 1970s when military officers with ties to the Bayano Corporation, the semi-autonomous government agency that controlled much of the Bayano land in that era, carried out logging activities, including some within the Madungandí reserve (Wali 1993; MIDA and INRENARE 1979). Because of political repression at the time, Ipetí residents reported that they were afraid to actively protest this logging. By the 1990s, the Panamanian government was no longer directly involved in logging in the Bayano and had shifted to a discourse of sustainability. Panama's 1998 Environmental Law authorized individual subsistence permits that allow individuals to cut down up to twelve fine wood trees per year, community permits that allow *comarcas* to sign logging contracts, and forestry concessions granted to private companies that can cover up to 5,000 hectares over a five-year period (Consorcio Louis Berger International Inc. and Delca Consultores S.A. 1998a; *La Prensa* 1993b). At the time of my fieldwork, I was unable to obtain information from the National Environmental Authority (ANAM) on the number and area of permits and concessions granted by the government, but one study suggested that in the 1990s approximately 7,000 hectares of rain forest were lost annually in the Bayano zone (World Bank 1997; *La Prensa* 1992b).

As Ipetí residents observed the logging activities of the military government and private companies in the 1970s, they started to reconceptualize their rain forests as a potential source of individual and community profit. Ipetí authorities began to sign contracts with logging companies to allow the extraction of valuable tree species (Wali 1993). Herrera (2002) estimates that in the mid-1990s, more land was being logged under this type of indigenous community permit than under private company concessions. Simmons's (1997) survey of the Bayano found little ethnic difference in participation in logging among *interiorano,* Kuna, and Embará communities.

The logging companies that have been active in the Bayano have links to important national economic interests and have generally taken the bulk of the profits from logging (*La Prensa* 1992d). NGO technicians familiar with the issue estimate that the twelve communities of Madungandí receive from $10,000 to as much as $50,000 per logging contract. In Ipetí, these funds are used to finance legal and political activities, in particular travel by caciques to Panama City on *comarca* business. Any leftover income is distributed to the community, generally several hundred dollars for each family.[18] In addition, during the dry season from December to April each year, as many as twenty to twenty-five young men from Ipetí are hired to cut trees at $10 a day, and some report earnings of $2,000 to $3,000 during this period (*La Prensa* 1992d).[19]

The involvement of Ipetí and other Madungandí communities in logging activities stands in tension with the discourse of sustainability Ipetí leaders have used to advance their land claims in national and transnational forums. Logging has also been frequently debated in Ipetí nightly congresses.[20] Residents who oppose logging in the *comarca* cite the environmental damage it causes and argue that it threatens the *comarca*'s long-term well-being. Supporters of logging note economic needs the *comarca* faces and argue that Ipetí has been able to sustain a lengthy lobbying campaign in favor of land and autonomy only with the logging income. At least for the moment, logging within the *comarca* has had a limited environmental impact, and almost all of the 183,000 hectares of land under Kuna control in the *comarca* is still forested (see Map 3.2). In contrast, the 129,437-hectare southern sector of the Bayano, occupied by *interiorano* migrants in the 1980s, is heavily deforested, with much of the land converted to pasture (Consorcio Louis Berger International Inc. and Delca Consultores S.A. 1998a:RE-12).

COLONIST VISIONS OF SUSTAINABILITY

On issues of environmental sustainability, *interiorano* settlers of the Bayano expressed views similar to those of the small farmers interviewed in Nicaragua and Costa Rica. These Panamanian agriculturalists emphasized that while they do not necessarily oppose environmental conservation on principle, meeting their economic needs is a greater priority.[21] Examples of comments from colonists in Wacuco, Loma Bonita, and Curtí include:

> We are Panamanians. We need to eat. (Curtí storeowner)
>
> They say we have to take care of the forest, but in order to live we have to cut down trees and grow crops. (Loma Bonita agriculturist)
>
> ANAM doesn't want people to cut down the forest, but we don't have any money to support ourselves (*para defendernos*). We are very poor. The forest doesn't benefit the campesino. (Loma Bonita agriculturist)

These colonists argued, in contrast to the collective model of the Kuna, that environmental protection could best be achieved by giving them full title to their land, including the land claims located within the *comarca* of Madungandí (see Consorcio Louis Berger International Inc. and Delca Consultores S.A. 1998a). In the late 1990s, 90 percent of Bayano residents outside the *comarca* did not have legal title to their land (Consorcio Louis Berger International Inc. and Delca Consultores S.A. 1998a:RE-6). In a perspective that resonates with dominant discourse of sustainability, the colonists argued that secure private property rights would allow them to invest in their land and thus avoid having to move further into the rain forest (Deininger and Binswanger 1999).

STATE ENVIRONMENTALISM

According to Madungandí's charter, *comarca* authorities must abide by national regulations and international accords and coordinate with ANAM in the exploitation of natural resources. Ipetí leaders suggested that to date, this state role in environmental oversight has not been a source of tension, likely because state agencies have rarely exercised this authority. While some lower-level ANAM officials have opposed the logging contracts signed by Kuna communities in Madungandí and Wargandí, higher-level government officials have avoided pressing the issue for several reasons—fear of the political costs of confrontation with these well-organized indigenous groups, the political power of logging interests, and the income logging fees provide to ANAM.[22] In the neighboring province of Darién, however, conflicts have emerged between the Embarás on one side and ANAM and environmental NGOs on the other over the creation of the 570,000-hectare Darién National Park and the limits this has placed on indigenous access and traditional activities such as hunting (*La Prensa* 1996b, 1996c, 1993b).[23]

As part of the shift to dominant sustainability, external funding for ANAM and sustainable development projects increased substantially in the 1990s (*La Prensa* 1995).[24] ANAM's presence in the Bayano has remained limited, however, and both Kuna and *interiorano* informants suggested that illegal logging continues. *Interioranos* were also highly critical of the agency's activities. Similar to campesino discourse in the Nicaragua and Costa Rica studies, the *interioranos* did not necessarily question the legitimacy of ANAM's expanded regulatory role over natural resources. Rather, they claimed that ANAM favors the interests of the wealthy over those of the poor. Juan, a small farmer from Curtí, stated, "The big ones (*los grandes*) can do whatever they want, but the small farmers can't get permission to cut even one tree." The settlers also pointed out the contradictory nature of government environmental policies that punish individuals who engage in logging even as certain government agencies have historically promoted logging in the Bayano. ANAM officials interviewed were rather skeptical that the colonists can easily become agents of sustainability. They cited the *interioranos'* deep mistrust of the government, lack of organization, low level of environmental knowledge, and desire for economic accumulation as factors in the failure of local sustainable development projects to meet their goals.

NEOLIBERAL REFORMS

State and international financial institution (IFI) support for indigenous collective land rights and environmental protection in Panama, as in the rest of Central America, has also been accompanied by neoliberal reforms. The

Panamanian government adopted its first structural adjustment program in the early 1980s and further deepened neoliberal policies in the 1990s with labor code revisions, tariff reductions, and the privatization of state industries, ports, and telephone and electric service (World Bank 1999a). On the one hand, in Ipetí the consolidation of land rights appears to have aided residents by providing them with a relatively stable means to meet basic needs beyond the uncertainties and risks of newly deregulated markets. While prices Ipetí residents have received for coffee, their principal commercial crop, have fluctuated, the Kunas also produce food crops—plantains, avocados, rice, and corn—for household consumption and sale in local and regional markets, where prices have been relatively stable.[25]

Kuna leaders at the national level have been critical of neoliberal reforms and free trade agreements.[26] In community-level interviews, however, residents expressed relatively little concern over neoliberal policies. Several factors might explain this. First, community experiences of neoliberalism are mediated by prior interactions with the state. Because Ipetí residents have been relatively neglected by the state in the provision of state services and have chosen largely to forgo bank credit and electricity for cultural reasons, policies of privatization and withdrawal of state services under neoliberalism may not necessarily be perceived as losses. Also, of all the case study communities, Ipetí leaders are the most single-mindedly focused on struggles framed in local and ethnic terms. They have had more limited engagement to date with broader economic or structural debates.

In addition to its impact on indigenous material well-being, neoliberalism also incorporates a cultural project. It imparts values and organizational forms of individualism, competition, and consumption, as well as an instrumental view of nature, which may disrupt and conflict with traditional indigenous collectivist orientations (Hale 2002; Assies, van der Haar, and Hoekema 2000). Critical consciousness in Ipetí, however, implicitly contests some of the basic tenets of neoliberalism. Neoliberal values of individualism and wealth maximization are countered by strong, ethnically bound norms and sharing, reciprocity, and prohibitions on conspicuous consumption within the boundaries of the community.[27] A more independent critical consciousness in Ipetí is also reinforced in Kuna efforts to maintain relative economic autonomy by utilizing *comarca* natural resources and avoiding indebtedness to and patron-client ties with non-Kuna economic brokers.

SUSTAINABLE DEVELOPMENT PROJECTS

In addition to state environmentalism and neoliberal reforms, in the third policy area, sustainable development projects, Panama's civil society organizations have historically been somewhat weak. It was not until the 1990s, in part as a response to post-invasion external funding opportunities, that NGOs became a substantial presence.[28] NGO personnel interviewed believe that, with a few exceptions, this sector has not emerged as a strong voice for alternative discourses of sustainability. NGO critical analysis of structural adjustment programs as well as activism on issues such as logging in Panama have been relatively muted, particularly in comparison with more vocal NGO sectors in Nicaragua and Costa Rica. Rather, a number of the NGOs and sustainable development projects in Panama are aligned most closely with the dominant vision of sustainability.[29] Panama's indigenous groups have been identified as priority beneficiaries of these projects because of both the high levels of poverty in Panama's *comarcas* and the overlap between indigenous territories and Panama's remaining rain forests (World Bank 2005b, 1999a).[30] A more cautious view, however, suggests that these types of multicultural development projects may serve to co-opt and demobilize well-organized, critical indigenous peoples like the Kunas by imposing external representations of the indigenous, promoting political participation that is more symbolic than substantive, and reinforcing neoliberalism as an economic and cultural project (Hale 2002). Ipetí residents, however, appear to have maintained a degree of internal unity and cultural coherence that has enabled them largely to avoid such external manipulations. Over the past several decades, half a dozen NGOs have worked with the community on sustainable development projects (see Table 8.1).[31]

During my fieldwork, Ipetí residents were working with the Darién Sustainable Development Program.[32] This $80 million program, financed by the Inter-American Development Bank (IDB) and administered through the Ministry of Economy and Finance, has been publicized as an example of the new, "green" multilateral policies (Potlatch 1998a).[33] The centerpiece of the program has been the paving of the dirt and gravel Pan-American Highway, which becomes impassable during Panama's long rainy season. For environmental reasons and to prevent the spread of foot-and-mouth disease, the IDB decided not to finance the extension of the highway to close the Darién Gap between Panama and Colombia. Even with the more limited paving project, however, the program's environmental impact study identified potential negative environmental consequences (Louis Berger Group, Inc. 2000). The report optimistically incorporated a series of mitigating measures to prevent or lessen the processes of deforestation that typically accompany road projects in Central America—most important, a program of territorial ordering (*ordenamiento*). IDB officials also linked funding for the highway to Panamanian government support of Embará collective land titling in the Darién and resolution of land conflicts in the Bayano (Huertas 1999). Outside of indigenous territories,

Table 8.1. Development Projects: Ipetí, Panama, 1993–2003

NGO/Government Agency	Project Titles and Activities	Dates
European Community	Agricultural Frontiers Program Sustainable agriculture and agroforestry	1996–2000
BMZ (German foreign aid), International Union for the Conservation of Nature	Management of conservation of native forests in eastern Panama; Sustainable forest management, training seminars	1993–1996*
Social Emergency Fund (government agency)	Akua Yala aqueduct, warehouse, schools	various dates 1990s
Patronato de Nutrición (government agency)	Nutrition program for children	ongoing
Napguana (indigenous NGO)	Community center	mid-1990s*
Inter-American Development Bank, Global Environmental Facility (GEF)	Darién Sustainable Development Program Comarca demarcation, mediation of land disputes	1998–present
World Bank, GEF	Mesoamerican Biological Corridor of the Atlantic Pilot projects in sustainable agriculture, reforestation	2000–

Note: *Dates are approximate.
Source: Field notes.

the program has supported individual land titling, social development projects, and greater integration into markets, with the goal of raising the well-being of local populations and discouraging environmentally destructive activities (Louis Berger Group, Inc. 2000).

The environmental impact study also found that both Kuna and Embará respondents viewed the highway in negative terms, while the region's non-indigenous respondents strongly supported the project (Louis Berger Group, Inc. 2000). Ipetí residents interviewed expressed concerns that the paved highway would attract more outsiders (*extraños*) to the Bayano, with a possible increase in road accidents, crime, drugs, and political violence of the type seen in neighboring Colombia. However, Ipetí leaders also saw in the highway project an opportunity to advance their demands to have the colonists removed from the *comarca*, leveraging the presence of the IDB and its discourse of sustainability against entrenched national economic and political influences on the Panamanian state.[34] Ipetí residents have threatened to protest and block the paving of the highway and bypassed state officials to bring their grievances directly to IDB officials. Government officials interviewed did not view this as a positive advance and claimed that IDB support had made Madungandí leaders more "radical" and intransigent in their position on the land conflicts.[35]

Postdevelopment literature has suggested that sustainable development projects such as this advance state and bureaucratic control, but in fact a series of factors has limited and contained the project's potential influence on Ipetí residents.[36] To non-indigenous project personnel with a very limited, sometimes stereotypical understanding of Kuna language and culture, the internal social and political dynamics of the *comarca* remain something of a "black box." For their part, some Ipetí leaders have guarded this ethnically and geographically bounded space from outside intrusions or interventions. Several project representatives, for example, expressed frustration that they were allowed to interact only with a small group of Kuna leaders, who served as a filter of information to community members, and that they were unable to get a more direct reading of community concerns and needs. In addition to controlling project personnel access to community members, leaders also employed a strategy of bypassing intermediate-level project personnel, whom they felt were not always responsive to their demands, and contacting IFI officials directly. One Ipetí resident, active in the Mesoamerican Biological Corridor Program, praised IFIs' new openness to direct consultation with Kuna leaders: "The World Bank has changed. Before, the World Bank financed projects without consulting with us [the Kunas]. Now they don't. Every time the government solicits money for a big project, they consult with us."

In contrast, several Kuna NGO technicians based in Panama City expressed concern as to whether the *comarcas* should participate in projects funded by agencies such as the World Bank, which in the past have financed projects harmful to indigenous interests and are currently supporting structural adjustment. They suggested that some Madungandí communities have agreed to participate in development projects simply to access money and other material benefits, not because they necessarily share the goals of the donors or the project. In such cases, projects are likely to have limited or no long-term impact on community income or agricultural or environmental practices. Several Ipetí traditional authorities suggested that sustainability projects, designed by outside interests, might bring problems rather than benefits to the community. Ventocilla and colleagues (1996) have also documented the divisive impact of influxes of large amounts of external funding on Kuna Yala–based organizations.[37] In Ipetí, individuals who have participated in sustainable development projects have faced suspicion from other community members that they are seeking personal gain and that their participation in projects is linked to particular political party interests. In addition, resources and funding for sustainable development projects may encourage the proliferation of indigenous NGOs and facilitate an alternative base of power to conflict with traditional authority structures.[38]

INTERNAL GOVERNANCE

The previous discussion highlights the importance of Ipetí's robust forms of self-governance in enabling the community to effectively manage interactions with external agents.[39] Of the three case study communities, Ipetí residents have the most formalized and extensive structures of community and inter-community self-governance.[40] At the *comarca* level, external pressures of the hydroelectric dam project and *interiorano* migrants, as well as encouragement from the Torrijos regime in the 1970s, accelerated coordination between Madungandí communities (Herrera 2002).[41] At the *comarca*'s twice-yearly gatherings or congresses, caciques and representatives coordinate common strategies on issues such as the removal of colonists from the *comarca*, demarcation of the *comarca*, and ongoing claims for compensation for land lost as a result of the hydroelectric dam project. At the community level, Ipetí holds nightly congresses that last from three to six hours. Both men and women attend the first part of the congress, during which traditional authorities recite religious chants and provide religious and social guidance. Only men are allowed to participate in the second part of the gathering, as pending community issues are discussed and debated. *Sailas* and caciques do not have fixed terms of office and may hold their positions until ill health leads to retirement or death (see Reverte 1961). They are also subject to oversight by male community members, who may force them to step down if residents are unhappy with their work.

These forms of intra- and inter-community governance have empowered Ipetí residents in several ways. The community is able to collectively define priorities, organize collective action, maintain a unified position when negotiating with the government, and resist government efforts to divide and co-opt community leadership.

The Madungandí and Ipetí leadership has also chosen a strategy of engagement with, rather than withdrawal from, the state as a means to advance Kuna interests. Caciques have persistently worked to expand opportunities for direct ethnic representation in Panama's dominant political institutions. They have also lobbied the Electoral Tribunal for the right to elect their own legislator and mayor, despite the *comarca*'s relatively small population (Aparicio 2004). Whenever possible, caciques have bypassed intermediate levels of power and insisted on direct and personal access to top government nexuses of power, in particular the presidency.[42] In addition, leaders have been able to parlay relatively strong ethnic solidarity and centralized leadership into political influence, as they have employed their ability to strongly influence voting at the community level as a bargaining tool with politicians.

In a context in which dominant political institutions and actors have greater access to material resources and control over work and income opportunities, the potential for the creation of dependency ties with indigenous communities is strong. Panama's post-1989 invasion political party system has been intensely competitive, although it is often difficult to identify substantive ideological differences between political parties (Perez 2000). Patterns of political patronage begun under military rule continue, and Ipetí residents' interactions with external government agencies have incorporated elements of this dominant political culture. Ipetí informants reported that in the 1999 and 2004 elections, debates within the community on which political party to support focused less on political ideology than on determining which parties would provide the most material benefits to the community in exchange for Kuna support. It remains to be seen, however, if conflicts will develop in Madungandí between these parallel governing structures—elected officials who respond to political party interests and traditional authorities—as has occurred among the Ngöbe-Buglés and to a lesser degree in Kuna Yala (Herrera 2002; Howe 2002).

DISEMPOWERMENT

Overall, I have suggested that land ownership, critical consciousness, and robust internal governance have contributed to the empowerment of Ipetí and to residents' ability to formulate claims, take collective action, and avoid potential external machinations of political parties or development agents. Several issues, however, may undermine this process of empowerment—the exclusion of women from direct participation in community and regional governance and a potential trend toward migration to urban centers. On the one hand, Kuna myths and cosmology give women high symbolic status, and women occupy a strong position in family and daily life (Tice 1995; Howe 1986). In Ipetí, fairly strict gender segregation exists in both daily labor and community activities, and women have a limited direct role in community governance. Although some Ipetí women have spent extended periods in urban centers, women's movements in public spaces and travel outside the *comarca* are more restricted than men's, and women are particularly discouraged from having contact with non-Kuna men (see Moeller 1997). Ipetí women sell their fruits and vegetables at a stand along the highway, and when non-Kuna men approach too closely or make sexually suggestive comments, women withdraw and refuse to continue the sale.[43] These restrictions and the fact that more than 25 percent of Ipetí women are monolingual mean that their knowledge of Panama's dominant culture is largely mediated by Kuna men (Vakis and Lindert 2000). Women have had little direct participation in past sustainable development projects, and even projects involving traditionally female activities such as sewing *molas* have been mediated in part by men.[44]

Moeller (1997) reports hearing Ipetí men comment that women are "weak" and less capable than men. During my fieldwork, several men and women suggested that because Ipetí women are not well-informed on issues and "do not have opinions," they have no need to participate in community governance.[45] As mentioned earlier, the passage of the *comarca* law further codified this exclusion of women from important aspects of *comarca* public life, an ongoing dynamic that contrasts with other, more democratic features of Kuna culture. In interviews and informal conversations, however, Ipetí women expressed less concern about political exclusion than about issues of family well-being and some men's perceived failure to provide adequately for their families. These women did not challenge traditional Kuna gender roles, perceived as complimentary, but rather called upon men to properly fulfill their traditional role and responsibilities of providing subsistence to their families. Women suggested that they wished to prevent the changes in family structures and responsibilities now seen in the *comarca* of Kuna Yala, where 55 percent of women are heads of households because of the abandonment or, less commonly, the death of a male partner (Alvarado 1995).

Ipetí residents, while agreeing that the community is still fairly unified, also identified a trend toward migration to urban centers as a potential challenge to the unity and cultural integrity of Ipetí. In Kuna Yala, 30 percent or more of the population now resides outside the *comarca* (World Bank 1998). In recent years, only a dozen or so Ipetí residents have left the community for extended periods, but the young men of Ipetí are seen as particularly vulnerable to the lure of urban life and relationships with non-Kuna women. In informal conversations, some Ipetí young people expressed curiosity about work, educational, and entertainment opportunities available in the capital. A World Bank study found that Kuna Yala residents migrate to urban areas for educational and economic reasons and that urban Kuna poverty rates are approximately half those of rural Kuna *comarcas* (Vakis and Lindert 2000).

Ipetí authorities interviewed view migration as a serious threat to community integrity and have developed a number of strategies to keep the population stable. Men who wish to travel outside Ipetí, other than those taking part in official missions for the community, must request written permission from the *saila*. Those who leave without permission are fined. Likewise, community authorities have contacted the Panamanian police and asked them to control young men drinking and watching television in non-indigenous stores and bars and not to allow Ipetí men without written passes to cross the Bayano Bridge. In nightly congresses, community authorities emphasize the importance and benefits of Kuna community life, and religious teachings highlight negative consequences of leaving the community in terms of personal health and well-being.[46] Moeller's (1997) study of Ipetí focused on millenarian discourse that emerged in Ipetí in the mid-1990s in which seers (*neles*) dreamed of the end of the world. He argues that this discourse has been an important control mechanism to maintain community cultural cohesion. Individuals who do leave Ipetí on a longer-term basis are obliged to pay money to the community to compensate for their lack of participation in communal labor activities; if they fail to do so, they risk having their possessions confiscated.

CONCLUSION

The Ipetí experience further illustrates the diversity of grassroots visions of sustainability and ways they may contest dominant discourse. Ipetí residents challenge the centrality of economic growth to community well-being. Rather, Ipeti residents collectively choose to place limits on economic growth, forms of consumption, and engagement in certain types of economic activities in favor of central values of cultural expression and a communal way of life. Residents view the *comarca*'s natural environment as essential to their way of life, not only as a means to meet material needs but also in cultural and spiritual terms. Ironically perhaps, it has been increased contact with markets, a policy promoted by dominant institutions, that has to a degree undermined environmental consciousness in the community and facilitated collective decisions to allow logging in the *comarca*.

The Ipetí experience also illustrates a relatively effective balance of community autonomy and engagement with the state and dominant development policies that has helped enable the community to advance land claims and access material resources. In addition, this case study provides further evidence that the outcomes of sustainable development encounters are shaped not only by top-down policies but also by the community's characteristics and degree of empowerment. While I have suggested that internal governance has been a key element of this empowerment, a more diffuse process of the advance of market forces and dominant Panamanian culture—infused with values of consumerism and the attractions of urban life—represents a key challenge to a form of empowerment constructed on a basis of ethnic difference.

Chapter 9

Bringing the Case Studies Together

I have argued that the adoption of a discourse of sustainable development by a wide range of institutions and actors signifies less an ideological and policy convergence than the opening of a new terrain of struggle over meanings and practices of sustainability. Sustainability encompasses not only environmental conservation but also economic and sociocultural transformations. The case studies, therefore, have approached sustainability from a contextualized and holistic perspective that locates the sustainable development interventions of dominant institutions in a broader context of neoliberal reforms and concepts of participation and empowerment. Dominant sustainability has been critiqued as a northern elite ideological project to depoliticize and demobilize the poor in Central America (Goldman 1998a; Ferguson 1990; Sachs 1993). The case studies suggest, however, that the dominant vision of sustainability has not achieved hegemony in rural Central America and that pockets of resistance, spaces of counterhegemonic discourse, persist or are in the process of formation.

COMMUNITY VISIONS OF SUSTAINABILITY

Several common elements can be identified in these alternative discourses of sustainability. First, these grassroots perspectives challenge the epistemological orientation of dominant discourse. Community residents do not frame their perspectives and claims in a technical or quantitative discourse but rather draw on lived experience and ethical, moral, and spiritual values and structures of understanding. Dominant institutions present their assumptions, values, and policy prescriptions as universally applicable (World Bank 2003d; Collier and Dollar 2002). Actors at the grassroots level, however, insist upon history and context, discourse and practices grounded in collective and local experiences. Likewise, communities do not necessarily view markets as natural and good. Instead, they articulate a more complex perspective that recognizes market processes as potential opportunities for household material advancement but also as potentially exclusionary and risky (see Table 9.1).

The livelihood orientation to sustainability resonates strongly at the grassroots level in all three case studies, with localized environmentalism also present in Costa Rica. However, within the Nicaraguan and Panamanian communities, these claims for land, resources, and power are framed somewhat differently. Miraflores residents employ a class-based discourse that draws a sharp dichotomy between the "rich" and the "poor" majority such as themselves and emphasizes values of social justice that take precedence over unfettered markets and absolute property rights. In contrast, Ipetí residents make claims to the state and international institutions on the basis of historical, ethnically bounded rights to resources and have placed less attention on articulating a broader critique of development models.

Economic Component

In contrast to dominant sustainability discourse that prioritizes macro-level economic growth, Miraflores residents are skeptical that national economic growth in and of itself will provide them with a pathway out of poverty and address their concerns about subsistence security and distribution. These individuals place priority on being able to meet their basic needs—food, medicine, housing, and education for their children—and argue that this requires not simply access to markets but also substantive redistribution of land and subsidies through an activist state. Like their Nicaraguan counterparts, Osa peninsula residents question the goal of maximizing economic output through, for example, large-scale tourism projects. Ecotourism entrepreneurs and environmental activists in Puerto Jiménez less strongly emphasize economic subsistence themes, perhaps because most of those interviewed do not face immediate subsistence threats. They have sought instead to exert local control over the forms and rate of growth to preserve their self-defined vision of quality of life on the peninsula—a mirror image of urban, industrialized society—which provides opportunities for close daily contact with nature.

Table 9.1. Community Visions of Sustainable Development

	Costa Rica	Nicaragua	Panama
Overview of Sustainable Development	localized environmentalism ethical, spiritual, emotional epistemology scope: broader structural trans-formations	livelihood orientation ethical, social justice epistemology scope: broader structural trans-formations	livelihood orientation ethnic identity ethical, social justice, spiritual epistemology scope: focus on sustainability at the local level
Economic Component	more well-off, less concern with subsistence needs support limits to economic growth	primary concern is meeting house-hold subsistence needs support redistribution of land and resources	alternative concept of poverty seek subsistence, limits to material accumulation
Social Component	distinct, evolving subcultures linked to farming, gold mining, and ecotourism value quality of life linked to nature	strong class-based identity as poor rural, *campesino* identity	distinct way of life key value of community well-defined and strongly defended ethnic identity
Environmental Component	nature has intrinsic and utilitarian value environmental destruction linked to poverty	utilitarian view of nature environmental destruction linked to poverty	well-being of nature and community linked environmental destruction linked to poverty

Ipetí residents also question the centrality of economic accumulation from a slightly different perspective. Although Ipetí, with an average monthly household income of $200, is represented by institutions like the World Bank as "poor," community members challenge this label (World Bank 1999a). They believe that because their access to the land and natural resources of the *comarca*, combined with community support networks, enables families to meet their food and housing needs, the community is not poor or even necessarily needy in an economic sense. Ipetí traditional authorities have also placed priority on cultural values and way of life and have limited income-earning activities, such as cattle ranching, and consumption seen to undermine that way of life.

Social Component

A second important component of sustainable development focuses broadly on social and cultural values and identity. The dominant discourse of sustainability incorporates collective identities and community ties primarily from a utilitarian perspective. Participation and community inclusion are seen as a means to implement development projects more efficiently and as a check on rent-seeking state elites (World Bank 2006a). In contrast, grassroots actors in these case studies view collective identities and social networks as intrinsically valuable and use them as imagined, bounded spaces within the expanses of globalization to nurture and enable mobilization.

Unlike Ipetí residents, Miraflores community members identify themselves as "poor"—an imposed condition, a state they seek to overcome and escape from—which at the same time provides an anchor of collective identity and mobilization against the "rich" and "large landowners." Poverty, from this perspective, is not an external label. Rather, it is a tool appropriated to make claims to the state and broader society, to organize for collective action, and to use as the most fundamental measuring stick of political and social programs—do they benefit the poor? Miraflores community residents also identify themselves as campesinos, people who live in the countryside and make their living from the land, with core values of independence and self-sufficiency. This identity in practice, however, appears to take second place to subsistence concerns, as Miraflores residents have chosen migration and non-agricultural employment to advance economically.

The Osa peninsula contains at least three distinct occupational subcultures—agriculture, gold mining, and ecotourism. Agriculturalists and gold miners are longer-term, more deeply rooted subcultures that draw on a more traditional instrumentalist perspective of the natural world and perceive their way of life as under siege from a combination of advancing environmental regulations and neoliberal economic policies. The growth of the peninsula's most recent subculture, ecotourism, however, has been linked to global processes—the emergence of environmental consciousness and a desire for contact with the natural world in the United States and Europe, as well as the Costa Rican government's transnationally influenced expansion of protected areas—that have been appropriated at the local level. Quality of life for this sector challenges some of the basic precepts of dominant sustainability and signifies distance from the stress and bustle of urban and industrial life, as well as featuring ongoing contact with the natural word.

In Ipetí, collective identity emerges as the most central value of sustainability. Residents identify first and foremost as Kunas and locate both ethnic and place-specific community loyalties before a broader, nationalist identity as "Panamanians." They have prioritized struggles for autonomy and land rights in part because the *comarca* is a space in which non-Kunas can be excluded and Kuna cultural traditions can be practiced, reinforced, and recreated. Note, however, that Ipetí residents' focus on ethnic identity does not exclude economic and environmental concerns and claims. Rather, they view cultural distinction, material subsistence, and environmental conservation as interlocking and mutually reinforcing for the community's overall well-being.

Environmental Component

In terms of the third component of sustainable development, environmental conservation, Miraflores residents, similar to dominant discourse, conceptualize the natural environment primarily in terms of its use and economic value, not its intrinsic worth. They express limited aesthetic or spiritual appreciation of nature. Although many prefer rural to urban lifestyles, "nature" to these families also represents discomfort and danger. Miraflores residents do not, however, actively engage in environmentally destructive activities, and on their own land they carry out a series of environmental conservation measures. These practices have emerged through contact with a more globalized environmentalist discourse, as mediated by sustainable development projects, and from economic interests.

In contrast to the Nicaragua case study, some Osa peninsula residents' localized environmentalism holds that all living things—including animals and plants—have intrinsic value and that human beings have an ethical obligation not to damage the environment. These Puerto Jiménez ecotourism participants and environmental activists link the long-term emotional and spiritual well-being of all human beings to the well-being of nature and prioritize maintaining this connection. In practice, residents have participated in grassroots environmental campaigns against the Stone Container wood chip plant and against logging in the Golfo Dulce Forest Reserve. At the same time, instrumental views of nature for profit—through gold extraction, farming, and ranching or through conservation of rain forests for ecotourism—also persist on the peninsula.

Ipetí discourse and practices also place central importance on the natural environment to meet a variety of daily needs in the areas of housing, diet, health, and handicrafts, as well as to tie the community together in collective cultural and religious activities. Ipetí conservationist practices are centered less on a sense of the intrinsic value of nature than on a belief that protection of the rain forest is crucial to the well-being of community residents as mediated through the spiritual world. And while respect for the natural world has deep roots in Kuna culture and religion, transformations in Ipetí over the past several decades also illustrate the dynamic nature of environmental beliefs and practices. Increased contact with dominant Panamanian culture, as well as the monetarization of community life, has influenced Ipetí residents to adopt less environmentally sustainable practices such as logging within the *comarca*.

A common perception across the three case studies is that environmental conservation is a matter less of consciousness or education than of the ability of households to meet their basic needs. Individuals engaged in environmentally damaging activities do not oppose environmental conservation in principle and are aware of the negative environmental impact of their activities. Yet in strikingly similar language across national borders, with phrases such as "we have to eat" (*hay que comer*), they argue that their poverty leaves them few options but to act against environmental sustainability.

COMMUNITY ENGAGEMENT WITH DOMINANT POLICIES OF SUSTAINABILITY

Market-Oriented Reforms

Dominant discourse and practices of sustainability have promoted neoliberal reforms as key to "pro-poor" economic growth, seen as central to alleviating poverty and associated pressures on the environment (World Bank 2006a, 2003d) (see Table 9.2). In Central America, the World Bank credits neoliberal reforms, implemented to varying degrees within the region, with facilitating relatively strong national economic growth in Nicaragua, Costa Rica, and Panama by the mid-1990s (World Bank 2006b, 2000, 1999a). Other studies, in contrast, suggest that these market-oriented reforms—a termination of crop price supports and lower barriers to agricultural imports in all three countries, as well as privatization of rural

Table 9.2. Engagement with Dominant Policies of Sustainability

	Costa Rica	Nicaragua	Panama
Market-oriented reforms	negative impacts of neoliberal reforms obstacles to competing in globalized markets want opportunities to participate in profitable activities	negative impacts of neoliberal reforms obstacles to competing in globalized markets want opportunities to participate in profitable activities	less affected by neoliberal reform *comarca* as a subsistence buffer
Sustainable development pathways	*Ecotourism* direct and indirect economic benefits to local people increased environmental awareness uneven geographic impact	*Shrimp Production* generates employment most economic benefits go to companies and large producers negative social and environmental impacts	*Indigenous Land Rights* economic benefits to local people contributes to social and environmental sustainability may only displace colonist patterns of deforestation
General attitudes toward government	governments corrupt, favor wealthy governments undermine community organization	governments corrupt, favor wealthy governments undermine community organization	governments corrupt, favor wealthy patronage ties to political parties
Government environmental regulation	government has effective environmental enforcement capacity community opinion divided on environmental regulation	government has weak environmental enforcement capacity environmental regulation not a major source of tension	government has weak environmental enforcement capacity environmental regulation not a major source of tension
Sustainable development interventions	"failed" projects on the peninsula demobilize population	NGOs are an important ally, fill in where state is absent NGOs provide material benefits, skills, critical discourse	ambivalent attitudes on the need for development projects more limited interaction and impact of NGOs

credit and an end to state benefits in Nicaragua—have benefited large commercial farmers and ranchers over the poor (Chase 2002; Enriquez 2000; Edelman 1999; Jonakin 1996).

The case studies suggest that even when national economic growth occurs, certain sectors of the rural poor may experience a deterioration of their income and subsistence security. It appears that those communities that received more state support and subsidies in the past most strongly perceive negative economic impacts from neoliberalism—a more general decline in agriculture on the Osa peninsula and increased inequality in Miraflores. A number of handicaps have impeded these Nicaraguan and Costa Rican campesinos from effectively competing in this increasingly global free market environment—difficult access to land, credit, and markets; a lack of legal titles to land; low intermediary prices for crops; and inexpensive food imports. In both case studies, residents draw a link between the economic pressures neoliberal reforms have placed on small and mid-sized farmers and an intensification of environmentally damaging activities, in particular deforestation of nearby protected areas.

In contrast, Ipetí residents perceive fewer direct negative impacts of neoliberal reforms, in part because historically they have received fewer government benefits in terms of technical assistance, credit, infrastructure, and subsidies. Community leaders have also framed their primary struggle as an inter-ethnic one over land rights and autonomy and have less actively engaged with broader discourses of critical political economy. Unlike their Nicaraguan and Costa Rican counterparts, who hold government and international financial institution neoliberal policies as at least partly responsible for their economic difficulties, Ipetí residents tend to view fluctuations in prices for their principle crops as more "natural" market occurrences and not necessarily a collective grievance to be acted upon.

Sustainable Development Pathways

The case study communities have also engaged in activities promoted by dominant institutions as promising pathways to sustainable development. These include two market-based activities linked to economic globalization—ecotourism and shrimp production as a nontraditional export—as well as state recognition of indigenous collective land rights. It appears that, as dominant institutions have suggested, both ecotourism and shrimp production have brought economic benefits to local communities, primarily through the creation of jobs and new income-earning opportunities. In both case studies, however, the distribution of economic benefits has been uneven. Profits from shrimp production have gone primarily to the large national and international companies that dominate both production and processing, while on the Osa peninsula smaller-scale foreign investors have dominated ecotourism investment. Residents in both case studies identified lack of access to land and limited capital, as well as state policies that have tended to favor better-off investors, as factors limiting more equitable participation in these activities.

In environmental terms, ecotourism has offered residents a material incentive to shift away from environmentally damaging activities such as logging and has been critical in drawing together a core group of environmental activists on the peninsula. In contrast, the expansion of semi-intensive shrimp production in the Estero Real has contributed to deforestation and environmental deterioration.

A third strategy of dominant sustainability, I have argued, is "indigenous exceptionalism," support for collective land rights for numerically and culturally delimited indigenous groups, a policy seen as not challenging the broader global economic model of individual property rights. On the one hand, Ipetí residents have successfully used this policy shift to advance their claims for state recognition and autonomy, contributing to some degree to environmental conservation and cultural diversity within the boundaries of the *comarca*. Yet Ipetí and the other two case studies also suggest a limitation of these activities and policies. Because they are constrained in scope—by geography, ethnicity, class, occupation, and similar factors—important population groups have been excluded from potential benefits. In essence, because broader dynamics of poverty and deforestation remain intact, environmental damage may simply be displaced to other, less protected zones.

States and Sustainability

The dominant discourse envisions a smaller, transparent, and accountable state that will provide market stability through sound fiscal and monetary policies and a stable regulatory framework (World Bank 2006a; Demmers, Fernández Jilberto, and Hogenboom 2004b). The case studies suggest, however, that in practice the state remains key in rural Central America in several ways. First, states continue to play a key mediating role as globalized discourses and policies of sustainability are applied in national and local settings. In particular, states have expanded their direct administration of large sections of rural territory and have increased their control over economic activities in the name of environmental protection. With largely external funding, governments also sponsor and oversee, and in some instances directly implement, sustainable development interventions.

The three case studies also draw our attention to the ways states remain central in community members' activism and claims making. Rather than withdraw, all three communities have persisted in engaging with their governments, not only in the local sphere but also at the national level in the case of Ipetí. They have sought out spaces for participation and attempted to influence government policy and employ government programs to their benefit. While Nicaragua, Costa Rica, and Panama followed distinct political trajectories in the post–World War II period, only converging politically in the 1990s with implementation of formal democracy, community members hold very similar perceptions of their governments and normative concepts of the state. Overall, even as they engage with their governments on a range of issues, residents of the three case study zones are skeptical and mistrustful of government officials. Somewhat ironically, they contend that the spaces of participation that have opened under formal democracy are in fact often used by political elites to attempt to manipulate and co-opt the rural population, particularly during election campaigns. They suggest that many, if not all, politicians have little interest in representing the interests of their poor constituents once they gain power. They characterize formal politics as an arena of self-interested individuals who are often captured by elite interests and use political offices to accumulate personal wealth and power. Importantly, however, individuals in the case study communities also identified political parties and individual politicians they believed were the exception to this characterization. Residents also contrast the relatively democratic spaces of participation they have nurtured within their communities with dominant political cultures, where they believe a formal rhetoric of consultation and inclusion often conceals exclusionary practices. True opportunities for participation have only come, they argue, with organized, persistent community pressure. In addition, all case studies suggest that state agents, in particular political parties, may seek to undermine the autonomy of community organizations and foment relationships of patronage and dependency.

In addition to the failure of democracy to live up to community members' increasing expectations, a common normative vision of the state emerges from these case studies. Residents of the three communities envision a role for the state qualitatively distinct from the limited state of dominant sustainability. They perceive government "neglect" as undermining their quality of life and express frustration that governments have failed to provide the types of basic infrastructure and services—roads, health care, and schools—that have been at the core of traditional development interventions. Grassroots actors call on their governments to play a more robust role in creating conditions that will buffer them from markets through redistribution of land, market interventions, and credit subsidies and to actively mediate social conflicts.

Government Environmental Regulations

Despite a substantial new inflow of international funding in the 1990s, the capacity of the Nicaraguan and Panamanian governments to protect national parks and reserves and enforce environmental laws and regulations has remained relatively weak in practice. Environmental protection in the case study zones has been undermined by a lack of funds for personnel and equipment and by elites who influence state apparatuses so they can carry out environmentally damaging activities. States in these instances are not neutral environmental arbitrators or enforcers but rather have shifted the costs of environmental protection disproportionately onto the poor.

In addition, even a relatively weak extension of state environmental control appears to intensify tensions between state agencies and local populations who have historically engaged in resource extraction and feel their subsistence security and localized way of life are threatened. An important exception to this has been the Osa peninsula residents more deeply entwined with ecotourism and a localized environmental discourse, who generally support the expansion of state environmental control as a buffer to the destructive impact of market activities. The case studies suggest that environmental knowledge and awareness may be advanced through both endogenous cultural processes, as in the case of the Ipetí, or interactions with external discourses. Communities may also act as agents of sustainability on several different levels: as caretakers of their own properties, by making sustainable use of nearby protected areas, and by acting as social and political advocates for environmental enforcement and conservation.

Sustainable Development Interventions

Both dominant and alternative discourses of sustainability have strongly emphasized nongovernmental organizations (NGOs) as key intermediary agents and implementers of sustainable development (Bebbington and Thiele 1993). The case study experiences with NGO-administered sustainable development projects can be located along a continuum, from the most empowering experiences in Miraflores to fairly positive outcomes in Ipetí and mixed experiences in Osa. In some instances NGOs have provided communities with basic infrastructure, technical assistance, and training. They have also served as political and social advocates for local communities and helped introduce or reinforce critical ideologies. In Miraflores, ongoing interactions with progressive NGOs have given men self-confidence and social skills that have enabled them to better articulate and defend their interests in a range of public and private arenas.

On the Osa peninsula, on the other hand, while local activists recognize that a few specific NGOs have contributed to individual and collective empowerment, they also identify projects whose perceived failures have undermined grassroots willingness to participate in collective activities. Some Ipetí residents also have ambivalent perceptions of NGO-administered development projects. They are drawn to projects for the potential material benefits they offer but are also wary of the potential cultural and social disruption development projects may bring. Overall, the case study communities have not been passive in their relationships with NGOs but rather have collectively and individually evaluated the costs and benefits of participation and selectively chosen to apply for or disregard NGO technical assistance and plans.

COMMUNITY EMPOWERMENT

Community Characteristics

Much of the critical literature on sustainable development focuses on the role of indigenous or traditional communities, seen as having a distinct way of life and strong place- and identity-based ties to local environments, as ideal environmental caretakers (see Table 9.3). This characterization can be applied to Ipetí, as over the decades community residents have accumulated specialized and unique knowledge about their natural environment and have a strong emotional and spiritual attachment to their *comarca*. In contrast, Puerto Jiménez and Miraflores are more open and fluid communities, to some degree more representative of contemporary rural Central America. Puerto Jiménez's network of ecotourism and environmental activists was formed with the arrival of globalized environmentalism and an ecotourism boom that have drawn Costa Ricans into a common geographic zone and a distinct way of life linked to contact with the natural world. Miraflores, the newest of the three communities studied, was an artificial creation of a 1980s government land reform program that brought together small farmers and agricultural day laborers with the incentive of land to farm. In the following years, a common pro-revolutionary political orientation, collective land management, and participation in sustainable development projects strengthened community shared identity and capacity to collectively confront a series of external challenges.

Community Empowerment

I have suggested that a material base of resources, as well as access to a critical ideology that enables communities to analyze their particular local circumstances and articulate alternative values and beliefs, are

Table 9.3. Community Empowerment

		Nicaragua	Costa Rica	Panama
Conditions of empowerment	Community characteristics	created with 1980s land reform	open, fluid community of migrants from other regions	deeply rooted, traditional community with strong place-based ties
	Critical consciousness	autonomous peasant land struggles; contact with revolutionary state	land struggles against TNC and state; contact with global environmentalism	historical resistance to state and dominant culture; ethnic identity
	Material base for activism	1980s land reform	ecotourism	collective landholdings
Community empowerment	Key strategies	economic diversification, political activism, social networking, participation in projects	NGO alliances, networking, political activism	persistent lobbying, direct action, frame claims in sustainable development discourse
	Practices that have reinforced empowerment	collective land management, land struggles; participation in sustainable development projects	1970s land struggles; environmental campaigns	land struggles, traditional governance structures
	Environmental consciousness	gained environmental knowledge through sustainable development projects	contact with globalized environmentalism	specialized knowledge of the local environment
Factors that undermine community capacity		increased intra-community inequality social and economic barriers to women's participation	past failed development projects social and economic barriers to women's participation	contacts with dominant Panamanian culture and markets social and economic barriers to women's participation

key elements in their empowerment as active agents of sustainability. The case studies illustrate, however, that there is no single path to empowerment but rather a diversity of processes communities may undergo. The Nicaragua and Costa Rica experiences suggest that external agents can play an important role in empowerment. In Nicaragua, the Sandinista land reform and a series of 1980s redistributive government programs and subsidies gave community members a critical material base from which to become active agents of sustainability. On the ideological level, contacts with revolutionary discourse in the 1980s provided community members with a critical, class-based lens through which to evaluate dominant discourse and practices. Personal and collective empowerment also advanced through opportunities to collectively administer land and through participation in NGO projects.

Miraflores residents describe empowerment as a cumulative process through which they have gradually overcome feelings of inferiority linked to social stigma, poverty, and lack of formal education and learned to interact with and confront individuals of higher social status. With an increased sense of self-confidence and efficacy, community members have collectively developed social networks, sought out development projects, planned strategies of legal defense against land claims, and acted in local politics. In the 1990s, Miraflores residents coped with increasingly difficult macroeconomic conditions by diversifying income sources, migrating to Costa Rica and El Salvador, and engaging in nonfarm employment.

On the Osa peninsula, ecotourism, linked to global sustainability, has provided income for local residents to enable them to maintain a way of life that contrasts with urban consumer culture and to undertake a series of environmental campaigns. Ideologically, community members have appropriated globalized environmental discourse and linked it to both national and local identities. Environmental activists articulate a complex, alternative discourse of sustainable development that focuses not simply on local issues but also encompasses broader policy and structural issues. In their collective mobilization against the Stone Container wood chip plant and, later, anti-logging campaigns, activists requested assistance from national and international NGOs and relied on word of mouth and informal social networks to organize. In both the Nicaragua and Costa Rica case studies, processes of empowerment have been not simply cognitive but also emotional and spiritual. While in Miraflores it was largely men who underwent empowerment experiences, in Puerto Jiménez many women learned from the 1990s environmental campaigns to overcome their fears and the limitations of traditional gender roles and to actively articulate and defend their interests.

In contrast to the Nicaragua and Costa Rica case studies, in Panama the process of empowerment has been more endogenous. In their struggles for autonomy and land rights, a key advantage of Ipetí residents has been their ability to present a consistent and unified position in negotiations with the colonists and the Panamanian government. Residents' capacity to define and act collectively rests in part on their traditional community- and regional-level governance structures, which are held accountable to community members. Community authorities and residents employ a variety of incentives, community norms, and sanctions to maintain physical and social cohesion. In addition to these largely internal processes, a group of younger men, who have spent time in non-indigenous environments and institutions, have applied their cross-cultural knowledge and Spanish- language skills to serve as intermediaries between elderly monolingual traditional leaders and government authorities. Empowerment has also been an ongoing process for these Ipetí activists. The highway protests in particular gave these men self-confidence, as they were able to overcome what they perceived as decades of Kuna passivity and directly confront the Panamanian state and its police force. In ideological terms, Ipetí residents have drawn on historical social justice narratives, reaching back 500 years to the Spanish Conquest, Kuna religious and cultural traditions, and a more globalized discourse of sustainability.

The case studies suggest that strategies of empowered sustainability will vary depending upon the repertoires of resistance of each community, as well as national and local political and power contexts. Relatively small-scale protests that have been effective in bringing government response in Panama and Costa Rica, for example, would likely be ineffective in Nicaragua's more polarized and violent political culture. The case study communities appear to have been successful in part because they have engaged in a wide variety of actions—lobbying government officials, engaging in traditional party politics, organizing meetings and protests, and participating in direct action techniques such as blocking roads. Community flexibility, as well as persistence in these collective mobilizations over months, years, and even decades, has also been key.

Community Disempowerment

The three case study communities illustrate not only processes of empowerment but also factors that may disempower communities, potentially undermining their material well-being and local ways of life and facilitating environmentally destructive activities. The activities of shrimp production companies in the Estero Real of Nicaragua and foreign gold mining companies and national loggers on the Osa peninsula have had direct negative environmental consequences (Rocha and Barahona 1999). The market-oriented activities of large national and transnational companies may place pressure on poor communities, leaving them few options but to engage in environmentally damaging activities, as in the case of the artisan gold miners in Costa Rica and the wood cutters of Nicaragua. In all of these cases, community residents contrast their subsistence needs with the companies' "greed" and "waste," contending that it has been economic necessity—framed in ethical terms as the need to feed their children—that has forced them to participate in deforestation. Additional key economic factors that have contributed to environmentally unsustainable activities by the poor include lack of land and credit, difficult access to markets, and competition from agricultural imports.

Of the three case study communities, Miraflores has experienced the most dramatic shifts, not only in terms of the sharp macroeconomic policy changes from 1990 onward but also in terms of the internal organization of the community. Families moved from a model of collective management of land and natural resources and relative equality in the 1980s to individual land ownership in the 1990s. While a few Miraflores families have advanced economically, other families—in particular single mothers, the elderly, and the handicapped—have sold part or all of their land and have chronic or seasonal difficulties meeting basic subsistence needs. These economic inequalities have also undermined capacity for collective action, as poor families have become mistrustful of households that are prospering. In addition, the poorest families are the least likely to participate in the types of development projects that in the past provided substantial support to Miraflores because of the open and hidden costs involved.

On Osa peninsula, a series of unsuccessful cooperatives and development projects have left some peninsula residents reluctant to act collectively. They are skeptical about the potential benefits of community projects and the honesty of community and political leaders. Osa peninsula residents also report that party politics tend to undermine community organization, as political party loyalties to Costa Rica's two major parties divide communities and create relationships of dependency that may weaken the autonomy of organizations.

Turning to Ipetí, while residents believe their community remains strongly united, contacts with the dominant culture and migration to urban areas are recognized as key challenges to community cohesion. Residents also note that some men now spend less time farming, both because agricultural land close to the community is largely controlled by older men and because they seek wage labor opportunities in agriculture and logging to obtain faster access to cash. This trend of increased use of money in Ipetí and contacts with the dominant culture and institutions has also contributed to community participation in logging. Although Ipetí residents recognize the environmental and potential cultural and spiritual damage logging may bring to the *comarca,* these concerns have been outweighed by a community desire for the income logging contracts provide. Another negative trend Ipetí residents identify is the potential for greater economic inequality and a weakening of the community's subsistence safety net. To date, cultural norms that encourage sharing food within and between households and prohibit purchase and use of certain consumer goods have helped maintain relative economic equity in Ipetí. Such norms of equitable distribution, however, are applied less consistently to more recent wage activity in logging.

A final factor that has undermined community empowerment in all of the case study communities has been gender inequity. In the Nicaragua and Panama case studies, women have had only limited direct participation in community decision making and sustainable development projects. In Miraflores, traditional gender norms have largely confined women's participation in development projects to the traditionally feminine areas of health care and family. In Ipetí, in addition to traditional Kuna gender norms that restrict women's movements more than men's, Ipetí women are more likely to be monolingual, and their contacts with government agencies, NGOs, and development projects tend to be mediated through men. In the Costa Rica case study, although women have taken a leadership role in collective action, they still have to deal with opposition from their husbands or *compañeros*, as well as negative social commentary, when they step outside traditional gender roles.

Overall, the findings of the three case studies illustrate multiple pathways to grassroots sustainability. They highlight an array of discourses ranging from environmentalist orientations that place intrinsic ethical, emotional, and spiritual values on nature, to livelihood views that focus on redistributive measures to enable the poor to meet their basic needs. The case study experiences suggest that under the right conditions, empowered communities are able to cope with, appropriate, and rework dominant discourses and practices. In Chapter 10, I evaluate these community experiences in the context of the broader theoretical debates of sustainability.

Chapter 10

Conclusion

In the twenty-first century, sustainability issues have moved to center stage in Central America. There has been a top-down convergence toward discourses of sustainability among dominant global institutions and donor governments (World Bank 2003a). Simultaneously, Third World grassroots movements have sought to articulate and put into practice alternative concepts of sustainability that bring together threads of poverty, cultural diversity, and ecological crisis (Guha and Martínez-Alier 1998; Peet and Watts 1996a; Friedmann and Rangan 1993). The discourses and practices of sustainability, indeed if such a thing as sustainable development can be achieved at all, remain deeply contested. More than merely an arcane issue of semantics, struggles over the meaning of sustainable development are closely linked to issues of power and material distribution. They have profound practical implications in terms of which groups in society are to bear the costs and reap the potential benefits of development (Adams 2001).

Much of the external project funding and many of the economic policies and forms of environmental protectionism in Central America since the 1990s have been linked to dominant constructions of sustainable development, as implemented and mediated through multilateral institutions, states, and nongovernmental organizations (NGOs). Dominant sustainability discourse retains the central goal of economic growth, taken from traditional development discourse, now reframed as "pro-poor" growth and accompanied by targeted poverty alleviation, participation and empowerment, good governance, and environmental conservation (World Bank 2006a, 2003d, 2001a, 2001b; Demmers, Fernández Jilberto, and Hogenboom 2004a; Sindzingre 2004; Wade 2004). I argue that while these different policy areas are not necessarily mutually reinforcing, they should be analyzed as a conceptually linked set that overlaps in implementation in grassroots settings. I explore the relationship between these components and the ways they impact and are appropriated, or resisted, by specific local communities embedded in common regional patterns of dependency, external interventions, and social and economic inequality, as well as unique local histories of resistance. In addition to these sets of policies from above, I have suggested that deeper forms of sustainability in rural Central America are linked to community empowerment built upon a material base of support, critical consciousness, and a capacity to act collectively. This analysis envisions a role for communities not limited to individual conservation measures on private property or to project activities but rather one that also encompasses collective engagement and social and political advocacy on a range of sustainability issues.

The case studies have explored several key questions. In what manner do these grassroots discourses concur with or challenge the assumptions, values, analysis, and related practices of the dominant model of sustainability? Second, how have multistranded, globally generated dominant sustainability polices—in the form of neoliberal reforms, environmental regulation, and development interventions and mediated through states and NGOs—influenced communities' capacity to act as agents of self-defined sustainability? Likewise, what localized, internal factors advance or undermine this process of empowerment?

POLITICAL ECONOMY IMPLICATIONS

World Bank reports frame the recent institutional adoption of sustainability discourse as a product of technical and economic knowledge and analysis and, implicitly, of good-faith efforts to address critics' social justice and environmental concerns (World Bank 2003d; Collier and Dollar 2002). International financial institutions (IFIs) have advanced economic liberalization as a means to promote economic growth that, in turn, should alleviate poverty in Central America and reduce the unsustainable pressures the poor place on their natural environments (World Bank 2001a, 2001b). From this perspective, at the very least the new discourse of sustainability represents opportunities for the rural poor to gain material support, new spaces for participation, and new ideological frames with which to make claims in national and transnational forums.

A body of critical literature has also emerged to challenge dominant discourse from political economy and ideological perspectives. The political ecology literature contends that dominant institutions' support for economic liberalization undermines social goals of sustainability, as vulnerable sectors of the population are further impoverished (Adams 2001; Bryant and Bailey 1997; Dore 1997; Utting 1996). In environmental terms, critics argue that because dominant policies fail to adequately address the underlying dynamics of environmental deterioration linked to processes of capitalist accumulation, their small-scale conservation projects are at best palliative or merely displace environmental destruction.

The case studies provide examples from rural Central America of the dynamics identified by critics. As neoliberal reforms are implemented and economic liberalization advances, Central America's rural poor must compete in market environments with a series of handicaps—lack of land, difficult access to capital, low levels of education, poor health, and limited state support (Proyecto Estado de la Nación 2003). Under these conditions, neoliberal reforms in the case study communities have perpetuated or deepened relative inequality or even undermined subsistence security in absolute terms (Ruben 2001; Barkin 2000; Lustig 1995; Painter and Durham 1995). In addition, new and intensified market activities that have advanced into more remote zones of rural Central America, particularly when combined with state subsidies to companies and weak regulation in ecologically fragile zones, may be linked to environmental deterioration (Ruben 2001; Reed 1996; Gibson 1996; Goodman and Redclift 1991a). The case study experiences emphasize that environmental education and knowledge, even if appropriated by local populations, are still not sufficient to prevent destructive activities if the underlying economic dynamics of poverty are not also addressed. In addition, World Bank poverty reduction strategies—essentially improved basic education and health care—while arguably important development goals in and of themselves, appear inadequate to address the more pervasive and systematic economic disadvantages experienced by Central America's rural poor (World Bank 2001a).

The critical literature, however, may fail to recognize the complexity of the relationships of poor rural and indigenous communities with expanded and intensified market processes in remote zones. Two new market activities deemed sustainable—ecotourism and shrimp production—have had unequal benefits but have generated new employment and income opportunities for local populations. In other words, even as relative inequality is perpetuated or deepened, local populations have received economic benefits in absolute terms. In these instances, it appears that residents are not necessarily anti-capitalist or opposed to participation in market activities, as livelihood critics might contend. Rather, they seek more favorable inclusion in the potential economic benefits of markets. In addition, while meeting basic needs remains an overriding concern for the very poor in particular, individuals and households also actively seek to move beyond subsistence toward economic accumulation, embracing the market processes at the center of dominant discourse. Grassroots claims for access to markets, however, also go beyond the IFI focus on better roads and transportation to demand interventions such as subsidies and distribution of assets that would help level the playing field.

GRASSROOTS CRITICAL DISCOURSES

Once firmly ensconced in the economic realm, IFIs in recent years have incorporated social and political concerns into their programs, in the form of support for participation and good governance (World Bank 2006a; Onis and Senses 2005; Sindzingre 2004; Demmers, Fernández Jilberto, and Hogenboom 2004a). A second important strand of the critical scholarship, articulated most fully in the postdevelopment literature, argues that such measures are not designed to advance empowerment but rather are an elite ideological and political project to demobilize and co-opt grassroots groups increasingly critical of, and mobilized against, economic globalization (Goldman 2005, 2001; Escobar 1995). This critique may overstate the unidirectional ideological influence of dominant institutions, however. Greater attention needs to be paid to the possibility that at least certain rural poor and indigenous communities can maintain or develop counternarratives and alternative concepts of sustainability. Such grassroots counternarratives, for example, may challenge the epistemology and many of the assumptions and values of dominant discourse. Community residents make claims in the name of social justice, cultural orientations, and nationalisms, not technical or scientific competency. Grassroots actors, discontent with the status quo, seek guided change or "sustainable development" that addresses the region's deep economic and social inequalities and provides for household subsistence needs through redistributive measures largely excluded from dominant practices of sustainability. These are not necessarily claims for a more radical egalitarianism but rather for a type of platform at the bottom through which to have basic needs met.

Although subsistence is a central theme of these critical grassroots discourses, the case studies provide evidence that essential human fulfillment or well-being is not universally achieved through greater material accumulation. Rather, once a threshold of subsistence or material well-being, as defined in particular social contexts, is reached, individuals and collective groups may choose to limit forms of economic growth in favor of other environmental or sociocultural priorities, such as contact with nature, way of life, dignity, or autonomy.

Another important theme that emerges in the grassroots discourses, which is virtually unrecognized in dominant discourse, is that of power. In contrast to dominant characterizations of markets and states, in which power is largely invisible, community discourses and life experiences highlight the embedded and very sticky power imbalances that frame and permeate their engagement with markets, development institutions, and the state. These discourses serve as a lens that enables local communities to evaluate external development programs and projects and to conceptually and practically connect their lived experiences of disruption, loss of power, and deterioration of quality of life to national and global patterns of capitalism and cultural modernization.

The Central American experiences also demonstrate that the degree to which the dominant discourse of sustainability moves toward hegemony, or is appropriated or resisted at the grassroots level, is linked not only to the characteristics of development institutions but also to the characteristics—prior local histories, repertoires of resistance, organizational forms—of communities themselves. In the case of the Kunas of Ipetí, the precondition of critical consciousness is largely endogenous, drawn from historical, locally nurtured ethnic difference and traditions of collective resistance. In Nicaragua, residents have developed a framework of class consciousness, linked to earlier campesino organization and contact with a revolutionary government. Studies by Wood (2003) and Lauria-Santiago and Binford (2004) of empowerment in rural El Salvador provide further evidence that the influence of leftist forces in Central America has not been confined to their waxing and waning fortunes in formal political arenas. Pockets of influence of historical revolutionary ideologies persist in the region and continue to influence consciousness and mobilization at the grassroots level. At the same time, it is important not to posit local and dominant institutional perspectives of sustainability as mirror-imaged, distinct. and dichotomized processes. The experience of the Osa peninsula illustrates the ways globalized discourses of sustainability may not simply be imposed but rather appropriated and adapted by organized grassroots actors to mesh with local realities. In this instance, residents' environmental interests were not necessarily historically grounded, predetermined, or fixed but rather were shaped by these development processes and interactions.

SUSTAINABLE DEVELOPMENT INTERVENTIONS

Proponents argue that sustainable development projects offer a number of potential benefits for the rural poor—material and organizational resources, knowledge and frames for interpreting social reality, and new forums and spaces for collective action. Sustainability has also enabled communities to bring local and national claims involving poverty and land rights to new global forums. Transnational institutions, now committed to "pro-poor," environmentally sensitive policies, can in theory be held accountable if they fail to address these issues. Likewise, transnational institutions may apply pressure to recalcitrant national governments, as in the case of Madungandí (Keck and Sikkink 1998). Even when participation in sustainable development projects is instrumental or constrained, participants may still be able to use these spaces to overcome fear and feelings of inferiority and gain skills that can be transferred to other settings and organizations. These case studies also suggest that empowerment is not merely a cognitive process of gaining new knowledge but also occurs through social interaction, as well as emotional and spiritual engagement and transformation.

Postdevelopment literature has been criticized for overstating the coherence of the elite development project and drawing the institutional-community dichotomy too sharply (Nustad 2001; Nederveen Pieterse 2000, 1998; Corbridge 1998). There is a broad convergence in Central America, and indeed globally, on the ideal components of a successful sustainable development intervention—participation, economic gains, environmental sensitivity, awareness of indigenous and gender rights. I argue, however, that in practice, important variations exist in the ideologies underlying development projects, the ways projects are implemented, and their outcomes. More empowering outcomes have involved a combination of a community already possessing at least some degree of critical consciousness and organization, combined with well-organized NGOs committed to deeper forms of participation and a more transformative vision of development.

Development encounters, however, are almost always undergirded by inequality. Central America's rural poor and indigenous citizens are well aware that NGO and government personnel possess greater control of material resources, institutional authority, and access to discourses of technical expertise. In IFI programs, grassroots communities now have an expanded role in proposing and approving local projects. However, the formulation of a program's fundamental mission, specific objectives, and parameters, as well as the control of funds, remains largely in the hands of program officials. The basic framework of sustainability is often predetermined at a higher institutional level, and fundamental issues, in particular contentious neoliberal reforms, may not be open to debate (World Bank 2005b, 2003c; Potlatch 1998a). Funding available for these projects may more subtly narrow local visions to "doable" small-scale interventions and separate "development" from the broader sociopolitical and policy context, thereby dampening and constraining the imagination away from broader issues of structural transformation. Project activity may also contribute to the appearance that social problems are being addressed, thus making it more difficult for communities to identify underlying causes and processes and act on grievances.

The landscape of rural Central America is also strewn with sustainable development projects that have not met their self-defined objectives. Community members have invested time and sometimes material resources, with few or no economic benefits at the end. Such experiences, intentionally or not, discourage participants from framing and acting upon collective solutions to their problems in the future. Overall, though, although there are risks for communities in engaging with dominant institutions and practices, it appears that the relative success of the three case study communities has occurred in part because they have not withdrawn. Rather, they have probed for openings and weaknesses in dominant discourses and practices and pressed forward into spaces of participation, however limited.

STATES AND SUSTAINABILITY

The advance of dominant sustainability, in particular the expansion of state-administered protected areas, should, I argue, be located within Central America's longer-term processes of modernization and the advance of market forces into largely unregulated periphery zones. Even in the absence of new environmental policies, pressures from the broader development model make it unlikely that such zones would have remained isolated and under local control. It is more useful, therefore, to evaluate the implications of expanded state environmental control not against a static form of local control but rather in comparison to a less regulated advance of market forces. The rural poor face a number of disadvantages in competing in these new globalized market spaces—difficult access to land and capital, low levels of education, and similar factors. The case studies suggest that the extension of state and bureaucratic control over land and natural resources is also not necessarily a neutral process. Rural residents are increasingly required to deal with government agencies in transactions that tend to involve open and hidden costs of time and money that make it difficult for the very poor to participate on an equal footing with those who are more affluent and to exercise their rights in practice. Likewise, as state environmental regulation expands, wealthy interests may exert influence over the government and evade regulatory controls. Dominant discourse now incorporates an advocacy role for organized citizens to rein in rent-seeking and environmentally damaging state elites (World Bank 2006a; Demmers, Fernández Jilberto, and Hogenboom 2004b). I believe that this approach, however, abstracts the state from its economic and social contexts. In fact, Central American states are embedded in market processes of accumulation and class formation. Poor and indigenous communities are contending not simply with the state as development apparatus but also with more fluid and intertwined powerful political and economic interests that operate both through and independent of the state.

Critics have suggested that dominant sustainability may be linked to a broader project to "scientize" and depoliticize development (Goldman 2005, 2001; Escobar 1995). However, because Central American states remain the proximate implementers of key dominant policies—neoliberal reforms and environmental protection in particular—rural populations may still perceive these issues as firmly within the "political" realm. What appears to have occurred in some circumstances, in fact, is that government agencies have served as a type of lightning rod for frustrations with the broader development model.

Neoliberal reforms and, more broadly, advances of economic globalization have increasingly constrained the functions and range of viable economic and social policy options available to Central American states (Robinson 2003). This raises the question as to why the rural poor continue to place their governments at the center of their claims and grievances. This continued grassroots focus on the state may reflect in part the success of the region's nationalist projects—whether led by populist military regimes, revolutionary governments, or a social welfare state—as well as politicians' populist discourse under formal democracy. Grassroots insistence on the centrality of the state, I believe, is also part of an implicit ideological struggle. In contrast to the IFI vision of a limited state, these citizens are reluctant to relinquish their more expansive claims and normative expectations of their governments even as they are skeptical that such demands will be met. This centrality of the state may also reflect a lack of alternatives for organized grassroots groups. Communities may be pressured by economic interests—logging, shrimp production, and tourism companies and investors—but have no channels of direct influence over these private actors and diffuse market processes. Although transnational networks have offered communities support on issues such as indigenous land rights, their links to transnational networks have been largely mediated through NGOs and remain somewhat distant and even superficial. For all the grassroots frustration with governments, politicians are more present (at least during election campaigns) in rural areas.

An additional theme of the case studies is that despite a democratic discourse of participation, government agents still tend to view autonomous grassroots mobilization as a threat. They attempt to control, channel, and pacify local grievances. In this sense, formal politics and civil society are not independent spaces, but rather they intersect along a continuum of state organizational and ideological efforts to penetrate rural community life. Such state agent efforts to channel more autonomous forms of mobilization are, I believe, linked to the type of broader elite project described in the critical literature and to politicians' more particular, personal interests. IFI project funding conditioned on community participation has increased pressure on governments to consult with communities. Community members emphasize that only through years of grassroots struggle—vis-à-vis participation in farmer advocacy organizations, environmental activism, and highway protests—have they been able to push these top-down openings toward more meaningful forms of participation. The Nicaragua experience, in turn, points out that hard-won gains of democratic participation are not a unidirectional process and that advances may be reversed if communities are not vigilant and persistent.

ROLE OF COMMUNITIES

Both dominant and critical discourses of sustainability have placed communities—bounded groups that construct, negotiate, and defend common identity and shared interests—at the vanguard of sustainable development (Guha and Martínez-Alier 1998; Peet and Watts 1996a; Friedmann and Rangan 1993). A core assumption of critical sustainability approaches is that local communities' cultural and emotional ties to specific places and specialized knowledge of their natural environments make them ideal environmental caretakers, in contrast to non-place-based actors such as national and transnational companies, which are more likely to exploit resources for short-term gain. Dominant sustainable development projects typically focus on instrumental mobilization of communities in project activities and conservation measures involving individual properties and neighboring protected areas (Hickey and Mohan 2004a). The case studies provide evidence, however, that in the face of weak state environmental enforcement, communities may play an important role as social and political advocates for sustainability.

These grassroots experiences, however, also send a cautionary note against romanticizing traditional and indigenous communities, seemingly intact and isolated from development processes. In Central America, modernization—in the form of roads, communication services, out-migration, off-farm labor, and government programs and regulations—has arrived in the most remote zones of the isthmus. Rural Central America is now populated with fluid and weakly rooted communities, and even strongly and self-consciously traditional communities such as Ipetí have come under increasing internal and external cultural and economic pressure. Market expansion is also an ideological and cultural process that brings values of individualism and consumerism, an instrumental view of nature, and transformations of traditions and ways of life. In Miraflores, a shift to individual farming and neoliberal reforms contributed to increased intra-community inequality, straining relationships of trust and making it more difficult to negotiate common interests. I argue that, in fact, neoliberalism is a powerful ideological force not only in its disciplinary effects but also because it offers hope, a sense of opportunity for individuals and households that may dissuade them from conceptualizing or acting on problems from a collective perspective. These ideological advances of market processes and cultural modernization also suggest that a strategy of leaving communities to their own devices and assuming that internally generated and self-sustaining processes of empowerment will occur is unlikely to be successful in many cases.

As I suggested in Chapter 1, my focus on communities as agents of sustainability carries important caveats. The formation of community collective identity is inherently a process of exclusion as well as inclusion, a drawing of boundaries and defining what a group is by also articulating what it is not. I have argued that dominant discourses of sustainability do not adequately conceptualize the role of entrenched patterns of power in development and market interactions. A community-based approach to sustainability, however, also needs to recognize the dynamics and relationships of power that permeate community spaces. Discourses and policies of sustainability influence the very processes of collective identity and community formation by recognizing and conditioning project resource allocation on the basis of poverty, largely as mediated by place-based and racial-ethnic collective identities. This process may suppress or make invisible others forms of difference and bases for shared identity and claims making. External development actors, for example, often interact with communities with an assumption that members share common interests. Community leaders themselves may employ populist and ethnic frames that leave unrecognized intra-community cleavages or potential cleavages, notably of wealth and gender.

Dominant sustainability discourses and policies may also directly elevate or undermine the power and status of particular subsectors within communities, through, for example, the promotion of particular forms of land and natural resource use and access. The dominant institutions' new focus on participation also incorporates spaces and forms of consultation that may favor certain intra-community sectors over others, as in the recognition and codification of Kuna, male-dominated traditional governance structures. The case studies suggest that even in these relatively egalitarian communities, processes of material and ideological empowerment may be uneven. The poorest of the poor and women, for example, tend to have the least participation in empowerment processes. Even on the Osa peninsula, where women have taken a leadership role in political mobilization, they have faced gender-specific challenges that have limited their participation in decision making and collective action and that are not clearly addressed by dominant sustainability.

CONCLUSION

What, then, does the adoption of a new discourse of sustainability by dominant institutions imply more broadly for sustainable development, defined here as a process of beneficial change guided by empowered communities in three key areas: (1) the meeting of basic material needs and economic accumulation; (2) social equity, cultural rights, and participation; and (3) environmental conservation in rural Central America? The most negative outcomes, from the case study communities' perspective, are linked to IFI policies of neoliberal reform, a carryover from traditional development discourse that is compatible with a broader elite project of economic globalization. The impacts of dominant social and environmental policies have been more mixed, however, bringing both constraints and opportunities for grassroots actors. Although environmental protection has advanced in rural Central America, the community experiences also highlight contradictions between the economic policies and environmental conservation goals of dominant discourse. A key determinant of the sociopolitical and cultural outcomes of sustainable discourse, in turn, is the nature of communities themselves. To the degree to which communities have an initial level of empowerment—a material base, critical consciousness, capacity for collective action—they are more likely to be able to take advantage of the potential openings and opportunities of dominant discourse to advance their interests. In contrast, grassroots groups with a weaker subsistence foundation, a less developed ideological base, and more fragile organization will be more at risk to suffer the disempowering sociopolitical outcomes outlined in the critical literature—cooptation, division, and demobilization.

This leads to a further question. What measures, beyond the limits of the current dominant discourse and policies, can be taken to advance more profound forms of empowerment and sustainability in rural Central America and elsewhere? I suggest that for many communities in rural Central America, such processes will not be entirely endogenous progressions and that external actors and resources have a role to play. Second, a basis of subsistence is necessary (if not sufficient) for any meaningful empowerment and sustainable development to occur. This implies, I would argue, more profound economic "leveling" measures on the part of states and development institutions than those contemplated in dominant discourse. In addition, processes of consciousness raising, of dialogue that negotiates and articulates not only immediate needs but also the deeper values and meanings of beneficial social change and sustainable development, as well as the connections between local experiences and broader structural processes, are essential. The case studies also offer a caveat about these processes. There is a tendency among dominant and often critical perspectives as well to approach sustainability from a managerialist or activist perspective, asking (understandably) what is to be planned and managed, what can be done. I suggest, however, that the complex dynamics detailed in the case study communities also involve more organic processes evolving over time, with strong elements of self-selection—dynamics not completely amenable to outside planning, intervention, or timetables.

Another important factor to consider is the ways relatively empowered communities, which have gained knowledge of and skills in organization and advocacy, can share and extend their experiences beyond their local settings. In other words, through what processes and mechanisms can these more localized experiences be linked to broader processes of change? Community members, as engaged and persistent as they are, emphasize that the scope of their activism and influence is limited by a lack of resources, formal education, time, and mobility. The case studies suggest that opportunities for grassroots actors to more directly and immediately effect change at the national or transnational level are linked to broader political opportunity structures (McAdam 1996). Supra-local organizations and movements may be a potential means to move social and political change beyond the local level and may (ideally) help connect more specific and local visions of sustainability, articulating common points for analysis and action.

On the one hand, when such broader movements are on an upswing of organization and activity, communities likely seek openings for participation in campaigns. When broader social movements are in ebb, grassroots communities may become "reservoirs" of resistance, occupying a space between active mobilization and passive accommodation. While not necessarily engaged in contentious policies, these communities may still serve as spaces of formation where counterhegemonic discourses and practices are nurtured. At the heart of this sustainability, I believe, is an expansion and deepening of the democratic practices nurtured (albeit imperfectly) in these communities. In the early 2000s, Central America's rural and indigenous poor no longer confront the crude political repression and state violence of earlier eras. Rather, they are presented with openings and opportunities, as well as more subtle elite efforts at control and manipulation. In this context, consciousness raising and empowerment will continue to be key at the grassroots level, as communities struggle from below to manage the complex linkages among economic growth, social justice claims, and environmental conservation.

Appendix

METHODS

To address my research questions on the discourses and practices of sustainability in rural Central America, I carried out fieldwork over an eighteen-month period in the countries of Nicaragua, Panama, and Costa Rica. Studies of sustainable development often focus on a single policy or program over a limited period of time. I chose instead to employ a case study methodology to obtain a more holistic and contextualized understanding of community histories, dynamics, and interactions with international financial institutions (IFIs), nongovernmental organizations (NGOs) and states, as well as of grassroots empowerment in a range of contexts. During this period, I conducted a total of ninety-two formal interviews in the three case study communities, held more informal conversations with key informants to detail significant events in the communities' recent histories, carried out participant observation, and gathered secondary data from NGOs and government agencies.

CASE STUDY SELECTION

The three case study communities were selected following a comparative and theoretical logic, not necessarily because they are "typical" of rural and indigenous communities in Central America. Rather, they offer an opportunity to explore in greater depth the ways rural grassroots actors may exercise agency and grapple with macro-level structural and policy shifts, with relatively positive outcomes. All three communities are located in geographically remote zones, on the edge of ecosystems now under state control and protection. Only in recent decades have these communities confronted intensified encroachment of market processes and state and bureaucratic controls. Communities were also selected because they have successfully struggled for economic subsistence and cultural integrity, while their interactions with local environments have been characterized more by stewardship than by predatory or unsustainable use. Internally, these communities exemplify a relatively high degree of democracy; and although inequalities, particularly of gender, persist, community decision-making processes have not been captured or manipulated by elites. An additional factor in the selection of Miraflores, Nicaragua, is the fact that I have carried out ethnographic fieldwork in the community over a period of fifteen years and am able to draw on these longitudinal data to explore community change and empowerment.

There are also important differences among the case study communities. First, they incorporate a range of national political contexts. In common with El Salvador, Guatemala, and Honduras, the Nicaragua context was one of repression and political exclusion, followed by a decade of a revolutionary government. In contrast, the Costa Rica experience has been one of democracy and that in Panama of a populist military dictatorship. In more recent times, however, all three countries have converged toward formal democracy. A second area of contrast is the nature of community. Much research has focused on indigenous and traditional place-based communities as at the forefront of sustainability (Guha and Martínez-Alier 1998; Peet and Watts 1996a; Friedmann and Rangan 1993). For comparative purposes, and in recognition of the processes of change and mobility in rural Central America, the case studies include an indigenous, long-established community, the Kunas of Ipetí, Panama, as well as more recently formed communities in Costa Rica and Nicaragua.

Finally, the goal of this book is not to attempt to identify a single pathway toward community sustainability but to expand our understanding of processes and identify patterns and the range of possibilities through which communities may be empowered as agents of self-defined sustainability. Therefore, case studies were selected to explore distinct strategies toward sustainability. Miraflores residents have drawn on a revolutionary class-based discourse and sought to consolidate and build upon land redistribution gains and to ally with NGOs. In Puerto Jiménez, residents have become active in ecotourism and have struggled to put into practice a localized environmentalism. In contrast, Ipetí residents have nurtured a distinct ethnic identity and have worked to consolidate semi-autonomous collective control over a 180,000-hectare *comarca*.

APPENDIX

INTERVIEW PROCESS

Because the concept this study explores, sustainability, is complex and abstract and not easily amenable to a quantitative survey instrument, I chose to carry out a series of semistructured interviews with community respondents, as well as interviews with key informants in government and NGO sectors. This semistructured format also facilitated clarifications of meanings. It allowed the interviews to have a more conversational flow, as in my experience rural Central Americans may be uncomfortable with more rigid interview structures. My interview guide consisted of open-ended questions on economic, social, and environmental issues of sustainable development. The goal of the interviews was to gather detailed information on community members' perceptions and attitudes toward sustainability, as well as to construct a holistic case study of communities' efforts to put into practice their particular visions of sustainability.

I also carried out participant observation in the three case study communities, with a particular focus on community interactions with government and NGO officials and use of natural resources. Where possible, I triangulated the data collected through interviews and observation with reports and studies carried out by governments and NGOs in the case study areas, as well as with census data. In the text, I incorporate descriptive statistics where available to enable the reader to evaluate the case study experiences within broader national and regional contexts.

IDENTIFICATION OF RESPONDENTS AND INFORMANTS

Overall, I conducted approximately thirty interviews for each of the three case studies. For each case study, I carried out two types of interviews: interviews with community members and interviews with government officials and NGO technicians who have worked directly with the community or have carried out projects in the case study zone. In the community-level interviews, just over half were carried out with residents of the principal communities: Miraflores, Puerto Jiménez, and Ipetí. For comparison, I also carried out a smaller number of interviews in neighboring communities—Río Hondo, Nicaragua; La Palma, Costa Rica; and Wacuco/Loma Bonita/Curtí, Panama–that are actively engaged in environmentally unsustainable activities such as logging and wood extraction. The breakdown of these interviews is detailed in Table A.1.

For the community-level interviews, I generally made the initial contact in person, at the individual's home or, in a few cases, at a place of work. I either arranged a future interview time or carried out the interview on the spot. Interviews with NGO and government officials, on the other hand, were almost all arranged over the telephone. Overall, with

APPENDIX

Table A.1. Interview Data

	Dates Interviews Conducted	Communities Practicing Sustainability (# of persons interviewed)	Communities Not Practicing Sustainability (# of persons interviewed)	Government and NGO Representatives (# of persons interviewed)
Costa Rica (n=32)	Oct–Nov 1999 April–June 2000	Puerto Jiménez: 17	La Palma: 6	Government: 5 NGOs: 4
Nicaragua (n=32)	July–August 1989 July–August 1998 Feb–March 2000 August 2000 June 2006	Miraflores: 19	Río Hondo: 5	Government: 4 NGOs: 4
Panama (n=28)	Ongoing from January 2000 to February 2001; December 2004	Ipetí Kuna: 11	Wacuco/Loma Bonita/Curtí: 5	Government: 5 NGOs: 7
TOTAL		47	16	29

Note: N=92.

the exception of some issues that arose in Ipetí, which I discuss in the Panama section of this appendix, the overwhelming majority of people I contacted agreed to participate in interviews. Because many of the individuals I interviewed were not functionally literate in Spanish, I asked for verbal consent. The interviews lasted anywhere from half an hour to an hour and a half, taking an average of forty-five minutes. Interviews took place in residents' homes and in government and NGO offices.

Gender considerations also came into play during the interview process. Originally, I had planned to carry out roughly half of the community-level interviews with men and half with women. In Costa Rica, I was able to achieve this. In Puerto Jiménez and La Palma, women appeared comfortable with the interview process and addressed questions at length. Based on my past experiences in Miraflores, I tried to schedule interviews with women at times when their male *compañeros* were not at home. In three cases, however, the husbands arrived home and essentially took over the interviews, with the women saying little or nothing more. While the men generally appeared comfortable with the interview questions, a few of the women appeared to find them confusing or intimidating. As I discuss in Chapter 7, Miraflores women have been largely excluded from organizing efforts and development projects, and for this reason they are less accustomed to speaking with outsiders or in formal circumstances. My discussion of Miraflores women's perspective of sustainable development is therefore based more strongly on participant observation and informal conversations with women than on their responses to interview questions.

In Ipetí, distinct gender roles are very sharply defined, and my role during my visits was at times that of an "honorary male." Many of my initial interactions with the community were with men, and during community activities residents often led me to the male side of the room rather than to the section where women and children were seated. At the same time, as a woman I was eventually able to spend time with female Ipetí residents. From the outset, several traditional authorities and other men discouraged me from including women in my interviews, arguing that women essentially believe what male community leaders tell them to and do not have opinions of their own. In part because of this reluctance of community authorities to have me speak with women and in part because women themselves at times preferred more informal conversation, I conducted only two formal interviews with women in Ipetí, both of whom were bilingual Spanish speakers. Where possible during my stays in the village, I did seek out opportunities to speak with women more informally about the issues addressed in this study.

INTERVIEW BIASES AND DIFFICULTIES

It is important to note that although I have lived and worked in Central America for a total of approximately eight years and speak fluent Spanish, I was still an "outsider" in the communities I visited. Only in Miraflores did I have partial "insider" status and the interesting experience of having respondents tell me stories about myself and things I had done in visits to the community years earlier. As an outsider, with Spanish as a second language, there was a greater possibility that I could misinterpret verbal and nonverbal communication cues and that key information might be withheld from me. In addition, because my years in Central America have been spent largely in mestizo rural zones and because of the language barrier, my lack of cultural knowledge contributed to several misunderstandings in Ipetí, which I discuss in the Panama section.

Another potential issue in the interviews was acquiescence bias. My past fieldwork experiences in rural Central America had suggested that there is a tendency by respondents to attempt to provide the answers they believe the interviewer—perceived to be of a higher social and economic status—would like to hear (see Horton 1999). To try to minimize this, I stressed before the interviews that there were no right or wrong answers and that as an outsider visiting the community, my wish was to learn as much as possible about the perceptions and experiences of residents themselves. Also, I placed the questions dealing more directly with the environment at the end of the interviews to lessen the impression that I was looking for "environmentally correct" answers.

Another difficulty in the interviews lay in the abstract nature of my research topic, sustainable development, or *desarrollo sostenible* in Spanish. At the community level, after some initial testing I stopped using the term "sustainable development" in interviews. Many people had not heard the term, and those who had were often unfamiliar with its meaning. Only community environmental activists in Costa Rica, who had higher levels of education and some of whom had participated in national and international conferences, brought up the term of their own initiative and in several cases offered detailed analyses of the concept. For other community respondents, however, I instead asked more concrete and specific economic, social, and environmental questions designed to draw out respondents' visions of sustainability.

An additional potential problem area in the interviews involved certain sensitive topics, in particular illegal activities such as poaching and unlicensed logging, as well as some households' wealth and land. Because better-off people are often reluctant to discuss their income, and because of the time required to obtain accurate economic data for households that rely on a variety of income sources, I did not ask detailed income questions of all community respondents. Rather, I talked in depth with informants about local wages, average crop prices, and other economic data. In terms of illegal activities, I never initiated the topic, but if respondents brought up talk of such activities involving either themselves or their neighbors, I would follow up with questions.

INTERVIEW STRUCTURE

In gathering the information for these case studies, I chose to use a semi-structured interview guide for several reasons. First, as mentioned earlier, I believe the major research questions involved in this study—the exploration of the concept of sustainable development and the sustainability strategies employed by communities—can best be addressed with open-ended questions. It would be very difficult, for example, to explore complex assumptions and values about the environment and the nature of development with a quantitative survey instrument. In addition, my previous research experience in rural Central America suggested that rural residents are generally unfamiliar with formal survey instruments and that highly structured interview schedules may leave some respondents uncomfortable, confused, or bored. While people often complete surveys out of courtesy, I believe a more conversational style of interviewing in rural Central America leads participants to respond with information of greater depth and quality. Also, as mentioned earlier, given that these interviews were conducted across significant cultural divides, a more fluid, semistructured interview format provided greater opportunity for building rapport with respondents and facilitated mutual clarification of meaning and correction of misunderstandings.

The community interview guide was divided into three main topic areas: economic, social, and environmental. I led with the economic questions because I believed that was the topic of greatest interest and concern to community members. I left the environmental questions until last because I did not want respondents to feel I was looking for certain "politically correct" environmental responses. I used the interview instrument only as guide, and when the opportunity presented itself, I varied the order of the questions following the lead of the interviewee. In the interviews with NGO and government officials, the questions varied according to the agencies and the particular activities in which they were involved.

COUNTRY-SPECIFIC ISSUES

This section describes in greater detail the research process for each of the three case studies, highlighting specific logistical and ethical concerns that emerged in each community.

Nicaragua

The process of identifying individuals to be interviewed was the easiest in the Nicaragua case study. I originally came to Miraflores as a volunteer on a Habitat for Humanity housing project in 1988 and spent six months living and working there. I returned in 1989 for four months and carried out some of the interviews cited in this study. I maintained contact with Miraflores over the following years and conducted interviews there in 1998, 2000, 2001, and 2006.

Because of the small size of the community, twenty-three households, I decided to interview one adult member of each household, striving for a roughly 50 percent balance between men and women. The only small logistical challenge was coordinating interviews with people's work schedules and other daily activities. Interviews with men in particular tended to take place in the evenings between 6 P.M., when they returned from the fields or visits to town, and 9 P.M., when most families retire to sleep. In general, the families, who have known me for many years, were receptive to being interviewed. Once word spread that I was doing interviews, several individuals sent messages to the house where I was staying asking that I come and talk to them, and several people asked to be interviewed more than once. Of the twenty-three households, I interviewed members from nineteen. One family was excluded for ethical reasons, discussed later, and three other families were away for prolonged periods or not otherwise available during my visits to Miraflores. In addition, I carried out eight interviews with NGO and government officials in the towns of Tonalá, El Viejo, Chinandega, and the capital, Managua.

I taped and took notes on all the interviews. I also had many informal conversations with individuals who served as informants on community and regional issues. For the neighboring community of Río Hondo, where I carried out five interviews, I first obtained information on which families were known to be actively involved in the extraction of mangrove wood, as well as members of a wood cutters' cooperative, and visited their homes to ask if they would participate in an interview.

The Nicaragua case study incorporates the most extensive participant observation of all the case studies, as over the years I have attended a variety of meetings and social functions in the community. At the same time, my extensive contact with the community raises ethical issues. Over the years, I have facilitated or directly provided financial support to the community. I am also a godmother to one of the families and since 1998 have provided substantial financial support to this family. Given this ongoing financial relationship and the particularly strong power inequality, I did not request a formal interview with this family, although I did have numerous informal conversations with the head of household about community issues. Also, because much of my time in Miraflores had been spent on personal, not research, visits, I felt tape recording the interviews would emphasize to respondents that I was acting in the role of researcher and that we were officially "on the record." I have attempted to limit the information about Miraflores included in this study to that gathered during research visits in 1989, from 1998 to 2001, and in 2006.

Costa Rica

In the Costa Rica case study, I conducted twenty-nine interviews in the communities of Puerto Jiménez and La Palma, as well as three interviews with NGO representatives in the capital, San José. Because Puerto Jiménez is the largest community included in this study, with a population of 6,102, I chose to interview a theoretically purposive sample of individuals actively participating in ecotourism activities. Employing "snowball" techniques, I initially contacted organizations and individuals I had read of in newspaper accounts of activism on the peninsula. I then gathered basic ethnographic data and information on ecotourism activities on the peninsula. I soon put together a list of a dozen individuals to interview, and at each interview I asked for suggestions of other individuals to speak with. For the six comparison interviews in La Palma, a much smaller community, I went house to house and also met individuals outside a local store. As in the Nicaragua community of Río Hondo, community members in La Palma are engaged in illegal activities—logging, gold mining, and hunting, in both the national park and the Golfo Dulce Forest Reserve. Again, I did not ask people directly about these activities but waited for respondents to bring them up in the interviews.

Of the three case studies, my participant observation was the most limited in the Costa Rica study. Because of a dispute between the two bus companies that operated on the peninsula during part of my fieldwork, I was at times forced to hitchhike on the single road up and down the peninsula. In the end, this aided my research, as the informal conversations I had with local residents who gave me rides provided further information about the peninsula.

I had originally planned to tape record my interviews in Costa Rica, assuming that given the country's relatively peaceful social and political context, this would not be a problem. However, several initial respondents were not comfortable with the idea. Some individuals felt threatened, not necessarily directly by the government but rather by logging and illegal drug interests active on the peninsula. In the Costa Rica interviews that I did not tape, I took detailed notes during the interviews, and generally within twenty-four hours I reviewed and typed up the notes. Overall, despite some cautiousness about taping, respondents and informants on the Osa peninsula appeared very open and forthcoming in interviews.

Panama

In Panama, the process of selecting respondents to interview was more complex. Because this study incorporates case studies in three countries, I decided from the outset that I would not attempt to gain fluency in Kuna but rather would rely on an interpreter when necessary. Although Ipetí is the most acculturated of the Madungandí Kuna communities, I initially overestimated the degree to which community residents would be bilingual in Kuna and Spanish. A Kuna representative from an NGO that has worked in Ipetí accompanied me and facilitated my initial contact with community authorities. I provided the traditional authorities with an oral summary of my project and a written copy in Spanish of my interview guide and was given permission to visit Ipetí and carry out interviews.

In subsequent visits, several issues arose. Although in the original visit the NGO representative emphasized that this was an individual, not an institutional, project, there appears to have been an assumption that as a North American I had access to substantial funding. Eventually, I decided that other than paying my interpreter for his services—which often involved him missing a day's work in other activities—I would not offer money to traditional authorities or respondents. My concerns were, first, that a thirty-minute interview in the home did not entail a substantial inconvenience or loss of income for respondents. Second, I had already done interviews with poor households in Costa Rica and Nicaragua, and in none of those cases had I provided financial compensation. Likewise, several community members discouraged me from offering money. Also, several Ipetí households were extremely hospitable and helpful from the outset and were very generous with their time and willingness to aid me in my project.

I was fortunate to find an excellent interpreter who had spent extended time outside the community. In addition to translation services, he shared his perspective and valuable insights on both Kuna and non-Kuna cultures. While I did learn some basic Kuna vocabulary, interviews were conducted in Spanish or in Kuna with translation into Spanish. In the latter case, which included all of the village authorities I interviewed, typically the person would respond at length in Kuna, and the interpreter would then provide a Spanish summary. Clearly, this situation was less than ideal, as much of the richness and nuance of the original Kuna discourse was lost.

In the end, I was able to carry out interviews with representatives of several key groups in the community—the traditional authorities and a group of younger males active in the land rights struggle. For these interviews I was not allowed to use a tape recorder, but I was able to take detailed notes. In addition, I had many informal conversations in which I gathered important background information about the community and the concerns of women in particular.

Overall, I have attempted through this methodological process to give voice as much as possible to community narratives, visions, experiences, and concerns. While inevitably the result is a partial and selective representation of a complex set of social realities and processes and a diverse group of actors, I believe the imperative remains to listen closely to those whose livelihoods are the most directly affected by "development" in all its permutations and transformations.

Notes

PREFACE AND ACKNOWLEDGMENTS

1. All names used in this text are pseudonyms, unless otherwise indicated.

2. The name of this community has been changed.

3. Key debates on globalization have centered around its degree of newness and qualitative distinctiveness, the role and authority of nation-states vis-à-vis deepening economic liberalization and the rising power of corporations, globalization's tendencies toward cultural homogeneity and local resistance to that tendency, its distributional consequences for the world's population, and the implications of globalization for social mobilization and change (Scholte 2005; Held and McGrew 2003; Giddens 2000; Mittleman 2000; Waters 2001). More recently, the globalization literature has tended to give greater recognition to its complexity, processes of cultural mediation, and the continued salience of the nation-state.

CHAPTER 1: CONTESTED VISIONS OF SUSTAINABILITY

1. A search of WorldCat in 2005 found over 27,000 books listed under the keyword "sustainable development."

2. Unless otherwise noted, all translations are the author's.

3. The World Conservation Union's 1991 definition, "to improve the quality of life while living within the carrying capacity of ecosystems," is also widely cited, although some critics suggest that this fails to explicitly incorporate concepts of justice and equity (cited in Agyeman, Bullard, and Evans 2003:5).

NOTES

4. This characterization of three discourses of sustainable development is inevitably a simplification, highlighting commonalities over differences. In practice, these models are not so much discreet units as located on a continuum.

5. The original Washington Consensus refers to the neoliberal orthodoxy of the 1980s predicated on individualism, market liberalism, outward orientation, and state contraction (Onis and Senses 2005). In the text that follows, I refer to the institutions that promulgate the post-Washington Consensus as IFIs and "dominant institutions."

6. This shift in discourse was also influenced by NGO and activist pressure on the U.S. Congress, the presence of reformers within these institutions, and recognition of the failure of IFIs in foreseeing and preventing the Asian crisis.

7. While the section "Dominant Sustainability Discourse" outlines in broad terms the common elements of the dominant discourse of sustainability as articulated in World Bank and IDB policy documents and reports, such policies have also been the subject of internal debate (Sindzingre 2004; Jacobs 1994). Low and Gleeson (cited in Adams 2001), for example, identify three currents in dominant sustainable development: market environmentalism, environmental modernization, and appropriate and intermediate technology. The discourse discussed here is linked most closely to policies as promoted and implemented in Central America and serves an instrumental function. It therefore represents a particular and, I would argue, selective interpretation and application of neoliberalism that may diverge in certain points from more academic neoliberal economic theory, for example.

8. Pearce (1989) characterizes sustainable economic growth as occurring when "real GNP per capita is increasing over time and the increase is not threatened by 'feedback' from either biophysical impacts (pollution, resource problems) or from social impacts (social disruption)" (143).

9. Wodon and Ayres (2000) discuss evidence that higher GDP per capita lowers national poverty rates, while Collier and Dollar (2002) argue that nations that have opened their markets have had the highest rates of economic growth in recent years. See Sumner (2004) for a critique of Collier and Dollar's methods and conclusions.

10. Neoliberal reforms also reflect a search for alternatives to the high inflation and stagnant export of Latin America's import substitution industrialization (ISI), the state-led development of earlier decades (Loker 1999).

11. The term "neoliberalism" is sometimes used interchangeably with "globalization" or "global capitalism" in the literature. In this book, however, I use neoliberalism more narrowly to include the specific policies listed earlier. Closely related to these policies are structural adjustment programs (SAPs) the International Monetary Fund requires of countries in debt as a condition for debt restructuring. SAPs are generally a combination of short-term measures aimed at economic stabilization and long-term structural reforms aimed at transforming state-controlled economies into market economies.

12. Studies by Roberts and Arce (1998), Stokes (2001), and Weyland (1998) explore the ways targeted poverty reduction programs and economic growth can build popular support for neoliberal reforms. Comaroff and Comaroff (2001) and Veltmeyer and O'Malley (2001) offer a more critical overview of neoliberalism in Latin America.

13. Key policies associated with pro-poor growth include targeted assistance to the poor, incentives for vulnerable groups to accumulate human capital assets such as education, health, and social capital, as well as funds for infrastructure projects, known in Central America as "social investment funds" (World Bank 2006a, 1999a).

14. An exception is IFI support for collective indigenous land rights, an issue explored in later chapters.

15. Collier and Dollar (2002) contend, for example, that there is no evidence of a decline of environmental standards in countries that have undertaken economic liberalization.

16. See Wade (2004) for a more detailed discussion of the evolution of World Bank environmental policy. Since the mid-1990s the World Bank has also managed the multimillion-dollar Global Environmental Facility (GEF) created specifically to finance projects in forestry, biodiversity conservation, water pollution, and protection of the ozone layer. In response to strong criticism from environmental NGOs over environmentally destructive projects in the Amazon, the IDB established an Environmental Protection Division in 1989, charged with evaluating the environmental impact of projects and recommending remedial actions (Bryant and Bailey 1997).

17. Local participation emerged as a key social component of mainstream sustainable development in international conference documents such as the 1987 Brundtland Report, the World Conservation Union's World Conservation Strategy for the 1990s, and the Agenda 21 Accord of the 1992 Rio Summit.

18. Fox and Brown (1998:2) conclude, for example, that "to a small and uneven but significant degree the bank [World Bank] has become more accountable as [a] result of external protests and empowering effects on inside reformers."

19. Additional factors that have limited shifts in World Bank practice are pressure to move funding quickly, career concerns of World Bank officials in a risk-adverse organizational climate, and resistance to policy implementation by national governments (Clay, Alcorn, and Butler 2000; Kolk 1999).

20. Political ecology emerged as a critique of neo-Malthusian views of population pressure on natural resources and the false homeostasis and apolitical nature of early ecological studies (Bryant and Bailey 1997; Peet and Watts 1996b). From the mid-1970s to the mid-1980s, political ecology drew on neo-Marxism and tended toward economic determinism, in which the state and world capitalism were viewed as monolithic forces. By the mid-1990s, Bryant and Bailey (1997) note, political ecology's attention had shifted toward local activities and had expanded to more eclectic sources such as social movement and feminist theory. For an overview of political ecology, see Adams (2001); Bryant and Bailey (1997); Peet and Watts (1996b); Rocheleau, Thomas-Slayter, and Wangari (1996a); Blaikie and Brookfield (1987); and Redclift (1987). Studies by Nygren (2000), Jansen (1998), and Stonich (1993) apply political ecology to the Central American context.

21. Important works in the postdevelopment literature include Escobar (2000, 1995); Goldman (2005, 2001, 1998a); Rahnema and Bawtree (1997); Sachs (1999, 1993); and Ferguson (1990). Studies by Nederveen Pieterse (2000, 1998), Corbridge (1998), and Everett (1997) offer a more critical perspective of postdevelopmentalism, including its tendency to represent development discourse as monolithic,

its focus on discourse and representation at the expense of political economy, its relative omission of the agency of the poor, and its lack of clear alternatives to development.

22. For example, as early as the nineteenth century, the creation of national parks in Africa was closely linked to policies of colonialism and racism in which local residents were punished and denied access to lands so whites could engage in hunting (Adams 2001; Redclift and Woodgate 1994).

23. Dore (1997) argues, for example, that sustainable development "is particularly favored by policymakers because it obscures ideological differences about the causes of ecological destruction and what should be done about them" (9). Goldman (1998c) states that the result of dominant sustainability "has not been to stop destructive practices but to normalize and further institutionalize them, putting commoners throughout the world at even greater risk" (23).

24. For details and case studies of grassroots environmental and livelihood movements in the South. see Dwivedi (2001); Guha and Martínez-Alier (1998); Johnston (1997); Peet and Watts (1996a); Rocheleau, Thomas-Slayter, and Wangari (1996a); Friedmann and Rangan (1993); and Ghai and Vivian (1992). Alternative visions of sustainability also find support in the North among ecology, peace, feminist, indigenous rights, and personal growth movements that in recent years have moved toward incipient synthesis (Adams 2001; Korten 1990).

25. In addition, while this analysis focuses on issues of sustainability in rural Central America, the concept of community becomes even more problematic when applied to the region's growing urban centers.

CHAPTER 2: POVERTY AND FORESTS: DEVELOPMENT AND (DIS)EMPOWERMENT IN CENTRAL AMERICA

1. I use the term "Central America" to refer to Guatemala, El Salvador, Honduras, Nicaragua, Costa Rica, and Panama, the six nations that currently participate in the Central American Common Market.

2. U.S. Marines occupied Nicaragua for over twenty years in the early twentieth century, intermittently during the period 1914 to 1936, waging war against nationalist guerrilla leader Augusto Sandino. Soon afterward, Anastasio Somoza, head of the National Guard, seized power and began what became a forty-year family dictatorship, with economic and military support from the United States. More recently, in the 1980s, the United States funded and trained contra rebels who fought against the FSLN. Likewise, in 1903 the United States aided the Panamanian independence movement and gained control of the Panama Canal Zone, a key North American military and economic enclave for almost ninety years. In 1989 the United States launched a military invasion of Panama to overthrow General Manuel Noriega and restore democracy to the country. In contrast to direct U.S. military interventions in Panama and Nicaragua, U.S. pressures on Costa Rica have been largely economic and political. In the late 1800s the North American United Fruit Company gained control of large tracts of Costa Rican land for banana production. The 1980s witnessed a dramatic increase in U.S. bilateral aid to Costa Rica and strong political pressures to support U.S. policies of low-intensity warfare in the region. Overall, in the peak years of the 1980s, the United States provided over $6.5 billion in economic aid and $1.5 billion in military aid

to Central American governments (Dunkerley 1994:145). For further details of the economic, political, and military impacts of U.S. interventions in Central America, see LeoGrande (1998), LaFeber (1993), Wickham-Crowley (1992), Sklar (1988), Robinson and Norsworthy (1987), Booth (1982).

3. Cherret defines empowerment as "a transformation of consciousness and self-perception which would enable them to understand their social situation and to see it as something they can, with others, struggle to change" (cited in Schmitz 1995:74). Korten (1990) defines empowerment as "a process by which the members of a society increase their personal and institutional capacities to mobilize and manage resources to produce sustainable and justly distributed improvements in their quality of life consistent with their own aspirations" (67).

4. The poverty line is calculated as the amount necessary to provide a minimal caloric intake, clothing, housing, and transportation.

5. Nicaragua's Poverty Reduction Strategy, negotiated with the World Bank and the International Monetary Fund, characterizes the 1960s as a period of macroeconomic stability and economic growth and identifies the roots of Nicaragua's contemporary poverty in the FSLN's economic policies of the 1980s (World Bank 2006b).

6. Traditional paternalistic landowner-worker relationships broke down, and historical patterns of land concentration in the region were reinforced. In some parts of the region's Pacific coastal zone and in El Salvador, with its high land-to-person density, rural families lost access to land altogether and were forced to migrate to the cities or the agricultural frontier. Other poor farmers combined temporary agricultural wage labor with subsistence farming in a form of functional dualism (Brockett 1990; Williams 1986).

7. Interviews with Miraflores residents and corroborated in Nitlapán (1990). The amount of land under cotton production in Chinandega and the neighboring department of León increased from 16,762 ha in 1950 to 217,592 ha in 1977 (Biderman 1982:179).

8. The following section on economic conditions in the Tonalá zone is based on Miraflores interviews and is corroborated in Brockett (1990), Gould (1990), and Williams (1986).

9. McAdam (1996) defines four dimensions of political opportunity: the relative openness of the institutionalized political system, the stability of elite alignments that undergird a polity, the presence of elite allies, and the state's capacity and propensity for repression (26–27).

10. These conditions shifted in the mid-1970s when a substantial sector of Nicaraguan elites turned against the dictatorship and the FSLN emerged as a potential external ally in a limited number of rural areas, including the Pacific coastal zone.

11. These interviews, conducted with community members from the late 1980s onward, also reflect Miraflores's exposure to revolutionary discourse and participation in Sandinista organizations in the 1980s. See Gould (1990) for details of the development of an autonomous peasant consciousness in the Tonalá zone.

12. Interviews with a Chinandega Ministry of Environment and Natural Resources official, NGO technicians, and residents of Río Hondo and Miraflores.

13. More broadly, in the department of Chinandega, forestland decreased from 78,161 ha in 1963 to 27,810 ha in 2001 (INEC 2004:13).

14. In Panama, indigenous *comarcas* are semi-autonomous, internally regulated administrative territories under the jurisdiction of the national government (Herlihy 1988).

15. Unless otherwise noted, the term "Ipetí" in this text refers to the indigenous Kuna community.

16. Of the total Kuna population of 61,707 in 2000, approximately half reside outside the rural *comarcas*, primarily in Panama City. The Ngöbe-Buglés, whose 186,861 members are located primarily in the western provinces, are Panama's largest indigenous group. Panama's third-largest indigenous group, the Embará, which numbers 22,485, is concentrated in the eastern province of Darién (PNUD 2002).

17. In the late 1800s, the majority of the Kuna population migrated to the archipelago of San Blas, which later became the *comarca* of Kuna Yala, while a smaller number of families remained on the Bayano mainland.

18. Evidence from Kuna mythology and Kuna place names suggests that at one time the Kuna occupied a large territory from Bayano to the present Colombian border, but several centuries ago, under pressure from the Spanish and escaped slaves from Colombia, the Kuna territory was reduced. The heavy rainfall and unhealthy climate of eastern Panama, as well as Kuna armed resistance, discouraged the Spanish from establishing permanent settlements in the region (Torres de Araúz 1977).

19. Interviews with Ipetí informants and corroborated in Moeller (1997).

20. Approximately 200,000 people were killed in Guatemala's civil war (Guatemalan Commission for Historical Clarification 1999). In El Salvador, around 75,000 people died (CIA 2001). In both cases Truth Commission reports attribute 85 percent or more of the deaths to government forces and right-wing death squads (Commission on the Truth for El Salvador 1993; Guatemalan Commission for Historical Clarification 1999). In Nicaragua, the 1978–1979 struggle to overthrow the Somoza dictatorship and the subsequent decade-long war between the FSLN and the U.S.-sponsored contra guerrillas led to around 60,000 deaths (Horton 1999).

21. Fewer than 1,000 people were killed under military rule in Panama. The Torrijos development model deepened Panama's transnational linkages in commerce and banking sectors in particular while simultaneously incorporating nationalist policies, such as the renegotiations of the Panama Canal treaty and nationalization of public utilities, including electric service (Gjording 1991).

22. Ipetí residents offered several explanations for this lack of more organized opposition to the dam—government officials deceived Madungandí leaders about the dam's true impact, and resistance would have been futile against the powerful institutions supporting the project.

23. Of the three displaced ethnic groups, the Kunas were the most organized and persistent in their negotiations with the government and received $1,500 per house lost and an average of $3,000 to $4,000 per family for lost crops (Wali 1989:67, 72). As additional compensation, in 1976 General Torrijos signed an agreement, known as the Farallón Accord, with the Bayano Kunas, extending the boundaries of the reserve another 28,120 hectares.

24. Interviews with Ipetí traditional authorities and corroborated in Wali (1989).

25. Interviews with Ipetí traditional authorities and activists.

26. In addition to deforestation, the focus of this book's case studies, other key environmental issues in rural Central America include soil erosion and agrochemical contamination. Twenty-eight percent of Central America's available land suffers from aridity, low rainfall, and high evapo-transpiration (Ruben 2001:142). Forty percent of Central America's soils are moderately to seriously eroded, and densely populated El Salvador in particular has been labeled an "ecological catastrophe," with over half its soils severely degraded (Carriere 1991:188). The expansion of cotton and banana production also contributed to the world's highest per capita rate of pesticide poisoning and deaths in Honduras and Nicaragua in the 1970s (Faber 1993:54).

27. Typically, an individual who settles on forested national lands and makes "improvements" *(mejoras)* to the land, such as paths, cleared land, and fences, gains usufruct rights over the land, with the option to establish legal title over the land in the future (Horton 1999). The small farms on the agricultural frontier are often unstable, however. Crop yields decline quickly once rain forest is cleared, and poor peasants often lack access to markets and credit. Poor migrants may then sell their land to wealthy ranchers who need pasture and migrate further into the agricultural frontier (Horton 1999; Maldidier 1996).

28. The following section on the history of the Osa peninsula draws on interviews with community informants and works by PDR (1995), Ramírez Avendaño and Quesada Camacho (1990), Barquero Barrantes (1988), García (1988), Lewis (1983), and Vaughan (1979).

29. Interviews with La Palma informants; also Van den Hombergh (1999), PDR (1995), Barquero Barrantes (1988), and Vaughan (1979).

30. The influence of these Costa Rican conservationists was enhanced by their transnational contacts, technical expertise, relatively elite backgrounds, personal relationships with high-level politicians, and their ability to mobilize public opinion (Campbell 2002; Steinberg 2001; Evans 1999; Wallace 1992; Vaughan 1979). While Costa Rican government officials maintained a degree of autonomy in the environmental arena to act against individual corporations, such as the OFP, in the interest of broader social stability, government policies overall were not anti-capitalist (Robinson 2003). State subsidies for infrastructure and cattle ranching in this era contributed to high rates of deforestation outside protected areas. In addition to park creation, the Costa Rican government has also taken the lead in innovative environmental initiatives such as debt-for-nature swaps, carbon offsets, bio-prospecting, and payments for environmental services (Brockett and Gottfried 2002).

31. In this and subsequent chapters, I use the term "Osa" as shorthand for the two communities of Puerto Jiménez and nearby La Palma.

32. Interviews with gold miners and corroborated in Wallace (1992).

33. A late 1980s survey by Barquero Barrantes (1988) found that 66 percent of respondents said their families had been harmed by the park, and 34 percent felt they had benefited from it.

CHAPTER 3: "ALL THE LAND BELONGS TO THE FOREIGNERS": ECOTOURISM AND SUSTAINABILITY

1. Costa Rica received over 1 million tourists in 2000, over half of whom visited at least one protected area (Zamora and Obando 2001). The tourism sec-

tor employed 12 percent of Costa Rica's labor force by the late 1990s and had overtaken coffee and bananas as Costa Rica's second-leading source of foreign exchange after microchips (Inman 2002; Zamora and Obando 2001).

2. The Costa Rican Tourism Institute estimated that 7 percent of Costa Rica's tourists visited the Osa peninsula in 2002, suggesting that it is still a somewhat remote ecotourism destination (cited in Inman 2002:32).

3. One of the founding principles of the Global Environmental Facility is the "development of environmentally sustainable nature-based tourism" (cited in Honey 1999:16). USAID began to fund ecotourism projects in the mid-1980s and a decade later had provided more than $2 billion in funding for programs with ecotourism components (Honey 1999:17).

4. Similar to other regions, the North American and European ecotourists who visit Costa Rica are relatively well educated and affluent—one survey found that 68 percent had college degrees and 36 percent had annual incomes over $100,000 (*Tico Times* 2002; Cheong and Miller 2000).

5. The section that follows on the economic impacts of tourism draws on interviews with Puerto Jiménez ecotourism operators and members of the Osa Chamber of Tourism and is corroborated in Furst and Hein (2002a), Stem (2001), Minca and Linda (2000), and COBRUDES (1997).

6. Interviews with *cabina* owners and corroborated in Ruíz (2002).

7. Ninety percent of Osa individuals surveyed by Ruíz (2002:323) listed employment opportunities as a primary benefit of ecotourism.

8. Ecotourism positions that require more specific skills and training generally pay higher wages, such as nature guides who earn an average of fifty dollars per day. The work is not entirely stable, however. During the high season, work hours may be long—cooks, for example, report shifts of twelve hours or more—while during the rainy, low season a number of eco-lodges temporarily lay off employees. The data that follow are drawn from interviews with members of the Osa Chamber of Tourism and Puerto Jiménez ecotourism operators and employees.

9. This section draws on interviews with female community activists and ecotourism operators.

10. In the late 1990s, women made up 62 percent of *cabina* workers but only 17 percent of hotel workers (Ruíz 2002:326).

11. Stem (2001) carried out an in-depth study of ecotourism in several communities on and near the Osa peninsula and found that only in Drake Bay did ecotourism offer local residents a viable economic alternative. In other cases, ecotourism projects were too small to have much impact on communities.

12. Local government officials and Chamber of Tourism representatives noted that to date, no systematic data exist on land tenure on the peninsula. Numerous informal and illegal land transactions along the coast and in the forest reserve in particular further complicate the situation (La Nación 2000a, 1997b). The Costa Rica Tourism Institute also estimated in the early 1990s that up to 80 percent of Costa Rica's beachfront property had already been purchased by foreigners (Honey 1999:134).

13. Cordero and van Duynen Montijn (2002) note similar patterns of ownership in Quepos, where foreigners owned 60 percent of the restaurants and 50 of 59 km of coastal land.

14. Campbell (1999) identifies similar dynamics in Ostional, Costa Rica.

15. Interviews with Ministry of Agriculture and Livestock and Agrarian Development Institute officials and corroborated in Van den Hombergh (1999).

16. One study found, for example, that 60 percent of sustainable tourism operations did not qualify for government subsidies because they were too small (Honey 1999:138).

17. Interviews with MINAE officials and local NGO representatives and corroborated in Fernández Morillo (2002b). From 1980 to 1995, approximately 16 percent of the peninsula's rain forests were cut down, primarily in the forest reserve areas away from ecotourism zones, while 32 percent of pastures were reforested (Rosero-Bixby, Maldonado-Ulloa, and Bonilla-Carrión 2002).

18. In addition to interviews, this section is corroborated in Ruíz (2002), Van den Hombergh (1999), and PDR (1995).

19. In Quepos, most saw tourism as contributing positively to the quality of life, but they also identified problems of increased drug use and prostitution associated with tourism (Cordero and van Duynen Montijn 2002).

20. Such suspicions have been fueled by a series of events on the opposite side of the gulf in the community of Pavones, in which a U.S. citizen, later arrested for drug trafficking and money laundering, bought up large tracts of land (*Tico Times* 1997c). Historically, in rural Central America alcohol abuse by men has been a serious social problem, but use of other types of drugs such as marijuana and cocaine has been limited.

21. In 1978 the government expropriated the last remaining Osa Forest Products land to create the 62,703-hectare Golfo Dulce Forest Reserve, where landholders have been allowed to remain, with government restrictions on land sale and use.

CHAPTER 4: "NATURE THAT GIVES THEM LIFE": GRASSROOTS SUSTAINABILITY ON THE OSA PENINSULA

1. Interviews with long-term residents in the Golfo Dulce Forest Reserve. Stem (2001) and Van den Hombergh (1999) identify similar environmental narratives on the peninsula.

2. See Vivanco (2002) for an exploration of the tension over the meanings of nature between Costa Rican peasants and foreign environmentalists and ecotourists in Monte Verde.

3. Interviews with ecotourism operators and environmental activists.

4. Stem (2001) found that ecotourism had a measurable positive impact on environmental attitudes and behaviors only in zones with significant ecotourism activity, a condition that would apply to Puerto Jiménez, the peninsula's ecotourism hub.

5. Interviews with Puerto Jiménez ecotourism participants; also González (2002).

6. See Sandoval García (2004) and Jiménez Molina (2002) on the roots of Costa Rican nationalism, which has accentuated differences with external "others" as a means to decrease the importance of internal class divisions and to unite against outside threats.

7. This section draws on interviews conducted with agriculturalists and gold miners in La Palma.

NOTES

8. Edelman (1991) documents the ways Costa Rican national peasant organizations have utilized a similar discourse of food sovereignty and nationalist symbols of rusticity.

9. See Edelman (1999) for a useful summary of government institutions and programs in rural Costa Rica. In the late 1970s the Costa Rican government provided subsidized credit and inputs, crop insurance, and extension services (Edelman 1999:68–69).

10. The Ministry of Natural Resources, Energy, and Mines (MIRENEM) was created in 1986. In 1996 MIRENEM was reorganized as the Ministry of Environment and Energy (MINAE), and the decentralized National System of Conservation Areas (SINAC) was created (Watson et al. 1998). For a detailed account of the passage of the Forestry Law, see Watson et al. (1998) and Fundación Arias (1997a).

11. Prior to 1993, the Osa Conservation Area received external support from the World Wildlife Foundation, the Swedish Authority for Development, and the Nature Conservancy. Since then it has depended almost entirely on government funds (MINAE and SINAC n.d.).

12. IDA administers 20,000 hectares inside the Golfo Dulce Forest Reserve and 19,000 hectares outside the reserve, land that has been distributed to peasants with the condition that owners are not allowed to sell the land for twenty years (PDR 1995:32). In total, 41,000 hectares of the reserve are occupied by families, only 5 percent of which had titles in the early 1990s (Arias Castillo, Chaves Quesada, and Luis Camacho 1993).

13. Local government officials reported that in practice, land transactions occur outside of the law, and because of the lack of official titles and paperwork, the sellers receive lower prices. Government officials, however, had little or no information on the extent of these land transactions.

14. For an excellent detailed account of Costa Rican forestry policy, see Brockett and Gottfried (2002).

15. For this reason, I have not listed the specific agencies, organizations, or individuals alleged by respondents to be corrupt. Costa Rica ranks 4.2 out of 10.0 on a scale of perceived corruption, tying with El Salvador for the best score among Central American nations (Transparency International 2005). Salazar (2000), Seligson (2002), and Rodríguez, Castro, and Rowland Espinosa (1998), however, present evidence that public perception of increased corruption over the past decade has contributed to an erosion of public support for the region's longest-lived democracy.

16. Along similar lines, Hagopian and Mainwaring (2005) argue that Latin America's democracies under neoliberalism have "underperformed" in economic terms and not fulfilled the expectations of the majority of the population. They suggest, however, that a series of political factors have mediated this popular discontent with government and maintained democratic stability (Hagopian and Mainwaring 2005).

17. Periods of recession that follow implementation of reform are seen as a temporary phase in a longer-term shift toward greater efficiency and productivity as Costa Rica develops new export products and forms of insertion into world markets (World Bank 2000).

18. During these protests, thousands of workers, students, and environmentalists took to the streets to protest proposed laws to privatize the telephone com-

pany and allow private companies to develop hydroelectric and geothermal projects in parks and reserves (Seligson 2001).

19. Such increased environmental consciousness, however, may be limited to zones of more intense ecotourism activity. Stem's (2001) study found that employment in small-scale ecotourism projects generally had little impact on environmental consciousness.

20. Interviews with environmental activists and corroborated in Van den Hombergh (1999).

21. See MAG-FOR (1999); CONADES (1998); MICE (1996a, 1996b); FACS and CEPAD (1993). This privatization of development through NGOs is supported by dominant institutions that seek to limit the role and decrease the size of the state, as well as scholars and activists on the left who view NGOs as inherently closer to the grassroots and more democratic, flexible, and creative than their government counterparts (Meyer 1999; Edwards and Hulme 1996b; Bebbington and Thiele 1993; Farrington 1993).

22. This section draws on interviews with Puerto Jiménez ecotourism operators and environmental activists and is corroborated in Van den Hombergh (1999).

23. Ecofeminists "posit a close connection between women and nature based on a shared history of oppression by patriarchal institutions and dominant Western culture, as well as a positive identification by women with nature" (Rocheleau, Thomas-Slayter, and Wangari 1996b:3). Debate exists, however, as to whether the connection is biological or socially constructed (see Rocheleau, Thomas-Slayter, and Wangari 1996a; Jackson 1994; Mies and Shiva 1993).

24. According to a project document, BOSCOSA "would differ from the traditional idea of conservation and emphasize instead the management of natural forests by local inhabitants, complimented by support from the public sector and NGOs" (Fundación Neotrópica 1991:7).

25. Several participants reported that their crops did not meet size or quality requirements to be shipped to the United States. A government official reported that the problems resulted from the personnel's lack of experience with exporting and from deceptive brokers in Miami.

26. Such commentaries may be based on hearsay and not on direct experience. As with charges of government corruption, it was beyond the scope of this study to investigate the veracity of specific allegations of NGO misconduct.

CHAPTER 5: "RIGHT BEHIND HIM ARE THE CAMPESINOS WITH AXES": DEVELOPING THE ESTERO REAL

1. IRENA was established in 1979. In 1996 it was converted to MARENA.

2. The protected status of the Estero Real allows scientific study and limited recreation in the estuary but prohibits land use without a management plan, as well as any development or hunting (IDR and CATIE 1999).

3. For case studies of nontraditional exports in Central America, see Thrupp (1997), Goldin (1996), Carter (1996), Murray (1994), Stonich (1993), Achong (1993), Carter (1996), and Barham et al. (1992).

4. This section draws on interviews with MARENA officials and an official in the Tonalá mayor's office and is corroborated in Rocha and Barahona (1999)

NOTES

5. In 2002, 21,351 hectares of land concessions had been granted—5,920 to the cooperatives and 15,431 to commercial enterprises—although not all hectares have been in actual production (Cato, Otwell, and Saborío Coze 2005:18). Some companies may also speculate with the land, paying the government $30/hectare and then selling access to the land at $2,500/hectare (Rocha and Barahona 1999).

6. In 1999, USAID initiated a $1.3 million technical assistance program to promote "healthy" and "environmentally safe" shrimp production that "provides jobs for thousands" (USAID 2002).

7. World Bank analysis (2003b) suggests that the strong growth in Nicaragua's agricultural exports was linked to a recovery from earlier declines, high commodity prices (until 2001), and expansion of the amount of land under cultivation.

8. It is not clear whether these are permanent or only seasonal positions during the growth (*crianza*) phase of production.

9. In addition, in the late 1990s, damage from Hurricane Mitch and the arrival of the White Spot Shrimp Virus ("*mancha blanca*") to the Estero Real affected around 75 percent of shrimp farms (Cato, Otwell, and Saborío Coze 2005).

10. Interviews with MARENA personnel and corroborated in IDR and CATIE (1999).

11. This paragraph is based on interviews with woodcutters and is corroborated in Paniagua and Aguilar (1996) and Rocha and Barahona (1999).

12. This paragraph draws on interviews with local government officials and NGO technicians and is corroborated in PROGOLFO (n.d.).

13. Government and NGO personnel and community members also reported that the zone's small farmer majority has little participation in soybean and peanut production, largely because of the amounts of capital required (INEC 2004). A MAG-FOR official estimated, for example, that the cultivation of peanuts requires an investment of $1,200 per hectare—an amount, given the credit squeeze of the 1990s and the privatization of Nicaragua's banking system, beyond the reach of most small and mid-size farmers (see Enriquez 2000; Jonakin 1996).

CHAPTER 6: "HE HAS BEEN TAUGHT NOT TO BE AFRAID": GRASSROOTS SUSTAINABILITY IN MIRAFLORES

1. Initially, the FSLN required peasants to join cooperatives and farm collectively to obtain access to land. In the mid-1980s, however, government recognition of growing rural opposition to the revolution and expansion of the contra forces in Nicaragua's interior led the Sandinistas to shift policy and grant individual land titles (Horton 1999; Bendaña 1991; Enriquez 1991). Sandinista policies requiring that certain food crops be sold to a state agency, as well as rationing measures, also caused resentment within the rural population.

2. This section draws on fieldwork and interviews conducted in Miraflores in the period 1988–1990 and is corroborated in Nitlapán (1990).

3. The information in this section on community visions of sustainable development is drawn from interviews carried out with male and female heads of household in the community of Miraflores and a smaller sampling of households active in the firewood trade in the community of Río Hondo. In addition, this chapter incorporates ethnographic data from stays in the community over a fifteen-year period. The caveats mentioned in the Costa Rica case study apply here

as well. While almost all of the Nicaraguan NGO representatives interviewed used the term "sustainable development," in community-level interviews I did not directly ask residents their opinion of sustainable development, nor did any respondents bring up the concept of their own initiative. Rather, the analysis here is drawn from residents' responses to questions on economic, social, and environmental issues. See the Appendix for further discussion of methodological issues.

4. One afternoon, for example, community member Alicia, her children, and I were resting in a large peanut field just outside Miraflores. A heavy chemical odor permeated the air, and several bags of herbicides lay discarded on the side of the path. Alicia's barefoot two-year-old daughter began to play in the dirt. I was about to comment that the child might accidentally eat some of this dirt, saturated with agrochemicals, when Alicia told me, "It [the peanut field] looks so beautiful, so clean," referring to the dirt rows completely free of weeds.

5. A World Bank (2001c) qualitative study of the poor in Nicaragua found that they believe poverty is "a vicious circle from which they cannot escape since it is inherited and perpetuated through generations" (13). The poor also broadly consider public institutions corrupt and nonresponsive.

6. While Miraflores was a relatively successful cooperative, it also faced issues common to other agricultural cooperatives, in particular illiteracy, lack of accounting skills, and issues of labor discipline (DEA-UNAN 1990). The UNAG leadership maintained close ties to the FSLN in the 1980s but still retained a degree of autonomy to pressure the government on issues of interest to agricultural producers. See Luciak (1995) and Serra (1993) for a discussion of the ties and tensions between the grassroots organizations of the 1980s and the FSLN.

7. Nicaragua has an extensive network of social development NGOs with strong grassroots ties, as well as a smaller environmental NGO sector highly dependent on external funding (Varela Hidalgo 1998).

8. By the late 1990s, polarization within Nicaragua's NGO sector had lessened. Following Hurricane Mitch, over 350 NGOs, social movements, and grassroots organizations formed a broad coalition to coordinate relief efforts and present social policy recommendations (Coordinadora Civil 1999). NGO representatives interviewed noted, however, that there have been strong tensions between NGOs and the government over ideological conflicts, control of material resources, and the role of NGOs in government policy formulation (see Close and Deonandan 2004).

9. In general, the government's review of land expropriations and the privatization of state-owned agricultural enterprises has been a closed process, with instances of cronyism (Everingham 2001). In the department of Chinandega I heard numerous complaints about government officials' inefficiency in the land titling process. One Office of Rural Land Titling employee explained that the lawyers who worked for the agency had no interest in resolving land cases because that only meant they would soon be out of a job. Studies suggest that approximately 20 percent of Nicaragua's lands have been in conflict. These conflicts include disputes between current and former cooperative members, as well as competing claims between wealthy landowners and poor peasants (Merlet and Pommier 2000).

10. Even those who are functionally literate may become victims. In 1999, I lost $100 in a series of transactions with a deceptive Chinandega lawyer while trying to help arrange a passport for a community member.

11. A few months later, the family member who had initiated the claims against Miraflores was shot and killed by his brother on the streets of Chinandega city. As of 2006, no other former owner family member had attempted to have the families removed from the land.

12. In 2004 Nicaragua was approved for relief of 80 percent of its external debt under the Highly Indebted Poor Country initiative (World Bank 2006b, 2001c).

13. Although the World Bank has focused on the FSLN's economic policies, the U.S. economic embargo and the ongoing civil war that caused widespread social and economic disruption in rural Nicaragua also strongly contributed to the economic crisis in the late 1980s (Horton 1999).

14. In the department of Chinandega, only 24 percent of agricultural producers obtained formal or informal credit in 2000 (INEC 2004:57). Nicaraguan private commercial banks generally do not lend money without a title as a guarantee or some other item worth a minimum of 160 percent of the loan (Rocha and Barahona 1999:30). The legal confusion over land titles has also added to small farmers' difficulties in obtaining loans.

15. Interviews with Ministry of Agriculture and Livestock officials and Miraflores and Río Hondo residents.

16. One of Miraflores's poorest families, whose soils were damaged by the contaminated runoff from Hurricane Mitch, was cut off by NGO credit programs, for example. The family has attempted for several years to grow corn without purchased inputs but reported that the corn generally does not even reach knee-high.

17. For example, the prices merchants pay households for their corn crop in September, when the department's main harvest comes in, are often less than half the amount families pay to buy corn a few months later, when it is more scarce.

18. This support for the FSLN was not uncritical, however. When the FSLN was in power in the 1980s, community members opposed its 1988 economic adjustment measures, and many expressed a strong desire for an end to the war and the military draft. See Horton (1999), Bendaña (1991), and Núñez (1991) for a discussion of peasant opposition to the revolution in Nicaragua's rural northern and central regions in particular.

19. Despite my long-term relationship with the community, it was difficult for me to obtain exact data on income levels and wealth there. Several of the better-off families in particular are sensitive to criticism by other community members about their post-1990 accumulation of land and cattle and are reluctant to share this information. Given Miraflores's self-defined revolutionary orientation, conspicuous displays of wealth within the community are still met with social criticism.

20. By the mid-2000s, an estimated 15 percent of Nicaraguan rural households received remittances from abroad, which made up 18 percent of Nicaragua's GDP (ECLAC 2005:24).

21. In contrast, Habitat for Humanity required that both men's and women's names be included on house titles, which has led to greater equity in the distribution of these goods.

22. See Deere and Leon (2001) and Luciak (2001) for a discussion of women's land rights in Nicaragua and El Salvador.

23. Plan International's foster parent plan is an example. Apparently without factual basis, rumors began to spread that sponsoring families were sending cash

in letters to their Miraflores and Tonalá "godchildren" and that two Miraflores residents were opening the letters and stealing the money. In another case, however, a member of a well-off Miraflores family was involved in corruption and lost his NGO position as a result.

CHAPTER 7: "BEFORE, THERE WERE ONLY KUNAS": THE STRUGGLE FOR THE COMARCA

1. Madungandí leaders have also strongly emphasized land issues in their discourse with the news media since the early 1990s (see González Pinilla 2005; Quintero de León 2005, 1993; Bonilla 1996; Alba 1992).

2. *Interioranos* here refers to individuals from Panama's rural central and western provinces who share a common lifestyle linked to music, dress, and a "cattle culture" (see Heckadon Moreno 1982). *Interioranos'* racial ancestry tends to range from light-skinned European to mestizo, with a more limited African presence.

3. From 1950 to 1970, the number of cattle in Panama doubled from 570,000 to 1.2 million, and the amount of land in pasture increased from 550,000 hectares to 1.1 million hectares (Heckadon Moreno 1982:18).

4. Census data from the district of Chepo that include the Bayano show that there were 3,373 head of cattle in 1970, 9,438 in 1980, 23,630 in 1990, and 42,923 in 1997 (Consorcio Louis Berger International Inc. and Delca Consultores S.A. 1998a: A/9-1).

5. Interviews with Ipetí leaders, also Moeller (1997) and Tejeira (1972).

6. Interviews with Ipetí protest participants.

7. This section draws on interviews with Ipetí protest participants as well as Quintero de León (1993).

8. This section draws on interviews with an indigenous legislative adviser and Kuna NGO technicians. Kuna authorities from Madungandí have also sought assistance from non-indigenous organizations such as the United Nations and the Smithsonian Institution, as well as from anthropologists and sociologists.

9. Since the mid-1980s, indigenous peoples have mobilized around a wide range of demands including self-determination, autonomy, territorial rights, access to natural resources, political reforms, control over economic development, and reforms of the military and police.

10. The World Bank's 2005 Operational Directive and Bank Policy 4.10 (which replaced a similar 1991 operational directive 4.20) states that the World Bank will only provide financing for projects that affect indigenous peoples when a process of "free, prior, and informed consultation results in broad community support to the project by the affected Indigenous Peoples" (World Bank 2005a).

11. Interview with a Kuna legislative adviser as well as Huertas (1999).

12. Interviews with Ipetí authorities and activists.

13. This section draws on interviews conducted in the *interiorano* communities of Wacuco, Curtí, and Loma Bonita and is corroborated in Azacarte and Huertas (1999).

14. Interviews with Kuna and non-Kuna NGO personnel.

15. A substantial Afro-Panamanian population resides in the province of Darién to the east of Madungandí, and some Afro-Darienita communities have

actively opposed both the legalization of the Kuna *comarca* of Wargandí and recognition of Embará collective lands (*tierras colectivas*) (Cordero 2003; Delgado 2001). For an insightful examination of Embará and Afro-Darienita tensions in Darién, see Kane (1994).

16. The indigenous NGO Dooba Yala played an important role, with funding from Spain, in providing legal and political support needed to bring the draft of the Wargandí *comarca* law to the National Assembly. Kuna lawyers working with NGOs and the Indigenous Affairs Commission of the National Assembly also worked out an agreement in which colonists in the immediate vicinity of Wargandí agreed to support the *comarca*.

17. The Ngöbe-Buglé *comarca*, however, incorporated only half of the land requested by the group. In addition, almost half of the Embarás still live outside the boundaries of their *comarca* and continue to campaign for recognition of smaller "collective lands" (Wickstrom 2003; Young and Bort 1999; Potlatch 1998a).

18. While in Panama both men and women are legally allowed to vote and hold political office, within the *comarca* of Madungandí women are not allowed to participate in *comarca*-level General Congresses or hold positions of traditional authority. The only reference the charter makes to the rights of women is to call for active female participation in local congresses.

19. The *comarca* charter also states that if Kuna law conflicts with Panamanian law, the latter will prevail; and *comarca* authorities are required to "coordinate" with government agencies such as the National Environmental Authority on the use of natural resources within the *comarca* (Gaceta Oficial 1996).

20. After nearly 200 residents contracted falciparum malaria in 2004, government officials had to negotiate permission to enter the community of Aguas Claras to examine ill residents, take blood samples, and spray pesticides for mosquito control (Molina 2004).

CHAPTER 8: "THERE ARE NO POOR PEOPLE HERE": GRASSROOTS SUSTAINABILITY IN IPETÍ

1. Similar to community interviews in Nicaragua and Costa Rica, the material in this section is drawn from discussions of the strengths, weaknesses, problems, and future of the community of Ipetí and the *comarca* of Madungandí. In addition, in the late 1990s the Panamanian government, with IDB financing, launched an $80 million Darién Sustainable Development Program whose centerpiece has been the paving of the dirt and gravel Pan-American Highway from Bayano to the town of Yaviza in the province of Darién. Much community debate and mobilization have centered on this road project as the embodiment of "development" and on the processes' deeper implications.

2. Such ambivalence was also expressed by a *saila* from the *comarca* of Wargandí who suggested there was no need for formal education in his community (Potlatch 1998b).

3. Stone throwing refers to the frequent protests and skirmishes between Panamanian high school and university students and the police in Panama City.

4. The 2000 census data show a wide variation in average household income among the twelve communities of the Madungandí *comarca* (Contraloría General

de la República de Panamá 2000). Median monthly household incomes range from a low of $50 in several interior communities to a high of $700 in Puerto Limón. This income variation may reflect different degrees of involvement with logging activities, a major source of cash for some communities, as well as greater opportunities for agricultural wage labor in communities closer to the highway. It is also unclear whether these income totals incorporate food crops, fish, wild game, and other resources from the rain forests that help sustain Madungandí households, particularly in communities farther from the highway.

5. Bennett's (1962) research suggests that as late as the 1960s, interior Madungandí communities were almost entirely dependent on agriculture and fishing for their survival.

6. This desire for improved health and educational services is echoed by Panama's other indigenous peoples. Rather than reject development in all its aspects, Ngöbe-Buglé and Embará leaders have called for the expansion of basic services such as electricity, potable water, and health care to their communities, as well as bilingual education, greater political autonomy, and legal recognition of land rights (*La Prensa* 1992e).

7. This section draws on interviews with community informants and is corroborated in Moeller (1997). See Ventocilla and colleagues (1996) and Alvarado (1995) for a discussion of this trend in Kuna Yala.

8. In comparison to men, Ipetí women have fewer opportunities to earn cash incomes. While in Kuna Yala the sale of embroidered *molas* is an important source of income for women, Ipetí women sew *molas* primarily for household use.

9. This section on Ipetí discourse and norms draws on conversations with Ipetí informants and is corroborated in Moeller (1997).

10. Such cultural revitalization also occurs in urban areas, where, for example, there is a self-conscious reappropriation of Kuna names (Sherzer 1994).

11. Open racism on television and in newspapers has in part been reduced because the Kunas have actively denounced negative representations of indigenous people in the media and advertising. Racist comments, however, can be heard in daily life in Panama, directed not only toward indigenous peoples but also toward other Panamanian racial and ethnic groups, such as people of Afro-Caribbean, Jewish, and Asian descent.

12. Although my interviews did not include health-related questions, residents often initiated discussions of this topic. I was told, for example, of an Ipetí woman who was injured in an accident and spent months in the Chepo hospital. Only when she returned to the *comarca*, however, were traditional healers able to cure her badly damaged leg. Moeller (1997) describes an incident in Ipetí in which a non-indigenous doctor made pejorative comments about a Kuna patient he was treating. See Molina (2004) on government-*comarca* conflicts over malaria control.

13. Such claims, however, exaggerate the material well-being of non-indigenous settlers in the Bayano, 68 percent of whom lay claim to fewer than 50 hectares of land (Consorcio Louis Berger International Inc. and Delca Consultores S.A. 1998c).

14. Interviews with Ipetí residents and corroborated in Moeller (1997).

15. According to Kuna tradition, the Great Father taught the Kunas about medicinal plants and carved wooden figures (*nuchus*) (Reverte 1961). Kuna healers

cure through the use of medicinal herbs, baths, smoke, and songs. For example, broken bones can be healed with *nia arsantuba* (a vine), headaches with *baila ukka* (a balsamic tree) (Reverte 1961).

16. Interviews with Ipetí residents and corroborated in Consorcio Louis Berger International Inc. and Delca Consultores S.A. (1998a).

17. Moeller (1997) notes that this discourse is part of a broader tendency in Ipetí to place responsibility for problems on oursiders.

18. In contrast, in communities in the neighboring Kuna *comarca* of Wargandí, households have received around $1,500 each (Núñez 1999). NGO technicians familiar with the communities suggest that logging has become their most important source of income, leading men to neglect agricultural activities.

19. Estimates in the mid-1990s suggested that logging in the Bayano generated 250 direct and 100 indirect jobs in high season (Barrios C. 1997:62).

20. Fieldwork and corroborated in Moeller (1997).

21. Interviews with colonist leaders and corroborated in Azacarte and Huertas (1999).

22. Interviews with ANAM and former ANAM officials.

23. Indigenous groups have also protested government support of mining concessions on indigenous lands (Herrera 2002). See Gjording (1991) for a detailed study of the 1980s conflict between the Ngöbe-Buglé and a government-sponsored copper mining project.

24. Panama passed its first comprehensive environmental law in 1998, and several years later the National Institute for Renewable Resources (INRENARE), renamed ANAM, received funding from the World Bank to strengthen its administrative and regulatory capacity.

25. Fieldwork and interviews with Ipetí leaders.

26. Interviews with Kuna NGO personnel.

27. The rest of this paragraph draws on fieldwork in Ipetí and Moeller (1997).

28. This section draws on interviews with NGO and USAID personnel in Panama. The preponderant role of the state under Torrijos, its efforts to co-opt leftist groups, and the increased military repression under General Manuel Noriega likely contributed to this weakness of civil society (Gjording 1991; Priestley 1986; Ropp 1982).

29. Panama's largest environmental NGO, the National Association for the Conservation of Nature, for example, has received funding from USAID and mainstream U.S. environmental NGOs.

30. In addition to the projects in Madungandí described in Table 8.1, Germany, the United Nations, and the Panamanian government funded a $13 million project for the Ngöbe-Buglé, and the European Community earmarked $675,000 for sustainable development in Kuna Yala (*La Prensa* 1994c).

31. Likewise, Ipetí residents, reluctant to work through intermediaries, be they Panamanian government officials or indigenous NGOs based in Panama City, with "air-conditioned offices," formed the Association of Producers of Madungandí to solicit project funds. The *comarca* of Madungandí has also created a small NGO, ORKUM.

32. In the early 2000s, Ipetí also participated in the World Bank–financed Mesoamerican Biological Corridor Program, which extended across Central Amer-

ica. The program's purpose was to promote "the participation of local and indigenous communities in activities of use and conservation of biological diversity" (*La Prensa* 2000). It employs discourse typical of dominant sustainability, identifying poverty as a key environmental threat and seeking "to integrate social needs with environmental priorities" by strengthening the administration of protected areas and promoting sustainable agriculture and ecotourism (Guzmán, Raine, and Rodríguez 2003:2).

33. For a discussion of IDB policy shifts toward the indigenous, see Deruyttere (1997). According to Deruyttere (1997), IDB indigenous policy incorporates structural adjustment and market-oriented reforms while seeking to minimize risks and maximize opportunities for indigenous social and economic development (16).

34. Interviews with Ipetí leaders and personnel of the Darién Sustainable Development Program.

35. Although the colonist land issue was still not resolved in 2006, the program did fund a formal demarcation of the *comarca* land. Initial studies indicated that with the natural boundaries set several decades earlier, the *comarca* of Madungandí incorporated not 180,000 hectares, as stated in the charter, but rather 200,000 hectares. Privately, some government officials have suggested that these "extra" 20,000 hectares could in fact be turned over to non-indigenous settlers. But apparently over concern of strong negative Kuna reaction, this idea had not been advanced during my fieldwork.

36. This section is based on interviews with Darién Sustainable Development Program personnel, observations of program activities, and interviews with Ipetí authorities.

37. A large influx of donations with little oversight weakened the Kuna sustainable development NGO PEMASKY (Study Project for the Management of the Wildlands of Kuna Yala), for example, and it lost credibility at the grassroots level (Ventocilla et al. 1996; Chapin 1991).

38. On Kuna Yala, tensions have developed between Kuna NGOs and traditional authorities (Martinez Mauri 2003; Herrera 2002).

39. In contrast, the Ngöbe-Buglés do not have clear leadership structures, a situation worsened by a series of political divisions in recent years (Herrera 2002; Mendoza n.d.; Young and Bort 1999).

40. See Howe (1986) for a detailed account of Kuna governance on Kuna Yala.

41. On the shift of power and authority from the extended household to more formalized authority at the village level in Kuna Yala, see Howe (1986).

42. This section on Ipetí internal governance draws on interviews with Ipetí leaders and government personnel of the Darién Sustainable Development Program.

43. Historically, Kuna males have viewed miscegenation as a serious cultural threat and have developed strong social norms to discourage it (Howe 1998; Moeller 1997).

44. In Kuna Yala, women have held several conferences and raised concerns about the high number of single mothers, the low prices women receive for their *molas,* men's unwillingness to work in agriculture, and a need to lessen restrictions on women's travel (*La Prensa* 1994a).

NOTES

45. Howe (1986) notes on Kuna Yala similar patterns of restricted movement and condescending male attitudes toward women.

46. One Ipetí resident who as a young man considered marrying a non-Kuna woman and living in Panama City, for example, reported that a community member practiced witchcraft on him and made him sick until he left his non-Kuna girlfriend and returned to live in Ipetí.

Bibliography

Achong Paz, Andés. 1993. *Las perspectivas de las exportaciones agrícolas no tradicionales para los pequeños y medianos productores centroamericanos*. Panama City: CADESCA.
Adams, William M. 2001. *Green Development: Environment and Sustainability in the Third World*, 2nd ed. London: Routledge.
Adger, W. Neil, Tor A. Benjaminsen, Katrina Brown, and Hanne Svarstad. 2001. "Advancing a Political Ecology of Global Environmental Discourses." *Development and Change* 32: 687–715.
AECO (Asociación Ecologista Costarricense). n.d. *Gestión productiva y sostentibilidad*. Unpublished report.
Agyeman, Julian, Robert D. Bullard, and Bob Evans. 2003. "Introduction: Joined-up Thinking: Bringing Together Sustainability, Environmental Justice and Equity." In *Just Sustainabilities: Development in an Unequal World*, ed. Julian Agyeman, Robert D. Bullard, and Bob Evans. Cambridge: MIT Press.
Alba, Rogelio. 1992. "Madungandí solicita demarcación de tierras." *La Prensa* (November 9, 1992).
Alemán Ortiz, Leyla, Rolando Mena Herández, and Laurent Dietsch. 1996. *Diagnóstico agrosocieconomico de cooperativas camaroneras*. ADAA-UCA Report. Managua: Universidad Centroaméricana.
Alvarado, Eligio. 1995. *El valor del ambiente en los Kunas desde una perspectiva de género*. San José, Costa Rica: UICN.
Aparicio, Gustavo O. 2004. "Indígenas kunas piden ejercer voto en Chepo." *Panamá América* (March 1, 2004).

Bibliography

Apostolopoulos, Yiorgos, Sevil F. Sonmez, and Timothy J. Dallen (eds.). 2001. *Women as Producers and Consumers of Tourism in Developing Regions.* Westport, CN: Praeger.
Arias Castillo, Elvis, Silvia Elena Chaves Quesada, and Juan Luis Camacho. 1993. *Recomendaciones para un ordenamiento territorial en la Península de Osa, Costa Rica.* Programa BOSCOSA. San José, Costa Rica: BOSCOSA.
Assies, Willem, Gemma van der Haar, and Andre Hoekema (eds.). 2000. *Challenge of Diversity: Indigenous Peoples and Reform of the State in Latin America.* Amsterdam: Thela Thesis.
Azacarte, Luis José, and Hector Huertas. 1999. *Mesas de Concertación Ipetí-Pariatí y Madungandí. Conclusiones y Plan de Acción. Informe Final.* Panama City: Programa de Desarrollo Sostenible de Darién.
Babb, Florence E. 2001. *After Revolution: Mapping Gender and Cultural Politics in Neoliberal Nicaragua.* Austin: University of Texas Press.
Barahona Najlis, Túpac, and René Mendoza. 1999. *Chinandega: el manejo de una reserva natural en un mundo de agricultores.* Managua: Nitlapán.
Barham, Bradford, Mary Clark, Elizabeth Katz, and Rachel Schurman. 1992. "Nontraditional Agricultural Exports in Latin America." *Latin American Research Review* 27(2): 43–82.
Barkin, David. 2000. "Wealth, Poverty and Sustainable Development." In *Rethinking Sustainability: Power, Knowledge, and Institutions,* ed. Jonathan M. Harris. Ann Arbor: University of Michigan Press.
Barquero Barrantes, Luis Alberto. 1988. *Diagnóstico ambiental y zonificación de la cuenca del Río Rincón.* B.A. thesis, University of Costa Rica.
Barrentes, Gilbert, Quírico Jiménez, Jorge Lobo, Tirso Maldonado, Mauricio Quesada, and Ruperto Quesada. 1999. *Evaluación de los planes de manejo forestal autorizados en el período 1997–1999 en la Península de Osa, cumplimiento de normas técnicas, ambientales e impacto sobre el bosque natural.* San José, Costa Rica: Fundación Cecropia.
Barrios C., Marta M. 1997. *Ordenamiento y tenencia de la tierra para un desarrollo sostenible en la cuenca alta del Río Bayano.* B.A. thesis, University of Panama.
Bartolomé, Miguel, and Alicia Barabas. 1998. "Recursos culturales y autonomía étnica. La democracia participativa de los kunas de Panamá." *Alteridades* 8(16): 159–174.
Baumeister, Eduardo. 1999. "Inciativas campesinas y sostenibilidad de los resultados de las reformas agrarias." Paper presented at the seminar Land in Latin America: New Context, New Claims, New Concepts (Amsterdam).
Bebbington, Anthony. 2000. "Globalized Andes? Peasant Organizations, Livelihoods and Landscapes." Paper presented at the Latin American Studies Association Twenty-Second International Congress (Miami, Florida, March 16–18, 2000).
———. 1999. "Organizing for Change—Organizing for Modernization? Campesino Federations, Social Enterprise, and Technical Change in Andean and Amazonian Resource Management." In *Traditional and Modern Natural Resource Management in Latin America,* ed. Francisco J. Pichón, Jorge E. Uquillas, and John Frechione. Pittsburgh: University of Pittsburgh Press.
Bebbington, Anthony, and Graham Thiele. 1993. *Non-governmental Organizations and the State in Latin America: Rethinking Roles in Sustainable Agricultural Development.* New York: Routledge.

Bendaña, Alejandro. 1991. *Una tragedia campesina: testimonios de la resistencia*. Managua: Editora de Arte.
Bennett, Charles F. 1962. "The Bayano Cuna Indians, Panama: An Ecological Study of Livelihood and Diet." *Annals of the Association of American Geographers* 52: 32–50.
Benton, Ted. 1994. "Biology and Social Theory in the Environmental Debate." In *Social Theory and the Global Environment*, ed. Michael Redclift and Ted Benton. London: Routledge.
Bernstein, Steven. 2001. *The Compromise of Liberal Environmentalism*. New York: Columbia University Press.
Biderman, Jaime M. 1982. *Class Structure, the State and Capitalist Development in Nicaraguan Agriculture*. Ph.D dissertation, University of California, Berkeley.
Biekart, Kees. 1999. *The Politics of Civil Society Building: European Private Aid Agencies and Democratic Transitions in Central America*. Utrecht: International Books.
Blaikie, Piers, and Harold Brookfield. 1987. *Land Degradation and Society*. London: Metheun.
Boas, Morten, and Desmond McNeill (eds.). 2004a. *Global Institutions and Development: Framing the World?* New York: Routledge.
———. 2004b. "Introduction: Power and Ideas in Multilateral Institutions: Towards an Interpretive Framework." In *Global Institutions and Development: Framing the World?*, ed. Morten Boas and Desmond McNeill. New York: Routledge.
———. 2004c. "Ideas and Institutions: Who Is Framing What?" In *Global Institutions and Development: Framing the World?*, ed. Morten Boas and Desmond McNeill. New York: Routledge.
Bonilla, Arcadio. 1996. "Las luchas de Madungandí." *La Prensa* (August 2, 1996).
Booth, John A. 1982. *The End and the Beginning: The Nicaraguan Revolution*. Boulder: Westview.
Bowers, C. A. 1995. *Educating for an Ecologically Sustainable Culture: Rethinking Moral Education, Creativity, Intelligence, and Other Modern Orthodoxies*. Albany: State University of New York Press.
Brandon, Katrina, and Michael Wells. 1992. "Planning for People and Parks: Design Dilemmas." *World Development* 20(4): 557–570.
Brenes, Luís Guillermo, et al. 1988. *Impacto ambiental de la explotación de oro en el Parque Nacional Corcovado, Península de Osa, Costa Rica*. San José, Costa Rica: FPN, SPN, ICI, CATIE.
Brizuela, Alvaro. 1972. "Agricultura y calenadario agrícola de los Kunas del Río Bayano, Panamá." In *Actas del II Simposium Nacional de Antropología, Arqueología y Etnohistoria de Panamá, abril de 1971*. Panama City: Impr. Universitaria.
Brockett, Charles D. 2005. *Political Movements and Violence in Central America*. New York: Cambridge University Press.
———. 1990. *Land, Power, and Poverty: Agrarian Transformation and Political Conflict in Central America*. Boston: Unwin Hyman.
Brockett, Charles D., and Robert R. Gottfried. 2002. "State Policies and the Preservation of Forest Cover: Lessons from Contrasting Public-Policy Regimes in Costa Rica." *Latin American Research Review* 37(1): 7–40.
Brohman, John. 1996. "New Directions in Tourism for Third World Development." *Annals of Tourism Research* 23(1): 48–70.

Brown, David. 2004. "Participation in Poverty Reduction Strategies: Democracy Strengthened or Democracy Undermined?" In *Participation: From Tyranny to Transformation: Exploring New Approaches to Participation in Development,* ed. Samuel Hickey and Giles Mohan. London: Zed Books.

Bryant, Raymond L., and Sinaed Bailey. 1997. *Third World Political Ecology.* London: Routledge.

Bryner, Gary C. 2001. *Gaia's Wager: Environmental Movements and the Challenge of Sustainability.* Lanham, MD: Rowman & Littlefield.

Bulmer-Thomas, Victor (ed.). 1996. *The New Economic Model in Latin America and Its Impact on Income Distribution and Poverty.* London: Institute of Latin American Studies.

———. 1987. *The Political Economy of Central America Since 1920.* New York: Cambridge University Press.

Campbell, Lisa M. 2002. "Conservation Narratives in Costa Rica: Conflict and Coexistence." *Development and Change* 33: 29–56.

———. 1999. "Ecotourism in Rural Developing Communities." *Annals of Tourism Research* 26(3): 534–553.

CAPRI (Centro de Apoyo a Programas y Proyectos). 1999. *Directorio ONG de Nicaragua, 1999–2000.* Managua: CAPRI.

———. 1990. *Directorio ONG de Nicaragua, 1990.* Managua: CAPRI.

Carriere, Jean. 1991. "The Crisis in Costa Rica: An Ecological Perspective." In *Environment and Development in Latin America: The Politics of Sustainability,* ed. David Goodman and Michael Redclift. New York: St. Martin's.

Carter, Michael R. 1996. "Agricultural Export Booms and the Rural Poor in Chile, Guatemala, and Paraguay." *Latin American Research Review* 31(1): 33–65.

Cato, James C., W. Steven Otwell, and Agnés Saborío Coze. 2005. *Nicaragua's Shrimp Subsector: Developing a Production Capacity and Export Market during Rapidly Changing Worldwide Safety and Quality Regulations.* Washington, DC: World Bank.

Chapin, Mac. 1991. "Losing the Way of the Great Father." *New Scientist,* August 10: 40–44.

Chase, Jacquelyn. 2002. "Introduction: The Spaces of Neoliberalism in Latin America." In *The Spaces of Neoliberalism in Latin America: Land, Place, and Family in Latin America,* ed. Jacquelyn Chase. Bloomfield, CT: Kumarian.

Cheong, So-Min, and Marc L. Miller. 2000. "Power and Tourism: A Foucauldian Observation." *Annals of Tourism Research* 27(2): 371–390.

CIA (Central Intelligence Agency). 2001. *The World Fact Book: El Salvador.* Available on the CIA Web site: http://www.cia.gov/cia/publications/factbook/.

Clay, Jason W., Janis B. Alcorn, and John R. Butler. 2000. *Indigenous Peoples, Forestry Management and Biodiversity Conservation: An Analytical Study for the World Bank's Forestry Implementation Review and Strategy Development Framework.* Washington, DC: World Bank.

Close, David. 2004. "Undoing Democracy in Nicaragua." In *Undoing Democracy: The Politics of Electoral Caudillismo,* ed. David Close and Kalowatie Deonandan. Lanham, MD: Lexington Books.

Close, David, and Kalowatie Deonandan (eds.). 2004. *Undoing Democracy: The Politics of Electoral Caudillismo.* Lanham, MD: Lexington Books.

COBRUDES (Consejo Bruqueño para el Desarrollo Sostenible). 1997. *Diagnóstico socioeconómico de la región Brunca.* Working Paper.
Collier, Paul, and David Dollar. 2002. *Globalization, Growth, and Poverty: Building an Inclusive World Economy.* Washington, DC: World Bank.
Comaroff, Jean, and John L. Comaroff (eds.). 2001. *Millennial Capitalism and the Culture of Neoliberalism.* Durham: Duke University Press.
Commission on the Truth for El Salvador. 1993. *From Madness to Hope: The 12-Year War in El Salvador.* Available on the United States Institute for Peace Web site: http://www.usip.org/library/tc/doc/reports/el_salvador/tc_es_03151993_toc.html.
CONADES (Consejo Nacional de Desarrollo Sostenible). 1998. *Inciativas y proyectos de desarrollo sostenible en Nicaragua.* Unpublished report.
Conniff, Michael L. 1985. *Black Labor on a White Canal.* Pittsburgh: University of Pittsburgh Press.
Consorcio Louis Berger International Inc. and Delca Consultores S.A. 1998a. *Informe de fase 1. Diagnóstico. Volumen 1. Tomos 1 y 2. Manejo integral de la cuenca del Río Bayano, subcuenca del Río Majé y áreas adyacentes al embalse.* Panama City, Panama, unpublished report.
———. 1998b. *Informe Bimestral 4. Estrategia y formulación de proyectos. Manejo integral de la cuenca del Río Bayano, subcuenca del Río Majé y áreas adyacentes al embalse.* Panama City, Panama, unpublished report.
———. 1998c. *Anexo 8. Población de la cuenca alta del Bayano. Manejo integral de la cuenca del Río Bayano, subcuenca del Río Majé y áreas adyacentes al embalse.* Panama City, Panama, unpublished report.
Contraloría General de la República de Panamá. 2000. *Censos nacionales de población y vivienda.* Available on the Contraloría General de la República de Panamá Web site: http://www.contraloria.gob.pa/censodepoblacion/index.htm.
Coordinadora Civil para la Emergencia y la Reconstrucción. 1999. *Convertiendo la tragedia del Mitch en una oportunidad para el desarrollo humano y sostenible de Nicaragua.* Managua: Coordinadora Civil para la Emergencia y la Reconstrucción.
Corbridge, Stuart. 1998. "Beneath the Pavement Only Soil: The Poverty of Post-Development." *Journal of Development Studies* 34(3): 138–148.
Cordero, Allen, and Luisa van Duynen Montijn. 2002. "¿Turismo sostenible en Costa Rica? El caso de Quepos-Manuel Antonio." In *Imaginarios sociales y turismo sostenible,* ed. Daniel Hiernaux Nicolas, Allen Cordero, and Luisa van Duynen Montijn. Available at http://www.flacso.or.cr/download/c123.pdf.
Cordero, Carlos Anel. 2003. "Darién podría desaparecer, sostiene Milanés de Lay." *Panamá América* (February 17, 2003).
Correa G., Carlos, Enoch Adames M., and Raúl Leis. 2001. *Gobernabilidad democrática y seguridad ciudadana en Centroamérica: el caso de Panamá.* Managua: CRIES.
CSE (Consejo Supremo Electoral). 2000. "2000 election results." Available on the CSE Web site: http://www.cse.gob.ni/elecciones/2000/escru/chinandega.htm.
DANIDA (Danish International Development Agency)-Manglares. n.d. *Estratégia para el desarrollo y la conservación del Estero Real.* Unpublished report.
Danielson, Anders, and A. Geske Dijkstra (eds.). 2001. *Toward Sustainable Development in Central America and the Caribbean.* New York: Palgrave.

Davis, Benjamin, and Marco Stampini. 2003. *Pathways towards Prosperity in Nicaragua: An Analysis of Panel Households in the 1998 and 2001 LSMS Surveys.* Washington, DC: World Bank.
Davis, Charles L., Roderic A. Camp, and Kenneth M. Coleman. 2004. "The Influence of Party Systems on Citizens' Perceptions of Corruption and Electoral Response in Latin America." *Comparative Political Studies* 37(6): 677–703.
Davis, Shelton. 2002. "Indigenous Peoples, Poverty and Participatory Development: The Experience of the World Bank in Latin America"' In *Multiculturalism in Latin America: Indigenous Rights, Diversity, and Democracy,* ed. Rachel Sieder. Houndsmills: Palgrave.
DEA-UNAN (Departamento de Economía Agrícola–Universidad Nacional Autónoma Nacional). 1990. *Cooperativas de producción en la región II: del acceso a la tierra hacia la eficiencia económica.* Managua: DEA-UNAN.
Deere, Carmen Diana, and Magdalena Leon. 2001. *Empowering Women: Land and Property Rights in Latin America.* Pittsburgh: University of Pittsburgh Press.
de Groot, Jan, and Ruerd Ruben (eds.). 1997. *Sustainable Agriculture in Central America.* New York: St. Martin´s.
Deininger, Klaus, and Hans Binswanger. 1999. "The Evolution of the World Bank's Land Policy: Principles, Experience, and Future Challenges." *World Bank Research Observer* 14(2): 247–276.
Deininger, Klaus, and Juan Sebastian Chamorro. 2002. *Investment and Income Effects of Land Regularization: The Case of Nicaragua.* Washington, DC: World Bank.
De Janvry, Alain. 1981. *The Agrarian Question and Reformism in Latin America.* Baltimore, MD: Johns Hopkins University Press.
Delgado, Nayra. 2001. "La lucha por la tierra." *La Prensa* (March 3, 2001).
Demmers, Jolle, Alex E. Fernández Jilberto, and Barbara Hogenboom (eds.). 2004a. *Good Governance in the Era of Global Neoliberalism: Conflict and Depolitisation in Latin America, Eastern Europe, Asia and Africa.* New York: Routledge.
———. 2004b. "Good Governance and Democracy in a World of Neoliberal Regimes." In *Good Governance in the Era of Global Neoliberalism: Conflict and Depolitisation in Latin America, Eastern Europe, Asia and Africa,* ed. Jolle Demmers, Alex E. Fernández Jilberto, and Barbara Hogenboom. New York: Routledge.
Deruyttere, Anne. 1997. *Indigenous Peoples and Sustainable Development: The Role of the Inter-American Development Bank.* Washington, DC: Inter-American Development Bank.
Donovan, Richard. 1994. "BOSCOSA: Forest Conservation and Management through Local Institutions (Costa Rica)." In *Natural Connections: Perspectives in Community-Based Conservation,* ed. David Western, R. Michael Wright, and Shirley C. Strum. Washington, DC: Island.
Dore, Elizabeth. 1997. "Capitalism and Ecological Crisis: Legacy of the 1980s." In *Green Guerrillas: Environmental Conflicts and Initiatives in Latin America and the Caribbean,* ed. Helen Collinson. Montreal: Black Rose Books.
Duffy, Rosaleen. 2002. *A Trip Too Far: Ecotourism, Politics, and Exploitation.* London: Earthscan.
Dunkerley, James. 1994. *The Pacification of Central America: Political Change in the Isthmus 1987–1993.* London: Verso.

Dwivedi, Ranjit. 2001. "Environmental Movements in the Global South: Issues of Livelihood and Beyond." *International Sociology* 16(1): 11–31.

ECLAC (Economic Commission for Latin America and the Caribbean). 2005. *Social Panorama of Latin America 2000–2001.* Available on the ECLAC Web site: http://www.eclac.cl/publicaciones/DesarrolloSocial/8/LCG2288PI/PSI2005_sintesis.pdf.

———. 2001. *Statistical Yearbook for Latin America and the Caribbean, 2001.* Available on the ECLAC Web site: http://www.eclac.cl/estadisticas/default.asp?idioma=IN.

Edelman, Marc. 1999. *Peasants against Globalization: Rural Social Movements in Costa Rica.* Stanford: Stanford University Press.

———. 1995. "Rethinking the Hamburger Thesis: Deforestation and the Crisis of Central America's Beef Exports." In *The Social Causes of Environmental Destruction in Latin America,* ed. Michael Painter and William H. Durham. Ann Arbor: University of Michigan Press.

———. 1991. "Shifting Legitimacies and Economic Change: The State and Contemporary Costa Rican Peasant Movements." *Peasant Studies* 18(4): 221–249.

Edwards, Michael, and David Hulme. 1996a. *Beyond the Magic Bullet: NGO Performance and Accountability in the Post–Cold War World.* West Hartford, CT: Kumarian.

———. 1996b. "Too Close for Comfort? The Impact of Official Aid on Nongovernmental Organizations." *World Development* 25(6): 961–973.

Elton, Charlotte. 1997. *Panamá: evaluación de la sostenibilidad nacional.* Panama City: CEASPA.

Enriquez, Laura J. 2000. "The Varying Impact of Structural Adjustment on Nicaragua's Small Farmers." *European Review of Latin American and Caribbean Studies* 69: 47–68.

———. 1991. *Harvesting Change: Labor and Agrarian Reform in Nicaragua, 1979–1990.* Chapel Hill: University of North Carolina Press.

Escobar, Arturo. 2000. "Beyond the Search for a Paradigm? Post-Development and Beyond." *Development* 43(4): 11–14.

———. 1995. *Encountering Development: The Making and Unmaking of the Third World.* Princeton: Princeton University Press.

Evans, Sterling. 1999. *The Green Republic: A Conservation History of Costa Rica.* Austin: University of Texas Press.

Everett, Margaret. 1997. "The Ghost in the Machine: Agency in 'Poststructural' Critiques of Development." *Anthropological Quarterly* 70(3): 137–151.

Everingham, Mark. 2001. "Agricultural Property Rights and Political Change in Nicaragua." *Latin American Politics and Society* 43(3): 61–93.

Faber, Daniel J. 1993. *Environment under Fire: Imperialism and the Ecological Crisis in Central America.* New York: Monthly Review.

———. 1992a. "The Ecological Crisis of Latin America: A Theoretical Introduction." *Latin American Perspectives* 19(1): 3–16.

———. 1992b. "Imperialism, Revolution, and the Ecological Crisis of Central America." *Latin American Perspectives* 19(1): 17–44.

FACS and CEPAD (Augusto C. Sandino Foundation and Council of Evangelical Churches for a Denominational Alliance). 1993. *Estudio sobre experiencias de los ONGs en proyectos de medio ambiente y desarrollo.* Managua: Impresiones y Troqueles SA.

FAO (Food and Agriculture Organization). 2003. *State of Forestry in the Latin American and Caribbean Region*. Santiago: FAO.

Farrington, John. 1993. *Reluctant Partners? Non-governmental Organizations, the State, and Sustainable Agricultural Development*. New York: Routledge.

Fennell, David A. 1999. *Ecotourism: An Introduction*. New York: Routledge.

Ferguson, James. 1990. *The Anti-politics Machine: "Development," Depoliticization, and Bureaucratic Power in Lesotho*. Cambridge, MA: Cambridge University Press.

Fernández Morillo, María Teresa. 2002a. "Dinámica de uso y tenecia de la tierra en la zona marítimo terrestre de dos áreas del Pacífico de Costa Rica." In *Turismo de larga distancia y desarrollo regional en Costa Rica*, ed. Edgar Furst and Wolfgang Hein. San José, Costa Rica: Asociación Ecuménico de Investigaciones.

———. 2002b. "Cambios en el uso y cobertura del paisaje micro-regional en relación a la actividad turística." In *Turismo de larga distancia y desarrollo regional en Costa Rica*, ed. Edgar Furst and Wolfgang Hein. San José, Costa Rica: Asociación Ecuménico de Investigaciones.

Fernández Quisbert, Edgar. 1997. "Reforma agraria y reversión de las grandes extensiones ganaderas de zonas bajas. Referencia sobre las condiciones de evolución, y limitantes de los sistemas de producción campesinos." Simposium del Estudio de Mercado de Tierras Rurales de Nicaragua (Managua, Nicaragua).

Fisher, William H. 1994. "Megadevelopment, Environmentalism, and Resistance: The Institutional Context of Kayapó Indigenous Politics in Central Brazil." *Human Organization* 53(3): 220–231.

Flores Coca, Julio, and Yuri Marín López. 1997. *Diagnóstico de la situación técnica, económica y adminstrativa de dos cooperativas camaroneros, Puerto Morazán, Chinandega*. Managua: Nitlapán.

Fox, Jonathan A., and L. David Brown. 1998. "Introduction." In *The Struggle for Accountability: The World Bank, NGOs, and Grassroots Movements*, ed. Jonathan A. Fox and L. David Brown. Boston: MIT Press.

Friedmann, John, and Haripriya Rangan (eds.). 1993. *In Defense of Livelihood: Comparative Studies in Environmental Action*. West Hartford, CT: Kumarian.

Fundación Arias. 1997a. *Una experiencia de incidencia para reformar la ley forestal: un caso de incidencia*. San José, Costa Rica: Fundación Arias, FECON.

———. 1997b. *Diagnóstico sobre la incidencia en Centroamérica*. San José, Costa Rica: Fundación Arias.

———. 1993. *Cooperación, solidaridad y filantropía en Centroamérica: viejos y nuevos significados en Centroamérica*. San José, Costa Rica: Fundación Arias.

Fundación Neotrópica. 1991. *OSA 2000: Una estrategia para la conservación biológica y el desarrollo sostenible en la Península de Osa de Costa Rica*. Unpublished report.

Furst, Edgar, and Wolfgang Hein (eds.). 2002a. *Turismo de larga distancia y desarrollo regional en Costa Rica*. San José, Costa Rica: Asociación Ecuménico de Investigaciones.

———. 2002b. "Potenciales y contradicciones del turismo en Costa Rica: un balance crítico de las implicaciones globales, nacionales, regionales y locales para el desarrollo sostenible." In *Turismo de larga distancia y desarrollo regional en Costa Rica*, ed. Edgar Furst and Wolfgang Hein. San José, Costa Rica: Asociación Ecuménico de Investigaciones.

Gaceta Oficial. 1996. *Decree Creating the Comarca of Madungandí*. December 8, 1996, Panama City.

Gale, Richard P., and Sheila M. Codray. 1994. "Making Sense of Sustainability: Nine Answers to 'What Should Be Sustained?'" *Rural Sociology* 59(2): 311–332.
García, Manuel. 1988. "Apuntes geohistóricos de la colonización agrícola en la Península de Osa (Costa Rica)." *Geoistmo* 2(1): 27–40.
Ghai, Dharam P., and Jessica M. Vivian (eds.). 1992. *Grassroots Environmental Action: People's Participation in Sustainable Development*. New York: Routledge.
Gibson, Bill. 1996. "The Environmental Consequences of Stagnation in Nicaragua." *World Development* 24(2): 325–339.
Giddens, Anthony. 2000. *Runaway World: How Globalization Is Shaping Our Lives*. New York: Routledge.
Girot, Pascal O. 1998. *El uso sostenible de recursos naturales vivientes en Centroamérica: hacia una síntesis*. Guatemala City: SUICA.
Gjording, Chris N. 1991. *Conditions Not of Their Choosing: The Guaymí Indians and Mining Multinationals in Panama*. Washington, DC: Smithsonian Institution Press.
Goldin, Liliana R. 1996. "Economic Mobility Strategies among Guatemalan Peasants: Prospects and Limits of Nontraditional Vegetable Cash Crops." *Human Organization* 55(1): 99–107.
Goldman, Michael. 2005. *Imperial Nature: The World Bank and Struggles for Social Justice in the Age of Globalization*. New Haven: Yale University Press.
———. 2001. "Constructing an Environmental State: Eco-governmentality and Other Transnational Practices of a 'Green' World Bank." *Social Problems* 48(4): 499–523.
——— (ed.). 1998a. *Privatizing Nature: Political Struggles for the Global Commons*. London: Pluto.
———. 1998b. "Introduction: The Political Resurgence of the Commons." In *Privatizing Nature: Political Struggles for the Global Commons*, ed. Michael Goldman. London: Pluto.
———. 1998c. "Inventing the Commons: Theories and Practices of the Commons' Professional." In *Privatizing Nature: Political Struggles for the Global Commons*, ed. Michael Goldman. London: Pluto.
González, Hector. 2002. "Cecropia Foundation." In *Sol de Osa*, December 2002 edition. Available on the *Sol de Osa* Web site: http://soldeosa.com/SOLDEOSA/ed7/cecropia.htm.
González Giraud, Carmen Rocío. 1992. *Impacto ambiental de la explotación de oro artesenal, Península de Osa, Costa Rica*. B.A. thesis, University of Costa Rica.
González Pinilla, José. 2005. "Families campesinas de Loma Bonita." *La Prensa* (April 22, 2005).
Goodman, David, and Michael Redclift (eds.). 1991a. *Environment and Development in Latin America: The Politics of Sustainability*. New York: St. Martin's.
———. 1991b. "Introduction." In *Environment and Development in Latin America: The Politics of Sustainability*, ed. David Goodman and Michael Redclift. New York: St. Martin's.
Gould, Jeffrey L. 1990. *To Lead as Equals: Rural Protest and Political Consciousness in Chinandega, Nicaragua, 1912–1979*. Chapel Hill: University of North Carolina Press.
Guatemalan Commission for Historical Clarification. 1999. *Guatemala: Memory of Silence*. Available on the American Association for the Advancement of Science Web site: http://shr.aaas.org/guatemala/ceh/report/english/toc.html.

Guha, Ramachandra, and Juan Martínez-Alier. 1998. *Varieties of Environmentalism: Essays North and South.* London: Earthscan.

Guzmán, Armando, Martín Raine, and Arsenio Rodríguez. 2003. "The Mesoamerican Biological Corridor: Multilateral Efforts to Promote Sustainable Development." *En Breve* 27: 1–4.

Gwynne, Robert N. 1997. "Globalization, Neoliberalism and Economic Change in South America and Mexico." In *Latin America Transformed: Globalization and Modernity*, ed. Robert N. Gwynne and Cristóbal Kay. New York: Oxford University Press.

Hagopian, Frances, and Scott P. Mainwaring (eds.). 2005. *The Third Wave of Democratization in Latin America: Advances and Setbacks.* New York: Cambridge University Press.

Hale, Charles R. 2002. "Does Multiculturalism Menace? Governance, Cultural Rights and the Politics of Identity in Guatemala." *Journal of Latin American Studies* 34: 485–524.

Hall, Colin Michael. 1994. *Tourism and Politics: Policy, Power and Place.* Chichester: John Wiley & Sons.

Harding, Robert C., II. 2001. *Military Foundations of Panamanian Politics.* New Brunswick, NJ: Transaction.

Hartwick, Elaine, and Richard Peet. 2003. "Neoliberalism and Nature: The Case of the WTO." *Annals AAPSS* 590(1): 118–211.

Hatch, L. Upton, and Marilyn Swisher. 1999. *Managed Ecosystems: The Mesoamerican Experience.* New York: Oxford University Press.

Heckadon Moreno, Stanley. 1982. "La colonización campesina de bosques tropicales en Panamá." In *Colonización y destrucción de bosques en Panamá,* ed. Stanley Heckadon Moreno and Alberto McKay. Panama City: Asociación Panameña de Antropología.

Heckadon Moreno, Stanley, and Albert McKay (eds.). 1982. *Colonización y destrucción de bosques en Panamá.* Panama City: Asociación Panameña de Antropología.

Held, David, and Anthony McGrew. 2003. *The Global Transformations Reader: An Introduction to the Globalization Debate.* Cambridge: Polity.

Herlihy, Peter. 1988. "Panamá's Quiet Revolution: Comarca Homelands and Indian Rights." *Cultural Survival Quarterly* 13(3): 17–24.

Herrera, Francisco. 2002. *Componente indígena del proyecto Corredor Biológico Panamá. Informe Final.* Panama City, unpublished report.

———. 1998. "Los indígenas, la sociedad civil, el ambientalismo y la justicia social." Paper presented at the Latin American Studies Association Twenty-First International Congress (Chicago, Illinois, September 1998).

———. 1972. "Politización de la población indígena en Panamá." In *Actas del II Simposium Nacional de Antropología, Arqueología y Etnohistoria de Panamá, abril de 1971.* Panama City: Impr. Universitaria.

Hickey, Samuel, and Giles Mohan (eds.). 2004a. *Participation: From Tyranny to Transformation: Exploring New Approaches to Participation in Development.* London: Zed Books.

———. 2004b. "Towards Participation as Transformation: Critical Themes and Challenges." In *Participation: From Tyranny to Transformation: Exploring New Approaches to Participation in Development,* ed. Samuel Hickey and Giles Mohan. London: Zed Books.

Hildyard, Nicholas. 1993. "Foxes in Charge of the Chickens." In *Global Ecology: A New Arena of Political Conflict*, ed. Wolfgang Sachs. London: Zed Books.
Honey, Martha. 1999. *Ecotourism and Sustainable Development: Who Owns Paradise?* Washington, DC: Island.
Horton, Lynn. 1999. *Peasants in Arms: War and Peace in the Mountains of Nicaragua, 1979–1994*. Athens: Ohio University Press.
Howe, James L. 2002. "The Kuna of Panama: Continuing Threats to Land and Autonomy." In *The Politics of Ethnicity: Indigenous Peoples in Latin American States*, ed. David Maybury-Lewis. Cambridge, MA: Harvard University Press.
———. 1998. *A People Who Would Not Kneel: Panama, the United States, and the San Blas Kuna*. Washington, DC: Smithsonian Institution Press.
———. 1986. *The Kuna Gathering: Contemporary Village Politics in Panama*. Austin: University of Texas Press.
Huertas, Hector. 1999. *Diagnóstico de la situación legal de las tierras de las comunidades indígenas de Alto Bayano. II parte*. Panama City: Programa de Desarrollo Sostenible de Darién.
IDR and CATIE (Instituto de Desarrollo Rural and Centro Agronómico Tropical de Investigación Enseñanza). 1999. *Estrategia para el desarrollo y la conservación del Estero Real, Nicaragua*. Serie técnica, Informe Técnica No. 312. Turrialba, Costa Rica: CATIE.
INEC (Instituto Nacional de Estadísticas y Censos). 2004. *III CENAGRO Chinandega*. Available on the INEC Web site: www.inec.gob.ni/cenagro/perfiles/30%20Chinandega.pdf.
———. 2000. *IX censo nacional de población y V de vivienda*. Available on the INEC Web site: http://www.inec.go.cr/.
Inman, Crist. 2002. *Tourism in Costa Rica: The Challenge of Competitiveness*. Working paper INCAE. Available at http://www.incae.ac.cr/ES/clacds/investigacion/pdf/cen653.pdf.
IRHE (Instituto de Recursos Hidráulicos y Electrificación). 1978. *Lago Bayano formación, manejo y control. Mesa redonda organizada por el IRHE*. Panama City: IRHE.
ITCO (Instituto de Tierras y Colonización). 1975. *Estudio de tenencia de la tierra, censo de ocupantes y actos de explotación de la Osa Productos Forestales en los lotes 10–11–12 y según plano aportado por dicha compañía*. Unpublished document.
Jackson, Cecile. 1994. "Gender Analysis and Environmentalisms." In *Social Theory and the Global Environment*, ed. Michael Redclift and Ted Benton. London: Routledge.
Jacobs, Michael. 1994. "The Limits to Neoclassicism: Towards an Institutional Environmental Economics." In *Social Theory and the Global Environment*, ed. Michael Redclift and Ted Benton. London: Routledge.
Jansen, Kees. 1998. *Political Ecology, Mountain Agriculture, and Knowledge in Honduras*. Amsterdam: Thela.
Jiménez Molina, Iván. 2002. *Costarricense por dicha: identidad nacional y cambio cultural en Costa Rica durante los siglos XIX y XX*. San José, Costa Rica: Editorial de la Universidad de Costa Rica.
Johnston, Barbara Rose (ed.). 1997. *Life and Death Matters: Human Rights and the Environment at the End of the Millennium*. Walnut Creek, CA: Altamira.

Joly, Luz Graciela. 1982. "La migración de los interioranos hacia la Costa Abajo." In *Colonización y destrucción de bosques en Panamá*, ed. Stanley Heckadon Moreno and Alberto McKay. Panama City: Asociación Panameña de Antropología.

Jonakin, Jon. 1996. "The Impact of Structural Adjustment and Property Rights Conflicts on Nicaraguan Agrarian Reform Beneficiaries." *World Development* 24(7): 1179–1191.

Kaimowitz, David. 1997. "Policies Affecting Deforestation for Cattle in Central America." In *Sustainable Agriculture in Central America*, ed. Jan de Groot and Ruerd Ruben. New York: St. Martin's.

———. 1988. "Nicaragua's Experience with Agricultural Planning: From State-Centered Accumulation to Strategic Alliance with the Peasantry." *Journal of Development Studies* 24(4): 115–135.

Kampwirth, Karen. 2004. "Alemán's War on the NGO Community." In *Undoing Democracy: The Politics of Electoral Caudillismo*, ed. David Close and Kalowatie Deonandan. Lanham, MD: Lexington Books.

Kane, Stephanie C. 1994. *The Phantom Gringo Boat: Shamanic Discourse and Development in Panama*. Washington, DC: Smithsonian Institution Press.

Keck, Margaret E., and Kathryn Sikkink. 1998. *Activists beyond Borders: Advocacy Networks in International Politics*. Ithaca, NY: Cornell University Press.

Knut, Walter. 1993. *The Regime of Anastacio Somoza, 1936–1956*. Chapel Hill: University of North Carolina Press.

Knutson, Julie. 2001. "Environmental Regimes in Nicaragua: Moving beyond Sandinista vs Somoza." *International Journal of Politics and Ethics* 1(4): 263–280.

Kolk, Ans. 1999. "Environmental Management and Organisational Change: The Impact of the World Bank." In *Growing Pains: Environmental Management in Developing Countries*, ed. Walter Wehrmeyer and Yacob Mulugetta. Sheffield: Greenleaf.

Korten, David C. 1990. *Getting to the 21st Century: Voluntary Action and the Global Agenda*. West Hartford, CT: Kumarian.

LaFeber, Walter. 1993. *Inevitable Revolutions: The United States in Central America*, 2nd ed. New York: W. W. Norton.

Lapa Rios. 2002. *Eco-Tourism and Lapa Rios: Goals and Action*. Available on the Lapa Rios Web site: http://www.laparios.com.

Lauria-Santiago, Aldo, and Leigh Binford (eds.). 2004. *Landscapes of Struggle: Politics, Society, and Community in El Salvador*. Pittsburgh: University of Pittsburgh Press

Leininger Mehroff, Allen, and José Vindas Carballo. 1988. *Diagnóstico y evaluación del potencial turístico y su impacto en el medio físico y humano del cantón del Golfito*. Heredia: Universidad Nacional.

LeoGrande, William M. 1998. *Our Own Backyard: The United States in Central America, 1977–1992*. Chapel Hill: University of North Carolina Press.

Leonard, H. Jeffrey. 1987. *Natural Resources and Economic Development in Central America: A Regional Environmental Profile*. New Brunswick, NJ: Transaction.

Lera St. Clair, Asunción. 2006. "The World Bank as a Transnational Expertised Institution." *Global Governance* 12: 77–95.

Lewin, Elizabeth, Karla Ceciliano P., Raúl Solorzano S., and José Daniel Cazanga S. 1993. *Evaluación Independiente del Programa Manejo Sostenible de Recursos Natura-*

les en Costa Rica. Una Inciativa Piloto. San José, Costa Rica: Ministerio de Recursos Naturales, Energia, y Minas and ASDI Suecia.

Lewis, Barbara E. 1983. "Reseña histórica de la población y los recursos naturales de la Península de Osa, Pácifico Sur, 1848–1981." *Revista Geográfica de América Central* 17–18: 123–130.

Loker, William M. 1999. "Grit in the Prosperity Machine: Globalization and the Rural Poor in Latin America." In *Globalization and the Rural Poor in Latin America*, ed. William M. Loker. Boulder: Lynne Rienner.

Long, Carolyn. 2001. *Participation of the Poor in Development Initiatives: Taking Their Rightful Places*. London: Earthscan.

Long, Norman. 2000. "Exploring Local/Global Transformations." In *Anthropology, Development, and Modernities: Exploring Discourses, Counter-tendencies, and Violence*, ed. Alberto Arce and Norman Long. London: Routledge.

Louis Berger Group, Inc. 2000. *Estudio de impacto ambiental. Categoria III. Proyecto: Carretera Panamericana tramos Bayano-Tortí y Tortí-Agua Fría No. 1*. Unpublished report.

Luciak, Ilja. 2001. *After the Revolution: Gender and Democracy in El Salvador, Nicaragua, and Guatemala*. Baltimore: Johns Hopkins University Press.

———. 1995. *The Sandinista Legacy: Lessons from a Political Economy in Transition*. Gainesville: University Press of Florida.

Lustig, Nora (ed.). 1995. *Coping with Austerity: Poverty and Inequality in Latin America*. Washington, DC: Brookings Institution.

MAG-FOR (Ministerio Agropecuario y Forestal). 1999. *Regionalización biofísica para el desarrollo agropecuario. Resumen ejecutivo Chinandega*. Managua: MAG-FOR.

Maldidier, Cristobal. 1996. *Frontera agrícola en Nicaragua*. Managua: Escuela de Economía Agrícola, Universidad Nacional Autónoma de Nicaragua.

Maldonado Ulloa, Tirso. 1997. *Uso de la tierra y fragmentación de bosques. Algunas áreas críticas en el área de conservación Osa, Costa Rica*. San José, Costa Rica: Fundación Neotrópica.

MARENA (Ministerio de Ambiente y Recursos Naturales). 1999. *Biodiversidad en Nicaragua: un estudio de país*. Managua: MARENA.

Martinez Mauri, Mònica. 2003. *Médiation et développement: l'emergence des ONG et des passeurs culturels à Kuna Yala (Panamá)*. Geneva: Institut Universitaire d'Études du Développment.

Matus L., Javier. 1994. *Monitoreo al mercado de tierras síntesis departamento de Rivas*. Managua: CCE.

McAdam, Doug. 1996. "Conceptual Origins, Current Problems, Future Directions." In *Comparative Perspectives on Social Movements: Political Opportunities, Mobilizing Structures, and Cultural Framings*, ed. Doug McAdam, John D. McCarthy, and Mayner N. Zald. New York: Cambridge University Press.

McMichael, Philip. 2000. *Development and Social Change: A Global Perspective*, 2nd ed. Thousand Oaks, CA: Pine Forge.

Mendoza, Oscar. n.d. "La lucha del pueblo Ngobe Buglé por la expansión, la implementación de la ley que establece la comarca Ngobe Buglé." From the proceedings of the *Taller Indígena sobre áreas protegidas y medio ambiente. Conservación, uso y manejo de recursos naturales*. Panama City.

Mendoza V., René. 1999. *Municipio de León: dilemas en la gestión del bosque seco y del área manglar*. Managua: Nitlapán UCA, CIFOR.

Merlet, Michel, and Denis Pommier. 2000. *Estudios sobre la tenencia de la tierra.* Managua: Institut de Recherches et d'Aplication de Méthodes de Développment.
Merry, Anelio (ed.). 1998. *Memoria: Taller de consulta sobre la situación ambiental en Kuna Yala.* Panama City: Congreso General de Kuna Yala, IDIKY, and Autoridad Nacional del Ambiente.
Meyer, Carrie A. 1999. *The Economics and Politics of NGOs in Latin America.* Westport, CT: Praeger.
MICE (Ministerio de la Cooperación Externa). 1996a. *Memoria de la cooperación externa 1990–1995.* Unpublished report.
———. 1996b. *Nicaragua: cooperación externa 1990–1995.* Unpublished report.
MIDA and INRENARE (Ministerio de Desarrollo Agropecuario and Instituto Nacional de Recursos Naturales Renovables). 1979. *Plan de acción inmediata para el manejo y conservación de la cuenca hidrográfica del Río Bayano.* Panama City: MIDA and INRENARE.
Middleton, Neil, and Phil O'Keefe. 2003. *Rio Plus Ten: Politics, Poverty and the Environment.* London: Pluto.
MIDEPLAN (Ministerio de Planificación Nacional y Política Ecónomica). 2003. *Plan Regional de Desarrollo 2003–2006 Región Brunca.* Available at http://www.mideplan.go.cr/cedop/2003/Plan_Regional_Brunca.pdf.
MIDINRA (Ministerio de Desarrollo Agrario y Reforma Agraria). 1980. *Diagnóstico soci-económico del sector agropecuario Chinandega.* Managua: CIERA.
Mies, Maria, and Vandana Shiva. 1993. *Ecofeminism.* London: Zed Books.
Minca, Claudio, and Marco Linda. 2000. "Ecotourism on the Edge: The Case of Corcovado National Park, Costa Rica." In *Forest Tourism and Recreation: Case Studies in Environmental Management,* ed. Xavier Font and John Tribe. Oxford: Oxford University Press.
MINAE and SINAC (Ministerio del Ambiente y Energía and Sistema Nacional de Areas de Conservación Area de Conservación Osa).
———. n.d. *Características Generales: Area de Conservación Osa, Zona Sur, Costa Rica.* Unpublished document.
Mittelman, James H. 2000. *The Globalization Syndrome: Transformation and Resistance.* Princeton: Princeton University Press.
Moeller, Eric J. 1997. *Identity and Millenarian Discourse: Kuna Indian Villages in an Ethnic Border Land.* PhD. dissertation, University of Chicago.
Moffatt, Ian. 1996. *Sustainable Development: Principles, Analysis, and Policies.* London: Parthenon.
Molina, Urania Cecilia. 2004. "Obstaculizan control de la malaria." *La Prensa* (June 2, 2004).
Moore, David B., and Gerald J. Schmitz (eds.). 1995. *Debating Development Discourse: Institutional and Popular Perspectives.* New York: St. Martin's.
Morales, José Tomás, Walter Aburto, and Arturo Aburto. 1999. *Diagnóstico municipal Puerto Morazán.* Managua: Alcaldía Muncipal, Plan Internacional, CODECOPMO.
Mosse, David. 2004. "Is Good Policy Unimplementable? Reflections on the Ethnography of Aid Policy and Practice." *Development and Change* 35(4): 639–671.
Mowforth, Martin, and Ian Munt. 2003. *Tourism and Sustainability: New Tourism in the Third World,* 2nd ed. London: Routledge.
Murray, Douglas L. 1994. *Cultivating Crisis: The Human Cost of Pesticides in Latin America.* Austin: University of Texas Press.

Myers, Norman. 1981. "The Hamburger Connection: How Central America's Forests become North America's Hamburgers." *Ambio* 10(1): 3–8.

Narayan, Deepa (ed.). 2005. *Measuring Empowerment: Cross-Disciplinary Perspectives*. Washington, DC: World Bank.

Nations, James D., and Daniel Komer. 1987. "Rainforests and the Hamburger Society." *The Ecologist* 17(4-5): 161–167.

Nederveen Pieterse, Jan. 2000. "After Post-Development." *Third World Quarterly* 21(2): 175–191.

———. 1998. "My Paradigm or Yours? Alternative Development, Post-Development, Reflexive Development." *Development and Change* 29(2): 343–373.

Nitlapán. 1990. *El doble rostro de la agroexportación: burguesía y campesinado en el occidente*. Managua: Nitlapán.

Núñez, Ubaldo. 1999. *Estudio de mercado y alternativas económicas*. Unpublished manuscript.

Núñez Soto, Orlando (ed.). 1991. *La Guerra en Nicaragua*. Managua: CIPRES.

Nustad, Knut G. 2001. "Development: The Devil We Know?" *Third World Quarterly* 22(4): 479–489.

Nygren, Anja. 2000. "Development Discourses and Peasant-Forest Relations: Natural Resource Utilization as Social Process." *Development and Change* 31: 11–24.

Olivas, Roger. 2006a. "Tranques en Chinandega: Protestan porque no les permiten más mangle." *El Nuevo Diaro* (May 28, 2006).

———. 2006b. "Policía desaloja a los que viven del mangle." *El Nuevo Diaro* (May 29, 2006).

Onis, Ziya, and Fikret Senses. 2005. "Rethinking the Emerging Post-Washington Consensus." *Development and Change* 36(2): 263–290.

Paige, Jeffery. 1997. *Coffee and Power: Revolution and the Rise of Democracy in Central America*. Cambridge, MA: Harvard University Press.

Painter, Michael, and William H. Durham (eds.). 1995. *The Social Causes of Environmental Destruction in Latin America*. Ann Arbor: University of Michigan Press.

Paniagua, Claudia, and Benicia Aguilar. 1996. *Diagnóstico socioeconómico del Estero Real*. Managua: Danish International Development Agency–Manglares.

PDR (Programa de Desarrollo Rural, Península de Osa). 1995. *Diagnóstico participativo de la Península de Osa*. San José, Costa Rica: Presidencia de la República, Ministerio de Agricultura y Ganadería and Instituto de Desarrollo Agrario.

Pearce, David W. 1989. *Blueprint for a Green Economy: A Report*. London: Earthscan.

Peet, Richard, and Michael Watts (eds.). 1996a. *Liberation Ecologies: Environment, Development, Social Movements*. London: Routledge.

———. 1996b. "Liberation Ecology: Development, Sustainability, and Environment in an Age of Market Triumphalism." In *Liberation Ecologies: Environment, Development, Social Movements*, ed. Richard Peet and Michael Watts. London: Routledge.

Perez, Orlando J. (ed.). 2000. *Post-invasion Panama: The Challenges of Democratization in the New World*. Lanham, MD: Lexington Books.

Plant, Roger, and Soren Hvalkof. 2001. *Land Titling and Indigenous Peoples*. Washington, DC: Inter-American Development Bank.

Potlatch. 1998a. *Dinámica Socio-demográfica y Tenencia de la Tierra*. Panama City: Programa de Desarrollo Sostenible del Darién.

———. 1998b. *Informe 3: Resumen de Talleres de Consulta (19–34) y Propuesta de Ordenamiento Territorial*. Panama City: Programa de Desarrollo Sostenible del Darién.
Pretty, Jules N., and Robert Chambers. 2000. "Toward a Learning Paradigm." In *Rethinking Sustainability: Power, Knowledge, and Institutions*, ed. Jonathan M. Harris. Ann Arbor: University of Michigan Press.
Priestley, George. 1986. *Military Government and Popular Participation in Panama: The Torrijos Regime, 1968–75*. Boulder: Westview.
PROGOLFO (Proyecto Golfo Fonseca). n.d. "PROGOLFO Estero Real report." Available at the CCAD Web site: http://www.ccad.ws/documentos/proyectos/progolfo/nicaragua/tecnico/ITproblematica.pdf.
Proyecto Estado de la Nación. 2003. *Estado de la región en desarrollo sostenible*. San José, Costa Rica: Proyecto Estado de la Nación.
Quintero de León, José. 2005. "Indígenas se sentarán a negociar." *La Prensa* (October 12, 2005).
———. 1996. "Indígenas enardecidos hieren a cinco policías." *La Prensa* (August 6, 1996).
———. 1993. "Indígenas toman rehenes." *La Prensa* (April 29, 1993).
Rahnema, Majid, and Victoria Bawtree (eds.). 1997. *The Post-development Reader*. London: Zed Books.
Ramírez Avendaño, Victoria, and Juan Rafael Quesada Camacho. 1990. *Evolución histórica de los cantones: Osa, Golfito, Corredores y Coto Brus*. San José, Costa Rica: Ministerio de Cultura, Juventud y Deportes.
Raventos, Ciska. 1997. "De la imposición de los organismos internacionales al 'ajuste a la tica': nacionalización de las políticas de ajuste en Costa Rica en la década de los años ochenta." *Ciencias Sociales* 76 (June):115–126.
Redclift, Michael. 1987. *Sustainable Development: Exploring the Contradictions*. London: Methuen.
Redclift, Michael, and Graham Woodgate. 1994. "Sociology and the Environment: Discordant Discourse?" In *Social Theory and the Global Environment*, ed. Michael Redclift and Ted Benton. London: Routledge.
Reed, David (ed.). 1996. *Structural Adjustment, the Environment, and Sustainable Development*. London: Earthscan.
Reilly, Charles A. 1992. "Who Should Manage Environmental Problems? Some Lessons from Latin America." In *Grassroots Environmental Action: People's Participation in Sustainable Development*, ed. Dharam Ghai and Jessica M. Vivian. New York: Routledge.
Reverte, José Manuel. 1961. *Río Bayano: un ensayo geográfico e histórico sobre la región de mañana*. Panama City: Imprenta Nacional.
Reyes, Yasmina. 1994. "Indígenas desalojarán a colonos de Bayano." *La Prensa* (January 17, 1994).
Roberts, Kenneth M., and Moises Arce. 1998. "Neoliberalism and Lower-Class Voting Behavior in Peru." *Comparative Political Studies* 31(2): 217–246.
Robinson, William I. 2003. *Transnational Conflicts: Central America, Social Change, and Globalization*. New York: Verso.
Robinson, William I., and Kent Norsworthy. 1987. *David and Goliath: The U.S. War against Nicaragua*. New York: Monthly Review.
Rocha, José Luís, and Tupac Barahona. 1999. *Puerto Morazán: la camaronicultura: una espejismo en tierra salada?* Managua: Nitlapán-UCA-CIFOR-Pro-tierra-INIFOR.

Rocheleau, Dianne, Barbara Thomas-Slayter, and Esther Wangari (eds.). 1996a. *Feminist Political Ecology: Global Issues and Local Experiences.* New York: Routledge.

———. 1996b. "Gender and Environment: A Feminist Political Ecology Perspective." In *Feminist Political Ecology: Global Issues and Local Experiences,* ed. Dianne Rocheleau, Barbara Thomas-Slayter, and Esther Wangari. New York: Routledge.

Rodríguez, Florisabel, Silvia Castro Méndez, and Rowland Espinosa (eds.). 1998. *El sentir democrático: estudios sobre la cultura política Centroamericana.* Heredia, Costa Rica: Editorial Fundación UNA.

Roldan Ortega, Roque. 1998. *Regimén legal general y territorial de las comunidades indígenas en Panamá.* Panama City: Unidad Regional de Asistencia Técnica, Unidad Ténico Nacional Panamá, and Proyecto Corredor Biológico del Atlántico.

Román, Isabel. 1994. "Costa Rica: los campesinos también quieren futuro." In *Alternativas campesinas: modernización en el agro y movimientos campesinos en Centroamérica,* ed. Klaus D. Tangermann and Ivana Ríos Valdés. Managua: Latino Editores.

Ropp, Steve C. 2000. "Panama: Militarism and Imposed Transition." In *Repression, Resistance, and Democratic Transition in Central America,* ed. Thomas W. Walker and Ariel Armony. Wilmington, DE: Scholarly Resources.

———. 1982. *Panamanian Politics: From Guarded Nation to National Guard.* New York: Praeger.

Rosero-Bixby, Luís, Tirso Maldonado-Ulloa, and Roger Bonilla-Carrión. 2002. "Bosque y Población en la Península de Osa, Costa Rica." *Revista de Biología Tropical* 50(2): 585–598.

Rowlands, Jo. 1997. *Questioning Empowerment: Working with Women in Honduras.* London: Oxfam.

———. 1995. "Empowerment Examined." *Development in Practice* 5(2): 101–107.

Ruben, Ruerd. 2001. "Economic Policy and the Environment: Structural Adjustment and Prospects for Sustainable Natural Resource Management in Central America." In *Toward Sustainable Development in Central America and the Caribbean,* ed. Anders Danielson and A. Geske Dijkstra. New York: Palgrave.

Ruben, Ruerd, and John Bastiaensen (eds.). 2000. *Rural Development in Central America: Markets, Livelihoods, and Local Governance.* New York: St. Martin's.

Ruíz, Keynor. 2002. "Mercado de trabajo y desarrollo social en las zonas de estudio: los casos de Tarmarindo y Puerto Jiménez." In *Turismo de larga distancia y desarrollo regional en Costa Rica,* ed. Edgar Furst and Wolfgang Hein. San José, Costa Rica: Asociación Ecuménico de Investigaciones.

Sachs, Wolfgang. 1999. *Planet Dialectics: Explorations in Environment and Development.* London: Zed Books.

——— (ed.). 1993. *Global Ecology: A New Arena of Political Conflict.* London: Zed Books.

Salazar, Roxanna. 2000. *Acciones contra la corrupción.* Available on the Transparencia International Costa Rica Web site: http://transparenciacr.org/publicaciones.php.

Sandoval García, Carlos. 2004. *Threatening Others: Nicaraguans and the Formation of National Identities in Costa Rica.* Athens: Ohio University Press.

Scheyvens, Regina. 1999. "Ecotourism and the Empowerment of Local Communities." *Tourism Management* 20(2): 245–249.
Schmitz, Gerald J. 1995. "Democratization and Demystification: Deconstructing 'Governance' as Development Paradigm." In *Debating Development Discourse: Institutional and Popular Perspectives*, ed. David B. Moore and Gerald J. Schmitz. New York: St. Martin's.
Scholte, Jan Aart. 2005. *Globalization: A Critical Introduction*. New York: Palgrave Macmillan.
Schurman, Frans J. 1993. *Beyond the Impasse: New Directions in Development Theory*. London: Zed Books.
Seligson, Mitchell A. 2002. "The Impact of Corruption on Regime Legitimacy: A Comparative Study of Four Latin American Countries." *Journal of Politics* 64(2): 408–433.
———. 2001. "Trouble in Paradise: The Erosion of System Support in Costa Rica, 1978–1999." *Latin American Research Review* 37(1): 160–185.
Seligson, Mitchell A., and John A. Booth (eds.). 1995. *Elections and Democracy in Central America, Revisited*. Chapel Hill: University of North Carolina Press.
Serra, Luis H. 1993. "Democracy in Times of War and Socialist Crisis: Reflections Stemming from the Sandinista Revolution." *Latin American Perspectives* 20(2): 21–44.
Sherzer, Joel. 1994. "The Kuna and Columbus: Encounters and Confrontations of Discourse." *American Anthropologist* 96(4): 902–924.
Simmons, Cynthia S. 1997. "Forest Management Practices in the Bayano Region of Panama: Cultural Variations." *World Development* 25(6): 989–1000.
Sindzingre, Alice. 2004. "The Evolution of the Concept of Poverty in Multilateral Financial Institutions: The Case of the World Bank." In *Global Institutions and Development: Framing the World?*, ed. Morten Boas and Desmond McNeill. New York: Routledge.
Sklar, Holly. 1988. *Washington's War on Nicaragua*. Boston: South End.
Steinberg, Paul F. 2001. *Environmental Leadership in Developing Countries: Transnational Relations and Biodiversity Policy in Costa Rica and Bolivia*. Cambridge, MA: MIT Press.
Stem, Caroline Jeanine. 2001. *The Role of Local Development in Protected Area Management: A Comparative Case Study of Eco-tourism in Costa Rica*. PhD dissertation, Cornell University.
Stiles, Kendall W. 2000. "Conclusion—Is There a Need for a New Theory?" In *Global Institutions and Local Empowerment: Competing Theoretical Perspectives*, ed. Kendall W. Stiles. New York: St. Martin's.
Stokes, Susan C. 2001. *Mandates and Democracies: Neoliberalism by Surprise in Latin America*. New York: Cambridge University Press.
Stonich, Susan C. 2000. *The Other Side of Paradise: Tourism, Conservation, and Development in the Bay Islands*. New York: Cognizant Communications.
———. 1998. "Political Ecology of Tourism." *Annals of Tourism Research* 25(1): 25–54.
———. 1993. *I Am Destroying the Land!: The Political Ecology of Poverty and Environmental Destruction in Honduras*. Boulder: Westview.
Stonich, Susan C., John R. Bort, and Luis L. Ovares. 1999. "Challenges to Sustainability: The Central American Shrimp Mariculture Industry." In *Managed Eco-

systems: *The Mesoamerican Experience,* ed. L. Upton Hatch and Marilyn Swisher. New York: Oxford University Press.

Stronza, Amanda. 2001. "Anthropology of Tourism: Forging New Ground for Ecotourism and Other Alternatives." *Annual Review of Anthropology* 30: 261–283.

Sumner, Andrew. 2004. "Epistemology and 'Evidence' in Development Studies: A Review of Dollar and Kraay." *Third World Quarterly* 25(6): 1167–1177.

Szok, Peter A. 2001. *La Ultima Gaviota: Liberalism and Nostalgia in Early Twentieth-Century Panamá.* Westport, CT: Greenwood.

Taylor, Ian. 2004. "Hegemony, Neoliberal 'Good Governance' and the International Monetary Fund." In *Global Institutions and Development: Framing the World?,* ed. Morten Boas and Desmond McNeill. New York: Routledge.

Tejeira, Bertilde. 1972. "Los congresos de las comunidades cunas del Bayano." In *Actas del II Simposium Nacional de Antropología, Arqueología y Etnohistoria de Panamá, abril de 1971.* Panama City: Impr. Universitaria.

Thiesenhusen, William. 1989. *Searching for Agrarian Reform in Latin America.* Boston: Unwin Hyman.

Thrupp, Lori Ann. 1997. "New Harvests, Old Problems: The Challenges Facing Latin America's Export Boom." In *Green Guerrillas: Environmental Conflicts and Initiatives in Latin America and the Caribbean,* ed. Helen Collinson. Montreal: Black Rose Books.

Tice, Karin E. 1995. *Kuna Crafts, Gender, and the Global Economy.* Austin: University of Texas Press.

Torres de Araúz, Reina. 1977. *Darién: etnoecología de una región histórica.* Panama City: Dirección Nacional del Patrimonio Histórico.

Transparency International. 2005. *Corruption Perceptions Index 2005.* Available on the Transparency International Web site: http://www.transparency.org/cpi/2005.sources.en.html#cpi.

United Nations Development Program (UNDP). 2002. *Informe de Desarrollo Humano 2002.* Available on the UNDP Web site: http://www.undp.org.pa/portal/lang_es/tabID__3465/Default.aspx.

United Nations Division for Sustainable Development. 2002. *Johannesburg Declaration on Sustainable Development.* Available on the United Nations Division for Sustainable Development Web site: http://www.johannesburgsummit.org/html/documents/summit_docs/1009wssd_pol_declaration.doc.

USAID (U.S. Agency for International Development). 2002. *Fomento de una camaronicultura saludable para el medio ambientey para seguridad económica.* Available on the USAID Web site: http://www.usaid.org.ni/historiadiesciocho.htm.

———. 2001. *Renewing a Partnership with Central America.* Available on the USAID Web site: http://www.usaid.gov/press/releases/2001/fs010607.html.

Utting, Peter. 1997. "Deforestation in Central America: Historical and Contemporary Dynamics." In *Sustainable Agriculture in Central America,* ed. Jan de Groot and Ruerd Ruben. New York: St. Martin's.

———. 1996. *Bosques, Sociedad y Poder.* Managua: UCA.

Vakis, Renos, and Kathy Lindert. 2000. *Poverty in Indigenous Populations in Panama: A Study Using LSMS Data.* Washington, DC: World Bank.

Van den Hombergh, Helena. 1999. *Guerreros del Golfo Dulce: industria forestal y conflicto en la Península de Osa, Costa Rica.* San José, Costa Rica: Departamento Ecuménico de Investigaciones.

Varela Hidalgo, Bladimir. 1998. *Limitaciones y tendencias en su relacion con la cooperación internacional.* Managua: CON FONG-INIES-REDD BARNA-KEPA Cooperación Finlandesa-SNV.

Vargas Ulate, Gilbert. n.d. *Evaluación ecológica de impactos ambientales en la explotación de oro: casos de Río Tigre y Agujas Península de Osa. Informe final.* Department of Geography, University of Costa Rica.

Vaughan Dickhaut, Christopher. 1979. *Plan maestro para el manejo y desarrollo del Parque Nacional Corcovado, Península de Osa, Costa Rica.* MSc thesis, Centro Agronómico Tropical de Investigación Enseñanza.

Veltmeyer, Henry, and Anthony O'Malley (eds.). 2001. *Transcending Neoliberalism: Community-Based Development in Latin America.* Bloomfield, CT: Kumarian.

Ventocilla, Jorge, Heraclio Herrera, and Valerio Núñez. 1995. *Plants and Animals in the Life of the Kuna.* Austin: University of Texas Press.

Ventocilla, Jorge, Valerio Núñez, Heraclio Herrera, Francisco Herrera, and Mac Chapin. 1996. "The Kuna Indians and Conservation." In *Traditional Peoples and Biodiversity Conservation in Large Tropical Landscapes,* ed. Kent Redford and Jane A. Mansour. Washington, DC: America Verde, the Nature Conservancy.

Vivanco, Luis A. 2002. "Environmentalism, Democracy, and the Cultural Politics of Nature in Monte Verde, Costa Rica." In *Democracy and the Claims of Nature: Critical Perspectives for a New Century,* ed. Ben A. Minteer and Bob Pepperman Taylor. Lanham, MD: Rowman & Littlefield.

Von Frantzius, Ina. 2004. "World Summit on Sustainable Development Johannesburg 2002: A Critical Analysis and Assessment of the Outcomes." *Environmental Politics* 13(2, Summer): 467–473.

Vries, Pieter de. 1997. *Unruly Clients in the Atlantic Zone of Costa Rica.* Amsterdam: CEDLA.

Wade, Robert. 2004. 'The World Bank and the Environment." In *Global Institutions and Development: Framing the World?,* ed. Morten Boas and Desmond McNeill. New York: Routledge.

Wali, Alaka. 1993. "The Transformation of a Frontier: State and Regional Relationships in Panama, 1972–1990." *Human Organization* 52(2): 115–129.

———. 1989. *Kilowatts and Crisis: Hydroelectric Power and Social Dislocation in Eastern Panama.* Boulder: Westview.

Wallace, David Rains. 1992. *The Quetzel and the Macaw: The Story of Costa Rica's National Parks.* San Francisco: Sierra Club Books.

Warford, Jeremy J., Mohan Munasinghe, and Wilfrido Cruz. 1997. *The Greening of Economic Policy Reform. Volume 1: Principles.* Washington, DC: World Bank.

Warren, Kay B., and Jean E. Jackson (eds.). 2003. "Introduction: Studying Indigenous Activism in Latin America." In *Indigenous Movements, Self-Representation and the State in Latin America,* ed. Kay B. Warren and Jean E. Jackson. Austin: University of Texas Press.

Waters, Malcolm. 2001. *Globalization,* 2nd ed. New York: Routledge.

Watson, Vincent, S. Cervantes, C. Castro, L. Mora, M. Solis, J. T. Porras, and B. Cornejo. 1998. *Making Space for Better Forestry: Policy That Works for Forests and People.* San José, Costa Rica: Centro Científico Tropical.

Weinberg, Adam, Story Bellows, and Dara Ekster. 2002. "Sustaining Ecotourism: Insights and Implications from Two Successful Case Studies." *Society and Natural Resources* 15: 317–380.

Weyland, Kurt. 1998. "Swallowing the Bitter Pill: Sources of Popular Support for Neoliberal Reform in Latin America." *Comparative Political Studies* 31(5): 539–568.

Wickham-Crowley, Timothy. 1992. *Guerrillas and Revolution in Latin America: A Comparative Study of Insurgents and Regimes Since 1956*. Princeton: Princeton University Press.

Wickstrom, Stefanie. 2003. "The Politics of Development in Indigenous Panama." *Latin American Perspectives* 30(4): 43–68.

Williams, Robert G. 1986. *Export Agriculture and the Crisis in Central America*. Chapel Hill: University of North Carolina Press.

Wilson, Bruce M. 1998. *Costa Rica: Politics, Economics, and Democracy*. Boulder: Lynne Rienner.

Wodon, Quentin T., and Robert L. Ayres. 2000. *Poverty and Policy in Latin America and the Caribbean*. Washington, DC: World Bank.

Wood, Elisabeth Jean. 2003. *Insurgent Collective Action and Civil War in El Salvador*. New York: Cambridge University Press.

World Bank. 2006a. *World Development Report 2006*. Washington, DC: World Bank.

———. 2006b. *The Republic of Nicaragua Poverty Reduction Strategy and Joint World Bank–IMF Staff Advisory Note*. Washington, DC: World Bank.

———. 2005a. *Operational Directive and Bank Policy 4.10*. Available on the World Bank Web site: http://wbln0018.worldbank.org/Institutional/Manuals/OpManual.nsf/0/0F7D6F3F04DD70398525672C007D08ED?OpenDocument.

———. 2005b. *Implementation Completion Report on a Global Environment Facility Trust Fund Grant in the Amount of 6.3 Million SDRs (US $8.4 Million Equivalent) to the Republic of Panama for an Atlantic Mesoamerican Biological Corridor Project*. Washington, DC: World Bank.

———. 2004a. *Nicaragua: Drivers of Sustainable Rural Growth and Poverty Reduction in Central America. Nicaragua Case Study* (2 vols.). Volume I: *Executive Summary and Main Text*. Washington, DC: World Bank.

———. 2004b. *Nicaragua: Drivers of Sustainable Rural Growth and Poverty Reduction in Central America. Nicaragua Case Study* (2 vols.). Volume II: *Background Papers and Technical Appendices*. Washington, DC: World Bank.

———. 2003a. *Nicaragua Poverty Assessment: Raising Welfare and Reducing Vulnerability*. Washington, DC: World Bank.

———. 2003b. *Agriculture in Nicaragua: Promoting Competitiveness and Stimulating Broad-Based Growth*. Washington, DC: World Bank.

———. 2003c. *Nicaragua Land Policy and Administration: Toward a More Secure Property Rights Regime*. Washington, DC: World Bank.

———. 2003d. *World Development Report 2003: Sustainable Development in a Dynamic World*. Washington, DC: World Bank.

———. 2002. *Memorandum of the President of the International Development Association and the International Financial Corporation to the Executive Directors on a Country Assistance Strategy of the World Bank Group for the Republic of Nicaragua*. Washington, DC: World Bank.

———. 2001a. *World Development Report 2000/2001: Attacking Poverty*. New York: Oxford University Press.

———. 2001b. *Making Sustainable Commitments: An Environmental Strategy for the World Bank*. Washington, DC: World Bank.

———. 2001c. *The Republic of Nicaragua Poverty Reduction Strategy Paper and Joint IDA-IMF Staff Assessment*. Washington, DC: World Bank.
———. 2000. *Costa Rica Country Assistance Evaluation*. Washington, DC: World Bank.
———. 1999a. *Panama Poverty Assessment Priorities and Strategies for Poverty Reduction. Volume I: Main Report*. Washington, DC: World Bank.
———. 1999b. *Panama Poverty Assessment Priorities and Strategies for Poverty Reduction. Volume 2: Annexes*. Washington, DC: World Bank.
———. 1998. *Panama: Atlantic Mesoamerican Biological Corridor Project*. Global Environmental Facility Document. Washington, DC: World Bank.
———. 1997. *Panama: Rural Poverty and Natural Resources Project: Staff Appraisal Report*. Washington, DC: World Bank.
———. 1995. *Republic of Nicaragua Poverty Assessment*. Washington, DC: World Bank.
World Commission on Environment and Development. 1987. *Our Common Future*. Oxford: Oxford University Press.
Yearley, Steven. 1996. *Sociology, Environmentalism, Globalization: Reinventing the Globe*. London: Sage.
Young, Melinda. 1994. *Preserving 'Pura Vida': The Environmental Movement, Costa Rica*. M.A. thesis, University of New Mexico, Albuquerque.
Young, Philip D., and John R. Bort. 1999. "Ngobe Adaptive Responses to Globalization in Panama." In *Globalization and the Rural Poor in Latin America*, ed. William M. Loker. Boulder: Lynne Rienner.
Zamora, Natalia, and Vilma Obando. 2001. *Biodiversity and Tourism in Costa Rica*. Available at http://www.unep.org/bpsp/Tourism/Case%20Studies%20(pdf)/COSTA%20RICA%20(Tourism).pdf.
Zimbalist, Andrew, and John Weeks. 1991. *Panama at the Crossroads: Economic Development and Political Change in the Twentieth Century*. Berkeley: University of California Press.
Zúñiga Villegas, Rodolfo Antonio. 1998. *Protected Natural Area Development: An Assessment of the Interrelationship between Park Biodiversity and Human Communities in Costa Rica*. MSc thesis, Cornell University.

NEWSPAPER ARTICLES

La Nación (Costa Rica)
2001. "Maderos sin permisos." March 6, 2001.
2000a. "Disputan lugareños y empresarios." June 25, 2000.
2000b. "Agonizantes." April 15, 2000.
1998. "Piden frenar la tala sin control." August 9, 1998.
1997a. "Decretos del poder judicial." October 6, 1997.
1997b. "Use de zona marítimo-terrestre." February 10, 1997.
La Prensa (Panama)
2000. Supplement. April 22, 2000.
1996a. "Pedirán veto para ley que crea comarca." January 5, 1996.
1996b. "Embarás se oponen a proyectos de ANCON." February 14, 1996.
1996c. "Disputa entre indígenas y ANCON." March 26, 1996.
1995. "Gobierno recibe 500 mil dólares por extracción de madera." July 7, 1995.

1994a. "Mujeres Kunas denuncian sus problemas." September 5, 1994.
1994b. "PRD presiona al congreso Kuna para que elija nuevo intendente." October 8, 1994.
1994c. "Comunidad Europea inicia proyecto en Kuna Yala." October 18, 1994.
1993a. Kunas piden se defina situación de comarca de Madungandí." April 12, 1993.
1993b. "Explotan irracionalmente la madera." October 27, 1993.
1993c. "La Declaración de los Indígenas." December 10, 1993.
1992a. Los problemas de Alto Bayano no terminan." May 6, 1992.
1992b. "Darién: hasta cuándo la deforestación?" July 23, 1992.
1992c. "Alto Bayano: un problema sin resolver." August 13, 1992.
1992d. "Arborcidio: el meollo del problema de Alto Bayano." August 20, 1992.
1992e. "Situación actual de los embará." September 8, 1992.

Tico Times (Costa Rica)
2004. "Poachers Ravage Corcovado Park." March 19, 2004.
2003. "Fiesta Premiere Resort Opens in Papagayo." November 7, 2003.
2002. "Ambitious Tourism Plan Unveiled." April 5, 2002.
2000. "Planning Proposals Spark Debate in Osa." November 10, 2000.
1999a. "Beach Park Imperiled by Overdevelopment." November 26, 1999.
1999b. "Manual Antonio: 2 Views of Development." December 3, 1999.
1997a. "Critics: Logging Probe in Reserve a 'Whitewash.'" August 1, 1997.
1997b. "3-Month Logging Ban in Osa." August 22, 1997.
1997c. "U.S. Rancher, C.R. Squatter Killed in Pavones Shootout." November 21, 1997.

Index

Active accommodation, 26
ADPESCA. *See* Fishery Administration
AECO. *See* Costa Rican Ecological Association
Afro-Panamanians, 104, 181–182(n15). *See also* Ethnic groups, Panama
Agrarian Development Institute (IDA), 58–59, 176(n12)
Agarian reform. *See* Nicaragua, Agrarian reform
Agricultural credit, 61, 90
Agricultural frontier: Central America, 33; Costa Rica, 35, 38; Nicaragua, 26, 173(n27); Panama, 98
Agriculture, employment in, 19
Agrochemicals, xii, 27, 179(n4)
Aguas Claras, 105, 182(n20)
Alternatives to development, 10, 11. *See also* Postdevelopment
ANAM. *See* National Environmental Authority
Anti-logging campaign. *See* Osa Peninsula: environmental activism

Bayano: deforestation, 31, 97–98, 116 (*See also* Ipetí: logging); ethnic conflicts, 106 (*See also* Ipetí: highway protests); migration to, 97–98 (*See also* Colonists); regional map, 28
Bayano Bridge, 125
Bayano Corporation, 115
Bayano hydroelectric dam: construction of, 27; economic impacts, 30–31; environmental impacts, 31
Bayano Lake, 31
BOSCOSA, 65, 177(n24)
Brundtland Commission, 2

Cabinas, 44
Caciques, 99, 105, 122
Campesino culture, 80, 94–95
Carate, 45
CARE International, 81
CAS. *See* Sandinista Agricultural Cooperative
Casitas volcano, 21
Cattle culture, 34, 181(n2)

211

INDEX

Central America: agro-exports, 19, 21–23 (*See also* Cotton production); authoritarian governments, 20, 30, 158; deforestation, 32–34; environmental deterioration, xv, 173(n26); environmental protection, 8, 37, 137, 151; external interventions, 20, 34, 170(n2); geographical characteristics, 32, 37; guerrilla movements, 25 (*See also* Sandinista National Liberation Front); Gross Domestic Product (GDP), 23; impact of neoliberal reforms, 60 (*See also* Neoliberalism); neglect of environmental issues, 32; peasant mobilization, 25; post-WWII development, xv,19–23; poverty, xiv, 19, 23–24; rural land tenure, 21–24; state repression, xv, 30, 172(n20)
Central American Common Market, 19
Central American System of Protected Areas, 37
Certificates of Tax Benefits, 71
Chamorro, Violeta, 86
Chepo, 100
Chile, 71
Chinandega province: agriculture, 21, 26, 70 (*See also* Cotton production); land tenure, 88; map of, 22
Colonists: agricultural practices, 98; communities, 28; environmental discourse of, 116; impact of hydroelectric dam on, 30; nationalist discourse of, 103–104
Colonos. *See* Colonists
Comarca status. *See* Madungandí
Community: advantages of studying, xiv; characteristics of, 15; definition of, 13, 153; participation, 11, 85, 136, 153
Corcovado National Park, 35, 43, 45, 58
Corruption, 59–60, 176(n15)
Costa Rica: deforestation 34–36, 49–50, 175(n17); economic development, 34; political culture, 66 (*See also* Costa Rican government)
Costa Rican Ecological Association (AECO), 63
Costa Rican government: democracy, 20, 58; social benefits, 60; state environmentalism, 58–59; structural adjustment, 60 (*See also* Neoliberalism)
Costa Rican Tourism Institute, 54
Cotton production: decline of, 70; environmental impacts, 26–27; harvests, 25; social and economic impacts, 22–25
Critical consciousness. *See* Empowerment: critical consciousness
Cultural diversity, 14
Curtí, 116

DANIDA. *See* Danish International Development Agency
DANIDA-Manglares, 77
Danish International Development Agency (DANIDA), 70, 77
Darién Gap, 119
Darién National Park, 117
Darién Sustainable Development Program, 102, 119, 182(n1)
DDT, 27
Deep ecology, 4. *See also* Ecocentric discourse
Depoliticization, 11, 152. *See also* Postdevelopment
Development, impasse of, xii
Development, sustainable. *See* Sustainable Development
Discourse, definition of, xiii
Dominant sustainability discourse: criticism, 8–9; economic component, 4, 6–7, 53–54, 145–146; environmental component, 6, 8; multiple strands of, xvi; optimism of, 6; origins of, 4–6; social component, 6
Drake Bay, 43, 45

Ecocentric discourse, 2, 4. *See also* Deep ecology
Ecofeminists, 177(n23)
Eco-lodges, 43–44, 47
Economic growth, 4. *See also* Dominant sustainability discourse: economic component
Ecotourism: comparison to mass tourism, 42, 47; control of land, 45–46, 59; critical perspectives, 42–43, 48; definition of, 42; economic impacts, 43–45, 134–135; employment, 44; environmental impacts, 47–48, 135; expansion of, 41–43; gender impacts, 44–45; role of foreign investors, 43; role of government, 46–47; sociocultural impacts, 48–50
Ecotourists, characteristics of, 42
Electoral Tribunal, Panamanian, 122
El Viejo, 76
Embarás, 30–31, 119–120, 181–182(n15), 183(n6)
Empowerment: critical consciousness, 20, 25–26, 62, 118, 140, 149; definitions of, xvi, 15, 20, 171(n3); link to development projects, 150; material base, 20–21, 49, 62; obstacles to, 64–65, 88–94, 141–143; processes of, 62, 138–141
Environment: instrumentalist perspective of, 52–53, 55–56; representations of, 52–53
Environmental Law of 1998, Panamanian, 115

Environmental protection. *See* Central America: environmental protection
Environmentalism: light green, 8 (*See also* Dominant sustainability discourse: environmental component); localized, 53–55; policing approach, 8
Estero Real: environmental characteristics, 21, 69, 177(n2); extractive activities, 27, 69–70; firewood, 74–76 (*See also* Río Hondo, firewood extraction); local access to, 73
Ethnic groups, Panama, 29. *See also* Afro-Panamanians; Embarás; Ngöbe-Buglés

Firewood cooperatives, 77
Firewood extraction. *See* Estero Real: firewood
Fishery Administration (ADPESCA), 71, 74. *See also* Shrimp production
Forestry Law of 1996, Costa Rican, 49
FSLN. *See* Sandinista National Liberation Front

GEF. *See* Global Environmental Facility
General Congresses, 99, 105, 122, 182(n18)
Global Environmental Facility (GEF), 10, 58, 169(n16), 174(n3)
Globalization, xiii, 13, 15–16, 101, 152, 167(n3)
Globalized environmentalism, 34
Gold miners: invasion of Corcovado Park, 37–38; protests, 37; way of life, 38, 49, 57–58
Golfo Dulce Forest Reserve, 47, 49, 55, 59, 175–176(n21)
Good governance: concept of, 6, 11, 91, 135; criticism, 91, 136–137
Grassroots autonomy, 65. *See also* Empowerment
Greenwash, 9. *See also* Dominant sustainability discourse: criticism
Guatemala, 71
Gulf of Fonesca, 73

Habitat for Humanity, 83–84, 180(n21)
Hamburger connection, 33–34
Highly Indebted Poor Country Initiative. *See* World Bank: highly indebted poor country initiative
Hurricane Mitch, 21, 82, 178(n9), 179(n8), 180(n16)

IDA. *See* Agrarian Development Institute
IDB. *See* Inter-American Development Bank
IFIs. *See* International Financial Institutions

Immanent development, 10
Imminent development, 10
Indigenous exceptionalism. *See* International Financial Institutions, indigenous exceptionalism
Innas, 29
Institute of Hydraulic Resources and Electricity, (IRHE), 31
Institute of Natural Resources (IRENA), 70
Integrated pest management, 81
Inter-American Development Bank (IDB), xiii, 30, 119–120, 185(n33)
Interioranos. See Colonists
International Financial Institutions (IFIs): description, xiii, 3; indigenous exceptionalism, 101–102, 135, 181(n10) (*See also* World Bank: indigenous land rights)
Ipetí: attitudes toward development, 109–110; basic indicators, 28–29; cultural identity, 112–113 (*See also* Kuna Indians: cultural practices); development projects, 120–121; environmental discourse, 102–103, 113–114; founding, 30, 110–111; gender inequality, 123–124; highway protests, 99–100 (*See also* Bayano: ethnic conflicts); intra-community inequality, 111–112; logging, 103, 111, 114–116 (*See also* Bayano: deforestation); migration, 124; political engagement, 122–123; poverty, 110–111; social controls, 112, 124–125
Ipetí River, 114
IRENA. *See* Institute of Natural Resources
IRHE. *See* Institute of Hydraulic Resources and Electricity
ITCO. *See* Land Colonization Institute

Johannesburg World Summit, 1

Kuna General Congresses. *See* General Congresses
Kuna health, 113, 183–184(n15)
Kuna Indians, cultural practices, 28–29, 102, 112. *See also* Ipetí: cultural identity
Kuna Yala, 29, 124, 172(n17), 185(n44), 186(n45)

Lai, Haydee, 104
Land Colonization Institute (ITCO), 36
La Palma, 45, 62
Large landowners, xi, 21, 23, 82
Leñeros, 75–77
León, 26, 76
Livelihood discourses: alternatives pathways, 14–15; characterization of the poor,

213

13–14; economic component, 55–56, 128; environmental component, 57, 131; epistemologies, 13; origins of, 2, 4, 12–13; role of community, 13; social component, 12, 57, 130; weaknesses of, 14–15
Loma Bonita, 116

Madungandí: comarca charter, 100, 105–106, 182(n19); comarca, definition of, 27, 29; comarca status, 98–99, 101–102, 104; land struggles, 106, 185(n35) (*See also* Ipetí: highway protests); origins, 29–30
MAG-FOR. *See* Ministry of Agriculture and Forestry
Manuel Antonio National Park, 47–48
MARENA. *See* Ministry of Natural Resources
Mass tourism. *See* Ecotourism: comparison to mass tourism
Matapalo, 45
Mesoamerican Biological Corridor Program, 121, 184–185(n32)
MIDINRA. *See* Ministry for Agrarian Development and Reform
MINAE. *See* Ministry of Environment and Energy
Ministry for Agrarian Development and Reform (MIDINRA), 86
Ministry of Agriculture and Forestry (MAG-FOR), 74
Ministry of Environment and Energy (MINAE), 38, 49, 57–59, 176(n10)
Ministry of Natural Resources (MARENA), 70, 73–74, 76, 177(n1)
Miraflores: basic indicators, 23; class conflict, 82–83; debt, 91, 93; environmental perspectives, 80–81; founding of, 80; gender inequality, 93, 95; interactions with NGOs, 85; intra-community inequality, 92–94; land invasions, 25; land privatization, 86–87; livelihood perspectives, 82–83; major development projects, 84; poverty, 21, 82
Molas, 28
Monge, Luis Alberto, 37
Monteverde, 44

National Assembly, Panamanian, 100, 104
National Environmental Authority (ANAM), 11, 117
National Guard, Nicaraguan, 24, 25
National Union of Farmers and Ranchers (UNAG), 83, 88, 91, 179(n6)
Nation-states, mediating effects of, xiv, 135. *See also* Globalization

Neoliberalism: definition of, 168(n11); economic criticisms, 61, 134, 147; environmental criticisms, 61–62; origins, 6; policies 6–7, 60–61, 118, 132–134, 146–147; protests against, 60; role of state, 7, 89; social criticisms, 10, 89–90, 94–95, 118, 154
Ngöbe-Buglés, 105, 123, 172(n160), 183(n6), 184(n23)
NGOs. *See* Non-governmental organizations
Nicaragua: agrarian reform, xi, 21, 70, 79–80, 179(n9); class conflict, 24–25 (*See also* Large landowners); democracy, 91–92; economic growth, 23; land privatization, 86–88; revolution, xi, 21, 79, 89 (*See also* Sandinista National Liberation Front); state repression, 24, 25
Nicaraguan Poverty Reduction Strategy, 72, 88
Non-governmental organizations (NGOs): criticism, 65–66; links to empowerment, 65, 83–84, 137–138; national characteristics, 63, 83, 118–119, 179(n8)
Nonplace actors, 12
Nontraditional exports, 65, 70–71, 75, 178(n13). *See also* Shrimp production

Oduber, Daniel, 35
Office of Rural Land Titling, 179(n9)
OFP. *See* Osa Forest Products
Ortega, Daniel, 89
Osa Forest Products (OFP), 34–36, 55–56, 62–63
Osa Peninsula: agriculture and ranching, 46; beachfront concessions, 45; early settlement, 34; environmental activism, 49–50, 55; land conflicts, 35–36, 59, 62–63; land speculation, 45 (*See also* Ecotourism: control of land); localized environmentalism, 52–55, 62, 131; map of, 35; squatter movements, 35–36; stratification, 46; women, obstacles faced by, 64–65; women's activism, 64
Ostional, 44

Panama: deforestation, 98 (*See also* Bayano: deforestation); democracy, 106; national identity, 112; pan-indigenist movement, 100; racism, 183(n11); state environmentalism, 117; state repression, 115; United States military presence, 103
Panamanian Legal Code of the Family, 105
Pan-American Highway, Panamanian, 27–28, 30, 97–98, 119–120
Patron-client ties, 26

214

PEMASKY. *See* Study Project for the Management of the Wildlands of Kuna Yala
Penetration roads, 33
Pesticides. *See* Agrochemicals
Pesticides, natural, xii
Plan International, 84–85
Political ecology, 9–10, 169(n20)
Political economy critiques, 9
Political opportunities, 25
Political patronage, 30, 66, 92, 123, 136, 152
Postdevelopment, 10–11, 15, 37, 121, 148
Post-Washington consensus, 3
Poverty. *See* Central America: poverty
Pro-poor growth. *See* World Bank: pro-poor growth
Puerto Jiménez: basic indicators, 34, 36; drug use, 48; ecotourism activities, 44 (*See also* Ecotourism: economic impacts)
Puerto Morazán, 24–27

Quepos, 44

Río Hondo: firewood extraction, 74–76; land conflicts, 88 (*See also* Leñeros)
Royal Estuary. *See* Estero Real

Sailas, 99, 105, 122, 124
San Blas. *See* Kuna Yala
Sandinista Agricultural Cooperative (CAS), 80, 86–87, 178(n1)
Sandinista National Liberation Front (FSLN), xii, 21, 79, 89, 180(n18)
SAPs. *See* Structural adjustment programs
Secretaries, Ipetí, 99
Shrimp production: cooperatives, 72; economic impacts, 72–73, 134–135; environmental impacts, 73–74; expansion of, 71; origins, 70; social impacts, 73–74
Social capital, 85–86
Socios, 80
Somoza family dictatorship, xi, 21, 24, 26, 80, 85
State and civil society relations, 7, 66
State environmentalism. *See* Costa Rica: state environmentalism
State repression. *See* Central America: state repression
Stone Container, 49–50. *See also* Osa Peninsula: environmental activism

Structural adjustment programs (SAPs), 168(n11). *See also* Neoliberalism
Study Project for the Management of the Wildlands of Kuna Yala (PEMASKY), 185(n37)
Sustainable development: definitions of, xii–xiii, xiv, 2, 167(n3); economic component, 2; environmental component, 2; goals of, 2–3; grassroots agency, xiv; origins of, xiii; political implications, xiii–xiv, 2–3, 145–146; social component, 2
Sustainable development projects, 65

Terratenientes. See Large Landowners
Tonalá, 21, 25–26, 76
Torrijos, General Omar, 30, 100, 112, 172(n21)
Traditional development. *See* Central America: post-WWII development

UNAG. *See* National Union of Farmers and Ranchers
United Fruit Company, 30, 34, 37
United States interventions. *See* Central America: external interventions
United States Agency for International Development (USAID), 71, 65, 174(n3), 178(n6)
USAID. *See* United States Agency for International Development

Vanguard Party, 36

Wacuco, 116
Wargandí, 104–105, 181–182(n15), 184(n18)
Washington Consensus, 6, 168(n5)
Women: connection to nature, 64; employment of, 44–45; obstacles faced by, 143
World Bank: civil society, 91; development expertise, 3; highly indebted poor country initiative, 180; indigenous land rights, 102, 119 (*See also* International financial institutions: indigenous exceptionalism); land titling, 86; neoliberal reforms, 60, 89, 132 (*See also* Neoliberalism); pro-poor growth, 6, 10, 132, 146, 169(n13) (*See also* Dominant sustainability discourse: economic component)

215